COCONUTS & WHITE BREAD

Brown on the Outside, White on the Inside

The Story of a First Generation Mexican-American

Albert Rodriguez, Jr.

PublishAmerica
Baltimore

PublishAmerica has allowed this work to remain exactly as the author intended, verbatim, without editorial input.

Hardcover 978-1-4512-9511-5
Softcover 978-1-4489-5245-8
PUBLISHED BY PUBLISHAMERICA, LLLP
www.publishamerica.com
Baltimore

Printed in the United States of America

This book is dedicated to all the Jose's and Carlos' that dream, but dream big.

Miguel Vizcarra,

De un coco a otro coco.

Dream But Dream
BIG!

A Rod

Foreword

I met Albert Rodriguez in a corporate boardroom when he and I were part of a special team. I had no idea nor expected that Albert was as gifted a story teller as he is a strategic corporate manager. We have been close friends ever since. I was fortunate enough to read "Coconuts and Whitebread," during the end of 2009 and it made an immediate impact on me.

I opened the file one mid winter Saturday. The first thing that hit me was that over four hours had passed without my noticing. "Coconuts and Whitebread," illustrates the multi-faceted challenges that immigrants face when coming to America. As a first generation American, born to Central American immigrants I have never read anything that captures the feelings that I felt as a Coconut growing up in Southern California. Racism, be it overt, clandestine or manifesting as group self-hatred was a constant in my life and the life of my Coconut friends. Albert shares stories that illustrate the pain that these events cause in the life of a child of Latino immigrants. The story shows the incredible resolve to be true to oneself and the value of continuous improvement of ones own lot in life. The reader gets an immersion into the difficult life of a migrant family. The fact that Albert is a 'success' in the eye's of any American is a testament to the resolve and tenacity that he has as a core value

The inner resolve of the immigrant is central to the building, maintaining and sustaining of America. I believe that this story could be written by the offspring of any immigrant. The desire to create a better life for oneself and ones' family is the common thread amongst them. Leaving behind friends, family, that which is comfortable for the unknown of our great country is a daunting proposition, yet as Albert states in his preface, "As you read this paragraph, a Mexican is coming to America looking for opportunity." This event happens every moment that you think of it and every moment you don't. They are all driven with an intense desire to make a better life for themselves and their family.

This book is a social commentary with all of the elements that make a good yarn. It is a family story, a story of abuse, challenges, determination and success. His story moved me in many ways. I felt compelled to share the story with my mother. She called me after the first evening telling me that she was moved to tears as she read past 2:00 am. She could not break away from the story. I trust that you will be moved by the images and the path that the protagonist takes on his way to becoming a respected leader in a major global corporation.

Con mucho gusto y respeto,

Mario Hernan Archaga de Fletez
American

Introduction

Being born in the United States does not make you an American. Being an American is a spirit that defines what a great country is built on. The foundation for that is opportunity. Our founding fathers came to this new land for that single reason. They came for the chance to raise their children free from religious persecution, free to exercise their minds as well as their hearts. They did not come to work and make money to send back home. Home was gone; now the wild forests of the east coast was their new home. The American Indians were their new neighbors. Try to imagine what it must have been like to have all your possessions in a tiny ship, leaving civilization, crossing an entire ocean just for opportunity. Standing on the bow of a wooden ship and not being able to see land for months, but knowing that somewhere out there was opportunity. The drive to find hope and a better life is what drove the Pilgrims to America. It is a similar feeling that drives people across a small river in the Southwestern United States today. As you read this paragraph a Mexican is coming to America looking for opportunity. He may have relatives already here, or maybe he is alone. He may have come across illegally or completed the documents that make him an official American. Either way he is experiencing the same feelings our forefathers felt several hundred years ago. Once here he will blend into the fabric of our society and quietly begin to take advantage of everything America is about: opportunity.

We see them every day yet we never notice them. They work at all your favorite restaurants, grocery stores, and even our schools. They build our homes, businesses, and roads. The next time you go to dinner look at the person who takes your order, cooks your food, and busses your table. Surprised? I'm not. Nor should you be. Think about your meal. Go way back, I mean way back, before the chefs and the kitchens.

They plant and harvest our crops. Raise our livestock and prepare everything we eat from the market. They place their hands on the food we consume at home and at the restaurants. The fruits, vegetables, and meats that our great lands produce are planted, harvested and cleaned by somebody.

The largest minority group in the United States is the Mexican-American, Hispanic, Latino, or Chicano. For easy conversation let's just say Mexicans.

We go about our day and take their hard work and determination for granted. That's okay, have you ever heard one complain? All these thoughts led me to write this book, "Coconuts and White bread." I want to bring awareness of the struggles the people, many of which are Americans, are facing and overcoming. Their spirit of seeking opportunity fosters more than just hard work and a will to survive. It creates a passion for life and a thirst for knowledge. My story also shows how that thirst is many times never satisfied because of petty human nature. Things like greed, jealousy, and ignorance from their family can dowse a flame of spirit faster than desperate economic conditions. Keep in mind, all these people want is the same thing you and I want.

Mexicans are in America to provide a better life for their family, the same way we want a better life for our children. They fight racism. There are people who will take their money and leave them to die in the desert in trailers that they smuggled them in. There are those that will hire them for projects and then call the Bureau of Immigration when the work is completed. Sadly, some of the people that abuse these immigrants are Mexicans themselves. There is also a different type of racism. While their children are being educated they get called names that sting. "Wetback" is the most common and it hurts, especially if you were not born in Mexico. This type of racism is ignorance. People have to remember that the only Native Americans are the Indians. We are all immigrants. There is however a type of racism that is worse than ignorance. It is the kind that comes from our own family and friends.

Mexicans that begin to excel in education or business suddenly get shunned for some reason. I remember a Mexican man telling his friends that a mutual acquaintance was doing well in his new business. His first response was that this person now probably wants to be White. "He thinks he is a White man now!" he said. I asked that person why he was being so judgmental. The man told me, "I bet that since he has business and a degree he thinks he is smarter than anyone else."

I said to him, "I have three degrees, does that make me better than you or just more determined?" Why can't people be happy when someone else is doing well? What is it about Mexicans that make some green with envy when their own relatives complete a challenge like a college education? I have seen relatives pat me on the back after I completed college and with the other hand point at me and call me a White man or a "coconut."

This type of attitude makes it easy to understand a question I have asked friends that are White as well as Mexican: Name a famous Mexican leader at a national level? No one could give me an answer. My Black friends were quick to point out that there are famous Black leaders such as Colin Powell, Condaliza Rice, Jesse Jackson, and Al Sharpton. Whether you recognize these people as leaders or not, is your opinion. We cannot disregard their power and influence as Black leaders. Where are the Mexican leaders? It is strange that such a large minority group has no national leaders. I believe it is due to the fact that as soon as someone begins to climb the ladder of success, others are ready to kick it out from underneath them. There have been people that were destined for success and overcame many obstacles and then did something foolish to tarnish their image. Henry Cisneros and Dan Morales come to mind.

Until Mexican Americans can join together and face the fact that America is great because it is called the "United" States of America, there will continue to be a lack of leadership that can support Mexican issues in this country. Who will that leader be? I do not have that answer. It will be someone that can overcome racism from others as well as our own people. I hope that future leader read my book.

My story is of hope, faith, and triumph. It is a journey through the fields and orchards of Texas and California. By sharing my dreams and struggles I hope people can see that America is made up of many people that take different paths to freedom. This journey takes a Mexican boy to small towns in America that challenge his identity and spirit. Join me in the travels of growing up first a generation Mexican-American in the United States.

Chapter 1
Betito and the Tomatoes

"Mommy, I want to go to college."

"Si mijito, but for now I need you to finish picking those tomatoes, and hurry, it's getting late." Actually it wasn't. The "blue norther" coming in over the Texas Panhandle made it appear later than it actually was. The temperature would hit the freezing mark tonight. If the crops were not picked in a hurry, they would freeze on the vine. That was not good. Frozen tomatoes are only good for ketchup. When the cold fronts rolled in we had to work faster. No matter how young or old you are, being cold, wet, and tired feels like a chilling spear through your spirit.

I still remember the blue sky and flat land of the Texas Panhandle around Plainview. I guess that's where it got its name. It is just a "plain view." It is perfect for growing crops but there was no scenic beauty from where I was standing. I was knee deep in mud and the world was not very scenic from there. At four feet tall and five years old, I could barely see over the plants we were harvesting. My mother had prepared me for the workday by dressing me in the best a migrant's pay could buy in 1969.

I was wearing the warmest clothes I had, which consisted of a pair of worn blue jeans with a patch on both knees. In fact they were so old, the patches had holes. My torn canvas sneakers made for my work shoes and for a jacket I had a red flannel shirt. I wore it every day and it was so thin that I had to wear two tee shirts underneath it. These clothes were from garage sales and the Salvation Army. My clothes were always clean until I got to work, then mud always found a way to get on me. The fields tend to do that to you.

I recall that scene because it stands out in my mind. I don't know if it was that beautiful dark blue sky creeping over the valley or the sight of me covered in mud, telling mom I would go to college. Looking back, it had to be funny. A little five-year old boy with a runny nose and a tomato in hand, ready to go to college. I stared at that tomato and replayed the events that led me to believe I was destined for something better.

I was attending a migrant preschool a few days a week but never went on consecutive days. We had work that needed to be done. The day before was a school day and a teacher had given me words that still move me to this day.

"Dream Betito, dream, but dream big!" He had told me. I had listened to the instructor as he read books to the children of our migrant camp. I carried those words in my head to work the next day. The falling temperature and the subtle hint of changing weather could not take those words away. "Dream, but dream big." I had asked the teacher what that meant and he tried as hard as he could to explain it to a five year old boy that could hardly understand English. He asked me what I wanted to do when I grew up. I told him I did not want to work the fields anymore. I wanted to do what he did. He told me that he was doing what he wanted because he went to college. I had to ask him what college was. He explained to me that it was where people went to get smart and fulfill their dreams. I must have stared at him with stars in my eyes. The teacher knelt down, looked into my dark brown eyes and said, "Dream, Betito. In your dreams you can do anything and go any where. Dream yourself away from the fields and then dream yourself into college. If you can dream it you can do it." He held my shoulders tight. "But promise me, when you dream, always dream big." Then he hugged me and I walked to my next class. I had shared my dream with my mother, the only person who would listen to me and not laugh.

After that huge proclamation I just kept on picking tomatoes. I would help my mother fill her basket, and when it was full, someone would take it away and bring an empty one. It was quite confusing to me. I worked so hard to get my mother's basket full, only to be rewarded several times with yet another basket to fill. There was no sense of accomplishment. This entire process never changed from sun up to sundown. Where exactly was this leading? I needed to find a place where someone of my intelligence could relax and enjoy the moment of my decision to get educated.

I found a large clump of tomato vines and hid in it. I squatted down real low where no one could see me. Green tomatoes hung down all around me and looked inviting. To this day, almost forty years later I can still smell the leaves as they rubbed against my face and tattered clothes. I spotted a big green juicy one. Yeah! Why wait for dinner? I was just going to have beans again anyway. I bit into that big, hard, sour tomato and I can still taste it. I could also feel a boot come across my rear end, as I would many times during my childhood. "Ponte a trabajar!" (get to work). I just introduced you to my father. We'll discuss him later. He actually did me a favor with his fierce kick. Big green tomatoes can give you a serious case of the runs. I felt my face hit the cold wet mud. It didn't mix well with my runny nose however. I did not let my tears become part of the mud. My body felt as cold as the winter soil.

My father's way of putting me back to work was very simple. He would grab me with one hand and kick or throw me over the row of vines to my mother. The message was always very clear: Get back to work! Once again I landed in mud. I knew it was no use to cry. After a while you just become numb. My hands were so cold and now my heart was colder. My mother tried to make it all better by saying "Mira, look at your brothers. They are working hard, why can't you?"

"But mommy, I told you, I am going to be smart someday. I'm going to college." I swallowed that large lump that was in my throat and went back to my basket.

"Pinche little coconut," I heard someone say with laughter from the other row of tomatoes. Apparently they saw what had happened to me. I couldn't understand why they were laughing. Why would they call me a coconut? My mother said it was because I was "hardheaded" like a coconut. That was the first time I would be called that, only that time I did not know it was supposed to hurt. How dare they laugh at me! I knew at any moment my parents would step up to my defense. But instead I heard my dad laughing loudly with the others when my mom told him of the good news. "Betito is going to go to college some day," I heard her tell him. He just kept on laughing. I thought to myself, how can it get worse? Then the cold front hit and the rain came.

In a strange way the weather was a blessing in disguise because work ended early. We were forced out of the fields by the cold rain, not for our benefit but to protect the plants. Walking in the deep mud would damage the crops and every step would tear the roots. The risk to the harvest was too great. The *Patron* (manager or landowner) blew the whistle. I loved the sound it made. It meant it was time to go home. So we all made a dash to the buses. There were about fifty of us, men, women and children running to the two old buses that would take us home.

As we filed into the bus, I remember seeing people's breath filling the air. I realized it was colder in the bus than it was outside and it would continue to be cold because the bus had no heater. We sat in family groups, usually in the same seat we rode to work in. We were all wet and tired. I saw other kids with red cheeks and noses. Mothers tried to hold their babies close to keep them warm. The workday had ended and I was excited to get out of the weather. I breathed on my hands and fingers and for some reason I couldn't get warm. I leaned closer into my mother to share her warmth. I knew better than to sit next to my dad. The ride home was bumpy and a few times I thought we would get stuck in the mud. Soon we were on a hard road. The ride was still not much smoother.

As we pulled up to the migrant housing projects, people began to stand up in the bus. I stayed next to mom. I could see the door to our tiny little apartment. The buildings were built of cinder blocks. It was as cold looking as the weather. The gray color of the bricks with brown doors spaced a few feet apart clashed with the color of the tin roof. It was still raining as we exited the bus. People were carrying lunch boxes and bags that had earlier held lunch for the day. Some people used these boxes and bags as umbrellas. They held them high as they made a mad dash out of the buses. The people looked funny. They reminded me of little trains because now everyone's breath was thicker in the cold wet air. As they ran it looked like the smoke of a train I had seen somewhere but could not recall where. I was standing behind my dad as he opened our door. I dared not get too close to him. He might hear my teeth chattering and get mad at me for showing weakness. We all ran through the door and my mother ran straight to our little gas stove. She lit every burner in hopes of warming our two-room apartment.

The main room was about twenty feet long and fifteen feet wide. It had another doorway that led to mom and dad's bedroom and a bathroom. The "main" room served as a kitchen, living room, and bedroom for the children. It had a small table with two chairs, a refrigerator, and our wonderful gas stove that was also a heater. My brothers and I kept our clothes in a few cardboard boxes under a cot where we slept. We got out of our wet clothes and changed. The clothes that we put on were not much better than what we had taken off, but I was so happy to be dry and a little bit warmer. All the clothes my brothers and I had were shared between us. It was just a matter of who got to the boxes first.

Jose, Carlos and I were spaced one and two years apart. I was five and named Albert but everyone called me Betito. That translates into "little Albert." My brother Jose was four, and Carlos was three. I didn't like Carlos, nor did I like any three-year old for that matter. "Que es college?" (what is college?) asked Jose. I told him it was where smart people went to school. "Like the school we go to?" he asked.

"No! Not the migrant preschool. College is where the smart people go," I said. At this point I could only speak Spanish.

I was starting to learn English from watching our television in the evenings. I would mouth the words I heard from the T.V. It was a small black and white ten-inch set we had bought at a garage sale for two dollars. I still remember moving the rabbit ear antennae with aluminum foil on the tips. It had to be a very interesting sight, three little boys sitting on a cot, mouthing English words while our feet dangled down and did not reach the floor. Our little faces would twist and contort as we tried to pronounce words like "cereal," "hamburger," and "Chevrolet," which was the hardest. To this day I still can not say it right. We sat glued to the T.V. while mom cooked beans for dinner.

I remember the beans being so good. My mom would soak them overnight then boil them for hours with a dash of salt and pepper and a clove of garlic. Soaking them helped reduce gas, I was told. From what I remember, it didn't work. The cooking beans made our little room smell so warm and cozy. She would then take the beans and fry them with lard and serve them with tortillas. Sometimes my mom would cook rice and beans. She would take a few ripe tomatoes from the field so she could use them to cook with. She would then slice the tomato in long wide sections. We would pretend it was a steak. The slices were flat and we would season them with salt and pepper. It made a nice addition to a plate of beans. Mom would also use them to make "boracho" beans, (bean soup) by adding onions and peppers in a broth. Mothers can always find a way to put extra love into a meal even when there is not enough food to create a meal. My mom came from a family of eleven brothers and sisters. Since she was the youngest she did all the cooking.

My mother was born in Mexico in 1946. She was the baby of the family and spent her early and teenage years taking care of all her brothers and sisters. This is how she learned to cook. While her family was out working in the fields, she stayed home with her mother and helped prepare all the family meals, clean the house, and do laundry. My mother used to tell us how she worked into the night with her mother making sure they all had food to take to work and have clean clothes to wear. At the age of fifteen my mother moved away to Texas, illegally to live with her aunt who was very sick. She took care of her aunt, and in exchange, her aunt helped her get her citizenship. She stayed with her aunt until she passed away two years later of cancer. In her later years my mother told me she pleaded to go to Texas so she could get away from the tremendous workload of caring for her family. She said she felt like a slave to her brothers and sisters. She thought that by going to America she could escape the hell that she was living. America to her was an opportunity for freedom and a new life. Instead she met my father and the cycle started over again. Once again my mom was in a kitchen cooking, cleaning, and doing laundry, after working in the fields. The only difference now was she had three boys that depended on her.

Every now and then my mother would prepare meats like chicken or pork. I still recall the smell of carne asada, (grilled beef flank steak) cooking on our little gas stove. I remember smelling it but never eating it. That was for the big folks I guess. They got to eat more because they picked more bushels. I could not wait to be big. I was getting tired of beans. No matter how good they are, you eventually run out of ways to prepare them before you have to start over again.

After dinner my brothers and I would watch more T.V. I looked forward to watching it after a hard day in the field. It made me think of other things that were more fun. The kids on T.V. were playing with toys and eating real food, like hamburgers. I had never had a hamburger before because mom said they were for rich people. I wondered if rich people ate beans also. T.V. may have given me the idea of going to college, at this point it is hard to recall. It did not hurt that my brothers and I were able to see a different life outside the one we were living. At our age we stayed inside a lot and were not allowed outside much.

We did not go outdoors because there was nowhere to play. We were at the "camp" to work, not play. The migrant camp looked like a long shed with doors. It was very plain. There were no trees to make it look nice. The area in front was gravel and had old cars parked in front of the doors. You could step out of your car and get to your front door in four paces. I remember the dirt was a reddish sandy brown color. It was all very dull and the colors to me seemed to suck the life from everyone. When the wind blew, the dirt was everywhere. You never stayed clean. When it rained the mud stuck to your feet, hands, and face. The camp was not there to look good, it was there for a purpose; it kept a roof over people's heads. However, if the wind blew too hard, the roof may blow off. I have no vivid memories of this place. Every memory seems to be in black and white. It may be that I do not want to remember this place because it was full of lifeless souls wandering in search of hope that would never come. No one ever got rich from working in the fields. Looking back, I can't believe no one had figured this out yet.

A main road passed in front of the camps or "projects" as the White people called them. I can still see little kid's faces pressed against the glass of cars as they drove by and stared at us. I see it in slow motion even though the cars went by very fast. The main road led to other housing camps and then disappeared into the horizon. I knew it reappeared at the fields where we worked. I did not know this for a fact, but could only guess because it was the only part of town I ever got to see. When we went to work it was still dark. Usually when we returned home it was dark again. I do remember that the best times were at the migrant pre-school. I loved that school! It was my first experience with White people, other than the *Patron*. Tomorrow was Monday and I would be going to school. We went to school two to three times a week from seven to four while mom and dad worked. We never went during the weekend because Saturday and Sunday we were needed in the fields. As we watched T.V. for the final hours before bedtime, mom and dad sat at the table and talked. Dad talked about money and working harder to make more of it. Mom would just listen and nod her head. The discussions usually went in that manner while dad drank his beer.

I heard my mom tell my dad how smart I was. I think he wanted to prove her wrong, or maybe right. "Betito will be smart enough to go to college someday," I heard my mother say to him.

"El flojo! (lazy one) Let's see how smart he is," my dad responded. "Pendeho, (stupid one) bring me a beer!" I went to the bare fridge, grabbed

17

a can of beer and ran it to my dad. I was careful not to shake it. My dad's boot would fly across my backside again if I made bubbles come out of the can. I was speaking from experience. After I handed the beer to my dad, he said, "Si, el tonto is pretty smart." I let out a five-year old sigh as my dad put the beer away in a few gulps. I went and sat down on the cot that I shared with my two brothers. Soon we drifted off to sleep. My mom put a blanket over us as we slept head to toe in our little cot. We kept each other warm that way. As I slept I dreamed of college, hamburgers, and a new day at preschool with the Anglo teachers and no *Patron*.

Some time during the night Carlos and I were awakened by something warm and wet on our feet. Jose wet the bed. This was the reason we slept head to toe; Jose was the head in the opposite direction. He could not help wetting the bed. We found out years later he had a medical condition and ended up having to get the problem fixed by real doctors, not the free clinic doctors that basically told mom to rub his nose in it. Anyway we got used to Jose wetting the bed. As we grew older Carlos and I got creative and would put mats under him. Mom and dad were at a loss for how to help him. Spankings didn't help, so they just gave up and dealt with the problem until we could afford a real doctor. That would not come until later in our lives when dad re-enlisted into the army. Until that time we worked the fields and traveled the harvest roads from Texas to California and even Florida and Georgia. Whatever crop was in season was fair game to my family. But nothing impacted me more than that little preschool in west Texas.

College students ran the migrant preschool. They came from the surrounding towns and I guess they worked there for internships and study hours for their degrees. I loved the days I got to spend with them. On the days we got to go, I was already up and digging in our cardboard box to put on my best clothes. I would be awake before my mom and dad. By the time they came into the main room I would be sitting at the table watching my brothers slowly waking up. My dad would ask my mom why I could not be that excited on the days that I had to work. Mom would just smile and start cooking breakfast on the little gas stove. We would have eggs and poppas, (potatoes), beans, and tortillas. She would always prepare more than we could eat so we could have that for lunch or a snack during the day. Mom would warm a tortilla and put a spoonful of eggs and beans in it and hand it to me. I can still remember how warm it felt in my hands. She would hand a taquito (taco) to my dad and he would eat it while also biting into big green jalapeno pepper. I think those peppers made him meaner. By the time my brothers started eating their tacos I was already at the door headed for the preschool bus stop.

The kids at the migrant camp totaled about twenty. They ranged from the ages of four to six. None of us spoke English very well, but I was able to speak it the best, and speak it first. I made sure I was the first one in line when the bus came so I could be the first one out. As you looked at the children of the camp you could not tell them apart from any other children in America. They were all beautiful and full of life. They would someday surpass their parent's achievements, and were all doing that now by going to school. My mother had never gone to school and I think my dad went up to the fifth grade. We all stood around the pole that had a light on it. It was still dark and cold. Some of us pretended to be grownups and smoked fake cigars and our breath was the smoke. None of us had jackets and some had clothes Goodwill would have thrown away. Jose and I stood close together and waited for the bus. Carlos was too young to go to school. Down the road we could see lights coming, but it was the bus that was taking mom and dad to work. Soon our big yellow bus came down "Project Road" and we started lining up. I once again made sure I was first. I heard a kid behind me tell someone, "My mommy and daddy said he's a pinche little coconut."

There are smells that you can recall from events early in your childhood. Mine are from the preschool. I remember the smell of cinnamon toast and oatmeal spice. As soon as we arrived we were fed breakfast. That was one of the first times I saw bread. I mean bread from a loaf, from a grocery store. Mom and dad never served this stuff. It was flat and had brown crusty stuff on the outside. You know, brown on the outside and white on the inside. Someone had covered it with something really sweet and good. They also served oatmeal. I was disappointed. I did not come here to eat, I came here to learn! As soon as I spotted one of the teachers I made a beeline for them. "Betito! Good to see you again!" I loved it when they spoke my name like that. I was important here.

"Buenos dias, George!" I shouted.

George's eyes flinched. I don't think he was as excited as I was that early in the morning. "Betito, tell me hello in English," George said to me. I thought to myself, okay, okay, I can do this, I can do this. I saw it on the television last night. In my best English I said, "Hello George, how you do?"

I was grinning from ear to ear.

George just patted my head, smiled and said, "You're getting better. Now eat your breakfast and we'll work on it later." I wanted to work on it now. I went ahead and had my toast and oatmeal. It was really good. It was a good change of pace. I knew that for some of the kids it would be the only time they would eat breakfast. There were actually kids poorer than Jose and I. I looked around and noticed Jose was already on his second bowl of oatmeal. Carlos and I swore he had a gusano (tapeworm) in his belly. He would eat and eat and never get fat. He was so skinny mom and dad gave him extra tacos. As the children finished their meal they were divided into different groups and led into the kitchen.

Before the lessons started all the kids were lined up in front of two sinks. We were handed a little paper cup with our name on it. In the cup was a toothbrush. We would walk up to the sink and the teacher would squeeze out toothpaste and they would show us how to brush our teeth. I only did this when I was at school. Mom and dad didn't make us brush our teeth. We had to work the toothbrush up and down in our little mouths until it got foamy. We filled the little cups to rinse with and spit in the sink. Then we had to smile real big for the teacher. George made me open my mouth wide and he would look at all my teeth carefully. "Albert," he would say, "some day what comes out of your mouth will be very important, so you must have pretty teeth." At the time I did not believe a word he was saying. I believed we all had bad breath and this was how they were fixing the problem.

I sat in the front row of all four classes that we had. We were taught reading, math, Basic English, and arts and crafts. As I sat in my English class I watched how the teachers' mouths formed words as they spoke. They all spoke beautiful English. The words flowed and they did not have to stop and think about words before they came out. Wow! I wish I could do that. "Albert, please come to the board," said George. I stood up and walked towards him. George had called me to the front of the class so I could pronounce my name in English. That was way too easy. I told everyone my name was Albert and how I loved coming to school. All the other kids really struggled to say their names in English. After class the teacher gave me a little book. It had a picture of a chango (monkey) on it along with the teacher's name (George). He told me the main character reminded him of me. I wondered if this had something to do with that whole coconut thing.

In the next class we learned to read. I tried to read the little book and a pretty young lady helped me figure out one of the long words. It took me forever to pronounce "curious." It was pretty close to the Spanish word curioso and it meant the same thing. The lady sat with me and helped me say that word over and over. Soon it was easy. Most of the other kids had easy books that talked about cats, dogs, and somebody running. My book had long words in it. I would let everyone back home know how smart I was, but only after recess. First in the playground got the Big Wheel!

When I got to the play area all the big toys were taken. Darn, I thought. I would have to wait my turn. I found a spot against the wall of the building and started to read about George the curious chango. Three boys came by and started asking me why I was reading a book and not playing. I told them I wanted to learn how to read better. That really took them by surprise. I told them I wanted to be able to read books with no pictures someday and go to college. "Oh, este es el pinche little coconut," said the first kid. The second kid responded, "El flojo?" They all turned away from me. "Si, el flojo," the third kid said. The first boy turned back towards me and shouted, "My poppy says you're lazy and you eat all the tomatoes."

"I don't care!" I told them. "I will go to college some day."

They just laughed and walked off. I heard one of them ask the other, "Que es college?"

Jose and I rode the bus home together. We talked about school and the other kids. Jose asked me, "Why do the kids call you coconut?" "I think it's because I am so hard-headed and I have brown hair," I told him. We both laughed it off and we sat quietly in the bus and looked at the funny pictures of the little monkey. "He looks like Carlos in this picture," I told Jose. We laughed again and finished the book. Carlos would be at my mom's side right now. He helped mom as best a three-year-old could. Carlos was very strong for his age and dad was happy that he worked harder than I did. I can visualize the entire scene now: Carlos covered in mud, pulling up the entire plant instead of the tomato and shaking the plant over the basket.

Looking back I can see myself on that bus, sitting in the front seat, leaning my head against the window. I guess I was searching for something as the bus drove through the projects. I was looking for something else, something more. I did not know exactly what it was. Now I know what I was looking for back then. I was looking for my future. Now when I drive through the country and see migrants working the fields I shed a tear for my past. My happy childhood history never happened. I left a little smudge on the glass where my head was pressed against it. I would have pushed my head harder if I could have seen hope on the other side of that little bus window. I catch myself daydreaming about the past, the same way I use to daydream about the future. I've heard it said that if you can see it, it can happen. In one way it worked. I use to pretend I was taller, no longer in the projects, and had on a suit and a nice car like the movie stars. I am now taller, don't live in the projects, wear a suit, and drive a nice car. However, I try to remember a happy little five-year-old, playing, riding a bike and going to school everyday. As hard as I try to see it, it will never happen, because it never did.

"Que se chinge! Tiene que trabajar!" (Too bad, he has to go to work) shouted my dad to my mom. When dad cussed in Spanish like that I knew it was not worth crying about. I was pretty tough for a five-year-old. It's sad that a child can harden at such a young age, but it prepared me for tougher things down the road. Today I wanted to go to school so bad. It was my turn to read to the class and I had been practicing so hard and I was so excited that I was up before my parents again. Mom had prepared her tacos and my brothers were already dressed. Dad was mad and was taking it out on us again, for some reason. He told my mother I would be going to work, not to school today. He wanted me and Jose to help my mother pick tomatoes. I think he counted on a few extra bushels with us helping her. That would add up to about five extra dollars in our paycheck for the week. My school day was being traded for beer money.

That night, we went for a long drive. I heard my dad tell mom that the county we lived in was dry. I knew it was dry. It's a desert out here. If it were not for irrigation nothing would grow in the Texas Panhandle. We would drive all the way to some "wet" county to this little store to buy beer. It may have been wet but it still looked dry to me. Anyway, I did not go to school that day and Jose and I ended up knee deep in mud picking those darn tomatoes again. I would however not be cheated. Someone would have to listen to me read somewhere. I took my little book to the field with me that day, after all I had two little brothers that needed reading lessons.

We started at sun up and stopped working for lunch around noon. I was starving. We all gathered around mom and she handed each of us a taco of beans and eggs. The tacos were cold but they were good. I finished it off quickly and mom gave me another one of beans and leftover rice from last night. My brothers and I shared a can of soda as my dad walked away to talk to the other men. I quickly finished off the other taco and told my mother and brothers I wanted to read to them. My mom smiled and told me to start when I was ready. I sat there and read my little book to my family. Jose understood a little and mom and Carlos looked at each other kind of funny. I didn't care, I just kept on reading. Jose was laughing at some parts of the book, and then Carlos and mom started laughing. I looked up from my book and told them I was not at the funny part yet. I kept reading until I got to the end, closed the book, stood up, and bowed. What a performance! My mom hugged me and congratulated me in Spanish. I knew she did not understand a word I had said. But I didn't care because I knew she loved me and wanted me to get smarter and she also noticed Jose and Carlos were paying very close attention. Off in the distance the *Patron* blew his whistle and it was time to get back to work.

As I picked the tomatoes I kept thinking about school; what were the kids doing today? Today was Friday so I would be working all weekend. This was the only time in my life I wished for Mondays. There was a sense of excitement in the air as we worked because Fridays meant payday. But it really did not matter to me because I wasn't getting paid anything. As the sun fell lower in the western sky I heard the whistle blow again and we slowly made our way to the buses. While we walked towards the bus Jose came up to me and asked me to show him my book. I told him to wait until we got in the bus because I was scared the book would fall in the mud. Another kid that also missed school walked up and started talking to me in English. "Albert, are you going back to school on Monday?"

I told him, "I hope I can go but it depends on my dad." I was excited to talk in English.

The orange sun was descending in the west as if it was falling off the edge of the world. That is exactly how I felt, like I had fallen off the edge and no one was there to catch me. I felt things a five-year should not. I felt so out of place, like I did not belong here. I wanted love, understanding, and a real family. I may have had no understanding of what a real family was, but I knew that this was not it. I needed to be picked up and read to, and I needed someone to share my love for school. I needed so much and had so little. The feelings were so deep I don't know how a child so young could describe them. I had wanted to go to school so bad today! When I watched T.V., I never saw any kids covered in mud and working all day. I must have been daydreaming because I felt someone grab me and shove me into our seat. "Sienta te!" said my dad. I had passed up the seat where we were all sitting. Once everyone was seated the bus driver revved up the old engine and we started rolling. I watched as people dozed off for the ride home. It put a lump in my throat. I looked up and Jose caught my attention.

"Albert, show me your book," he said in his best English. I reached into my red flannel shirt and handed him my book. My dad's head whipped around and in Spanish he asked me, "What did Jose call you?" I told him I had an American name now, and the migrant teachers said my name was Albert, and that I had learned to read the best in my class. In less than one minute I told him how I was becoming so smart and how much I loved school. He was about to say something bad. I knew this because his eyebrows were touching each other. I was glad I was sitting down because he would not be able to kick me. I tensed up and my eyes squinted; I knew what was coming! Then I saw something I had never seen before. My mother reached over and gently touched his arm. I knew she was also scared of dad. He looked at her with his dark eyes and heavy brow. His lips were dark and scrunched together. Her eyes were warm and soft. They were light brown and for that brief moment they were moist, not like a tear, but more like a plea. "Beto, dejalo," (leave him alone) she said softly. My dad wanted to say something but did not. Instead he sat back in his seat and looked at my mother. His eyes began to relax and his brow dropped. My dad was mean, but he loved my mother. I relaxed my shoulders and looked at mom and dad. I knew I better pretend like nothing happened because next time I might not be so lucky.

I still do not know what I did wrong. All I did was talk about school and my new American name. My dad knew how to speak English but rarely did. He used to tell us stories about how he used to run with a gang, fight, drink, and smoke. I remember he told me later in life that if a man did not drink and smoke, he was not a man at all. If that is really the case, dad was one hell of man. He smoked about two packs of cigarettes a day and drank at least two six packs of beer a day. He told us that by the time he was five he was already a man because he was drinking and smoking. I clearly remember that discussion because I got smacked when I asked him why he didn't go to school instead of doing all that bad stuff. Dad's vices would later come back to literally cripple him, but right now the rocking of the bus had put him to sleep. His head was hung down on his big chest. As I looked at my dad I felt no pride or shame for what he was. To me he simply existed. He was my father because of fate and circumstance.

Dad was born in the Mexican border town of Reynosa in 1944. His family was large like most families. There were six brothers and four sisters. I believe he was number three in the order they were born. I don't know very much about his family because I have never met them all and they are not a close family. Sometimes when dad would drink he would tell us stories about growing up in much the same way we were. He never had anything good to say about his dad, just like me. From his stories I guess he grew up poor and sacrificed an education to help support his younger brothers and sisters. His dad was dying of leukemia, which might have been caused by all those cigarettes that made him a man too. I was not sure what caused this disease, but dad said it kept him in and out of hospitals for ten years and he was not supposed to have lived more than two once he was diagnosed. Since his dad could not work he had to drop out and help support the family by working in the fields of South Texas. That is where dad learned his trade. From a young age he worked the fields and even learned how to operate tractors and bulldozers. He sent his money to his family in Mexico. Eventually the entire family would move to Texas with the money he his brothers had earned.

In 1960, his family finally settled down in a small town in the Rio Grande Valley. He had an opportunity to go to school but chose not to. I had heard him tell his mother that it was her fault he had not gone to school. She asked him whose fault it was that he stayed out all night and drank beer and could not go to school the next day? It was a never-ending blame game when my grandmother and her son met. She talked about the times she had to beat him with a stick when he came home drunk. She would start all over again the next morning because he would not go to school. I don't really know if my dad was whipped like we were for just being boys, but I do know my grandmother tried to straighten him out at a young age, however she failed. I don't know if dad ever experienced love from his parents because he never knew how to show anything but anger towards his sons. The man had no sensitive side and to this day I can never recall him hugging us or even saying something as simple as "I love you." Any type of praise would be a shock to us even today. The only person that understood him was my mother, maybe because their lives ran parallel to each other.

My dad never got past the fifth grade. He ran around with gangs and started smoking and drinking more and more. He still brags about beating and stabbing people, but I guess he never realized it didn't impress us. The whole bad boy image might have been what attracted my mother to him. They met when he was eighteen and she was sixteen. My mother and father had a short romance but it was long enough that my mom was expecting her first baby at the age of seventeen. I was supposed to have been the second oldest, but my sister did not live more than a week. She was born severely premature. I have heard it may have stemmed from stress that my mother experienced during her pregnancy. Regardless of whatever happened, dad and mom were married and a year later I came along. Dad was in the army at the time I was born. He had been drafted into the Viet Nam war. When he came back it was the first time I had ever seen him. I was not yet one year old. During his tour of duty he would come home for weeks at a time on leave. That was how my brothers came along. When his tour was over he came back to the Valley and started working in the fields again with my mother and three kids. People said that Viet Nam had affected my dad really bad and that was what made him mean. He never actually went to war but was stationed stateside the entire time he was in the army. That excuse just did not work for me once I was old enough to find out the truth. I do have uncles that were drafted into the service and stayed in. They are very successful businessmen and are doing well. So what happened to my dad? I was thinking this as I watched my dad sleeping, and I snapped out of my trance when he began to snore.

I took advantage of this and squeezed in between my two brothers and continued our reading lessons. Carlos and Jose were like two little Mexican sponges: they kept interrupting me as I read to them. "Que es that word?" they kept asking.

"If you stop asking questions I will tell you!" I told them in a whisper. The bus hit a bump and dad snored louder. Mom was also asleep. She was always tired. We knew she did not sleep much when dad drank because he kept mom up. I knew this because sometimes we could hear her cry through the thin walls of the apartment.

I was so happy to be sharing my book with my brothers. Carlos was catching on well for a three-year-old and Jose was already reading the big words. That's how my brothers learned to read, from the bus, to the fields and then to the school. We learned and relied on each other. To this day we are still close. Not a week goes by that we don't call one another, a bond that comes only from people that share adversity.

Chapter 2
The California Experience

"Mommy it's hot back here!" Carlos complained to my mother.

"Yo se mijo, (I know son)" she replied. We were somewhere in the Mojave Desert on our way to California. My parents were following a dream. They thought they could find a job there and make lots of money to support their three boys. They did not know that fieldwork was the same in every state. From Texas we had gone to Florida for a few months, then back to Texas. Now we were headed out west. I don't blame my parents for trying to better their lives, but at what cost to us? They were headed to California on blind faith. My dad had an uncle who told him he could get him a job, so here we go again. I wondered how long this would last. We left Florida when my dad had gotten drunk and had an accident.

We actually had a family outing at a small lake in Florida. I don't remember the name of the city it was close to. It was on a Sunday and for some reason we did not work that day. We were fishing with cane poles. My dad had made one for each of us and we were sitting on the bank and having a great time. He was drinking beer in the car. When it was time to go my dad called us in to the car. Jose and Carlos got to the car first but I was slow in putting my pole down. Dad told us to leave them for the next kids. By the time I was walking and getting close to the car my dad yelled that he was going to leave me to the alligators and drove off. I ran and grabbed the car door and for a split second I held on. My dad kept driving until he felt a thump under the rear tire. I had lost my grip and the car had run over my leg.

I can still remember the pain and the blood as I screamed.

It turned out to be only a small cut and no broken bones. The emergency room doctor was not buying my mom's story that I had fallen out of the car. My dad was too drunk to go in to the hospital. As soon as we got home dad quickly made plans to head back to Texas. They would not be able to find him there if they chose to follow up on mom's story. Since we had no permanent address we would be difficult to locate. I will never forget that feeling of pain as my dad drove off and left me standing there or the feeling of the car running over my right leg. I can still remember the smell of the emergency room and that cold table where the doctor examined me. I recovered on the road back to Texas. The doctor told my mom he would be filing a police report but by the time the police had that report my dad had traded our car for a truck. That truck would take us back to Texas and on to California.

California would be the culmination of several things for my family. My father's addiction to alcohol would reach a new high. We would stop following the migrant lifestyle and I would begin to develop resentment towards those who hurt me mentally as well as physically. We lived in California for two years. It was the most beautiful state we had ever lived in.

I was called a "wetback" and other words like "greaser" while attending public schools in California. There were very few Hispanics in non-migrant schools in the rural areas where we lived. It was different for the White children to see a little Mexican boy in the same class as them. I guess we Hispanic children were not supposed to be as smart as the White children. I had it set in my mind I would change that. At six years old I could read and write as well as any White child in my classes and in some cases even better. This was my first exposure to regular public schools. In a few classrooms I was the only non-White child. I had started school in migrant classes and the attention I received from the teachers there was paying off. I owe those college kids so much. Their attention to me had helped me prepare for public school. However no one prepared me on how to deal with racism at such a young age.

Racism came from both directions: the more I learned the less Hispanic kids wanted to be around me. I was striving to get smarter while the Mexican kids seemed to be going to school for other reasons. Some were going to school so their parents would not be arrested for not allowing them to go to school. As soon as they reached high school they would drop out. They were not even trying to learn anything. I wanted to get to high school as fast as I could. The kids would talk to me and notice that my English was becoming very clear and polished and take offense to that. I was told by one child that I was turning into a "White boy."

Whites that scorned me in elementary school did not bother me at all. I now know that children only hate other races because it is a learned behavior. They do not develop words like "wetback" on their own. Someone had to have said it first for them to repeat it.

We were riding in the back of an old pickup truck. It had a camper shell now and the window to the cab of the truck was open. Through the window mom would keep watch on us. It was over a hundred and fifteen degrees. We had all the sliding windows open to draw in the hot dry air, but all it did was circulate the heat. We had already taken off our shirts and jeans and were we were in our little white briefs in the back of an old truck. Dad had put boards on the inside of the pickup bed so it would not be as hot. We were raised up off the bed of the truck and we had more storage area. This helped a little bit and least we were not sitting or standing on the hot metal. Luckily I had heard California was very cool. It would be about a two to three day ride in that old truck.

Our life savings were in that old truck. Underneath the slats of wood were boxes of pots and pans and our clothes and blankets. It was very uncomfortable lying on the boards, but we made due. It is hard to imagine that a family of five does not have enough belongings to fill up half the bed of a pickup truck, but Mexican's are survivors. Looking back we made due with so little and every penny we made was accounted for. We spent money only on food and necessities; there was no excess anywhere, except beer and cigarettes. Those were needed. Remember, you could not be a man without those two things. Mom would buy groceries and make them last a long time. She would buy beans, potatoes, flour, and make a feast out of them. If we were lucky we would get to share a soda but most of the time we drank water. During our road trip mom had prepared a box of food that would last the entire trip. She had prepared tacos for the short term. She must have prepared at least four to five dozen tortillas. The good thing about a tortilla is you can wrap it around anything and you have a pretty good snack. She had also boiled two dozen eggs and about five pounds of potatoes. We ate boiled eggs and potatoes with tortillas all the way from Texas to California. It was not a pleasant experience at all in that camper.

My brothers and I made the time pass by reading anything we could. I had a few books from the preschool and we even read labels on cans and boxes of food. We talked about how things were going to be different in California, and hoped we would go to school every day once we got there. I was now six and speaking more English every day. My brothers had learned to read from me and no longer needed help. We slept during the day and watched the lights of the cars at night. We stopped at a few roadside parks to eat and use the bathroom. The desert was different from the fields of Texas. There were more plants here. There were huge cacti, spiny shrubs, and dry brush every where. When we stepped out of the camper we were quick to put our jeans back on. At one stop mom opened a box of clothes and she pulled out our jeans and cut the legs off them for each of us. She just grabbed a pair of scissors and eyeballed the length and cut the legs off those pants. We now would not have to wear underwear in the back of the truck.

When my father stopped at night to sleep, he would first find a store. He would buy a couple of six packs of beer so he could wind down from the stress of driving. My mother would not complain because she could not drive. For some reason all the women from the migrant camps we lived in, did not know how to drive. I don't know if it was a cultural item or the men found it easier to control the women that way. If the women could not drive away, they were stuck to deal with whatever the men dished out. At the roadside park we would crawl out from the camper in our new shorts and stretch our legs. We had to quickly put on our sneakers because the ground was so hot. Most of the parks had no bathroom facilities so we would quickly look for a big bush to hide behind to relieve ourselves. We had to be very careful because some of the bushes were actually cacti. I came close to squatting on one our first night in the desert. We also watched out for snakes and scorpions.

The desert has so much life in it once you walk away from the road. So much of the wildlife in the desert can hurt you if you are not careful. Most of the animals and insects came out at night. From squatting on a cactus to stepping on a scorpion, every rest stop became an adventure. From behind my cactus I heard my mom calling us for dinner.

Mom had laid out dinner for us on the concrete picnic table. The sun was still high in the western sky. There was no shade even though the table had a canopy over it. Dad decided to move the truck closer so it would block the sun. We sat down and had a dinner of tortillas, boiled eggs, and potatoes, again. Dad was drinking his beer and eating a bag of corn nuts. He would take a big swallow and then take a mouthful of nuts. We could hear the crunching as his powerful jaws bit down into them. He was looking off into the horizon. His eyes were squinted and his brow seemed large and dark. In between the beer and nuts he would take a puff from his cigarette. I remember this scene, silhouetted against the desert sunset. Dad had a way of looking larger than life and very powerful with just his facial features. He knew how to use his dark eyes to his advantage. At the time it terrorized me and my brothers. Later as we got older we just laughed it off. He looked down and saw that we had finished our meal and ordered us back into the camper. I asked to stay outside longer and walk around the campsite. He started to stand and I quickly made for the truck. Jose and Carlos were already crawling through the narrow opening of the camper door. I was a little too slow. I felt a boot connect squarely on my rear end, the force of which slammed me against the tail gate of the truck. I was then lifted by one arm and flung inside the camper. I was fortunate my brothers broke my fall.

I looked out of the camper window and my mother had lowered her head like nothing had happened. Like me, she was just numb to the whole thing. My mother cleared the table and dad just sat there and drank his beer and smoked. After the table was done she came to the truck and reached under the wooden slats and took out a heavy blanket. She laid this across the top of the table to form a bed. She lay down and covered her face with her forearm. I don't know if she was doing this to cover her eyes from the orange sunset or to cover her tears. Dad continued to just sit and empty the cans of beer. He would wander into the brush from time to time to use the desert facilities. Secretly, I wished he would fall into a cactus. I told Jose my wish and he laughed. "Do you think the cactus would die if it stuck poppy?" he asked.

"No, but I wish he would." I realized from that point forward I had no feelings of love for my father. The emotions bottling up in me were slowly reaching the boiling point. It would take years for them to fully explode. For now they would sit in me and fester, simmer, and crawl upwards from my subconscious to my conscious being. My brothers and I lay in the camper and whispered to each other. We did not want to draw attention from our father. We listened to noises from the desert. We could hear owls, coyotes and various insects. Those noises slowly put us to sleep. By the time we woke up we were moving again.

The desert gradually gave way to greenery. We could see fields of plants as we came over the hills of dry scrub brush. I wondered if we would be working in those rows of fruits and vegetables. I was not looking forward to that. I was growing weary of the dirt and mud. The truck began to slow down and we pulled into a convenience store. Dad got out and walked over to a pay phone. That was the first time I had ever seen him use a phone. We had never had one in our homes. He spoke into the phone for a few minutes but we were too far away to understand what was going on. I saw him laugh and chuckle. He hung up the phone and came back to the truck. He told mom that someone would come get us soon. We waited in the heat. I noticed that it was no longer dry; it was now sticky and we were sweating. The humidity had made the blankets that we had been laying in smell pretty bad. The boiled eggs and potatoes had not helped much either. I knocked on the glass to get my mom's attention. Instead I got my dad's. I just wanted permission to get out of the camper. The air was no longer flowing in and we were getting very uncomfortable. I was once again greeted by a look that to this day gives me nightmares. I lowered my eyes and crawled backwards away from the glass window.

A small import car pulled in and the occupant waved to my dad. The young man was strikingly handsome. He was taller than my dad and was very clean cut for a Mexican. I say that because he was totally different from what I had seen at the migrant camps. He walked with his head up and his step had an air of confidence. Most of the men at the camps walked with their heads low. Their hair was long and uncombed. The clothes were worn and never truly clean. This man was different. His hair was cut short and parted to one side and it fit his face well. His clothes were simple but clean. He had on nice denim jeans and a white tee shirt. The shirt had no holes or stains on it. His boots were clean and had no mud caked on his soles. This Mexican was totally different. He had an infectious smile. He walked, smiled and waved at the same time. I thought to myself that he must be a movie star. No Mexican could be that happy. He walked up to the truck and shook hands with my dad. He told him in English to follow him. I was about to ask if I could ride with him instead of riding in the oppressive camper. I decided against it. I did not want to bring the wrath of my dad in front of this person.

We followed the young man through farm land that was different from what we were used to in Texas. There were fields and fields of trees. I would later learn the fruit trees were peaches, plums and nectarines. The orchards gave way to a small town nestled in a valley. I remember crossing a railroad track, and it bounced us around in the truck. I thought the jolt would break the wooden boards we were laying on. I think my dad did that on purpose. We drove through a neighborhood of clean white framed wooden houses. They were well kept and all had nice green yards and some had big trees in the front and back yards. This was truly foreign to me. Where were the migrant shanty towns and cheap apartments? Surely we were in the wrong place. We slowly rolled into the driveway of the biggest house I had ever seen. It was huge! The house looked like two homes stacked on top of each other. It was white and had lots of windows. The windows actually had glass in them! The apartments back in Texas had no glass, or windows for that matter. The roof was pointed like a triangle and it was not metal. The big trees provided shade over the house. There was also a smaller house behind the big one. Wow, the Mexicans must live in the little house and the *Patron* lives in the big house. Slowly the truck came to a stop and dad turned off the motor.

The young man honked the horn and within in seconds people came out of the house. They were all Mexicans! Surely the *Patron* would not let all these people in his house. My mom and dad were shaking hands and hugging them while we lay on our bellies and looked out. Finally this big man pointed to the truck. He must have seen our little sweaty faces peering from the camper. The whole clan walked towards the truck. The family consisted of the mother and father and five children. The young man we had followed was about twenty years old. The next two sons were about eighteen and fifteen. The daughter was almost fourteen and the youngest boy was about eight. He had grabbed his mother's skirt, hiding behind her. I think he was frightened by what was hiding in the old truck's camper.

We arrived at my dad's uncle's house a few pounds heavier from all the eggs and potatoes, but at least we had on shorts instead of underwear. My dad called the big man "Tio Marko." He was a large man and towered over my dad. He was built like a big barrel with arms and legs. He opened the camper door and helped us out, asking each of us our name as we crawled over the tailgate. I came out first and told him my name was Albert. He reached under my arms and lifted me out like I was nothing. This man was so strong but so nice. I said my name in English so my brothers did the same thing. Out of the corner of my eye I saw my dad's dark stare bore a hole in me because he wanted us to say our names in Spanish. I didn't care because somehow I knew he would not hurt me with this giant around. My legs were cramped riding in the back of the truck so I was glad to get out. I noticed the teenage girl's nose wrinkled when we walked by. I don't know what her problem was. Maybe Jose's breakfast was catching up with him. He had eaten three tacos of boiled eggs this morning. With the introductions complete we made our way into the house.

My dad said his tio looked like my grandfather. I couldn't remember my grandpa; he was in heaven. One thing I do remember about Tio Marko is that he was always smiling. I thought that to be very strange. His kids were the same way. They all walked around with a smile. I was so confused about this. I talked to the youngest one and asked him, "when do we go to work?"

He looked at me like I was crazy. "I don't work. Mom and dad work. We go to school, you big dummy." He turned around and walked away towards Tia Concha. That was Marko's wife. Concha said something to my mom. I don't know what was said but we all ended up in the guesthouse taking showers. Jose, Carlos and I were all in the shower at the same time. I told them that Marko's kid did not work. Jose said, "Are they lazy like you?"

"No! They don't have to work." That was really strange. They attend school every day?

After our shower I got dressed in clothes I had never seen before. Mom had laid them out on the bed in the guest house. The guest house was the nicest house I had ever been in. It turned out the clothes belonged to the kid that had called me a big dummy. His name was Jimmy and he also had an English name like me. I was getting bigger every year and I was almost as big as Jimmy even though I was only six. My shoulders were getting very wide and my arms were getting thicker. All that hard work had made us strong and tough, which would soon come in useful. I also noticed no one had made any comments about my hard head. Jose and Carlos still had to wear our old clothes. The family did not have any clothes that would fit my brothers.

Some of the migrant camps we had lived in did not have showers. They had old tubs that we had to fill with a water hose. I remember my mom boiling water and pouring it in the tub to get it warm. The closest we had to a shower was another water hose that hung over a tree limb. Someone had built a plywood wall around the water pipe. We would turn it on after entering the cover of the four wooden walls. We could turn the water on and off by turning the little handle on the spout. The water was always very cold. We never used that "shower" in the winter only in the summer. But this place also had a real bathroom inside. We looked behind a door and there was a real working toilet inside, just like the one at the preschool. I reached over and pushed the handle down just to hear the swooshing sound. We had outhouses at some of the camps we had lived at and you never hear a "swoosh" when you used the outhouses, just a "plop."

Jose and I walked around the guest house and we both stopped and looked down at the same time. What was this stuff we were standing on? Part of the house had wooden floors but the bedroom had fuzzy stuff on it. Carlos walked over and started looking at the floor also. We kneeled and rubbed it with our hands. "What is it, Betito?" Carlos and Jose asked.

"I think its fake grass," I told them. I was grasping for anything to appear smart since I was the oldest. All three of us were on our hands and knees rubbing the carpet. We suddenly heard a girl laughing so loud I thought she was going to burst.

"We call it carpeting! Where are you guys from, Mexico?" she asked in between her laughs. I didn't want to tell her that one camp we had lived in had dirt floors inside the houses. "Let's go eat," she said after she stopped laughing

That dinner was like a feast! The grownups sat at a table in a big room with paintings on the wall. My mom commented on the art work and how the portraits of the family were so beautiful. Tia Concha said that Jacob had painted them in college. My head snapped around so fast at those words I almost spilled my food on the floor. College! I thought to myself. Did she say college? I had a huge plate of food and I was walking to the kid's table when I heard Concha say those words. I had to find out who Jacob was. I turned around and took my plate to the grown up table and began looking for an open chair. I walked past my dad's spot and purposely did not meet his gaze. All the sudden I felt my hair being ripped off the top of my head. My dad had reached over and pointed me in the direction of the kids table with my scalp as a steering wheel. The only problem was I was facing one way and my scalp was pointing in the other! I turned in the same direction as my dad's hand and walked back towards the kids table. My eyes turned and filled with tears that gave away the pain as I sat down to eat. I was sure I had a bald spot on the top of my head. A tear fell into my plate but I did not cry; I was too hungry and I was sure the food would be good.

My plate was fully loaded with chicken that had this crusty stuff on the outside along with rice, beans and tortillas. I picked up the chicken and asked Jimmy, "What is this type of chicken called?" Jimmy said they called it "fried chicken." I took a bite carefully, not knowing what to expect. It was so good! I took another bite, and then tore into it. I almost choked. I heard Jenny, the fourteen year old girl say, "Chew then swallow!" She did not realize we had been surviving on beans, eggs and potatoes for so long, and this was the best food I had eaten in ages. I looked over and Jose and Carlos looked like they needed the same advice. They both had chicken coming out of the corners of their mouths. Then I noticed that Jenny and Jimmy were not eating. They just sat and watched us as we ravenously took huge bites of chicken. Instead of eating they bowed their heads, placed their hands together and closed their eyes. I watched this with a mouthful of fried chicken. What in the world were they doing? Soon we would be finding Christ through this wonderful family. But for now I had discovered fried chicken

My brothers and I finished our plate of fried chicken and we did not eat much of the beans and rice. We already had plenty of that. I looked down and my leftovers looked like a chicken graveyard. Jenny and Jimmy were giggling at all the bones that were piled up in front of me. I laughed with them and so did Jose and Carlos. "You don't have any room for dessert now," said Jenny.

"Desert, I don't like desert. It is way too hot and there are snakes there." Jimmy lowered his head and almost spit out the food he had in his mouth because he was trying not to laugh so hard.

Jenny looked at me and said, "I said dessert, like cake and pies." I still had a blank look on my face. I looked back at her with a frustrated face and she pushed her chair back and left the room. Jimmy now had tears coming out of his eyes as he was tried not laugh. My brothers and I continued to wonder why they wanted to give us back to the desert. Jenny walked back into the room with three little plates that had a wedge-shaped object on it. She placed it in front of me after taking the chicken carcasses back to kitchen. I had seen something like this on T.V. once.

I lowered my nose to smell the glossy brown object. It smelled good. I got a bit too close and my nose touched the thick shiny stuff on top of the cake. I raised my head and Jimmy let a spray of chicken all over the table. I had a patch of brown stuff stuck to the tip of my nose. Jenny quickly set him straight. She said Christians should not laugh at each other. Jenny looked at me and stuck her finger in the top of her cake and then stuck her finger in her mouth. Carlos and Jose stared at me waiting for my approval. I rubbed my finger against my nose and looked at the stuff on it. I closed my eyes and stuck my finger in my mouth. My eyes opened in excitement. Jose and Carlos thought I was probably poisoned because my eyes were open so wide. I looked down and stuck two fingers into the wedge and stuck them in my mouth. Carlos and Jose did the same. Jenny was losing her patience. By the time she got our attention we had chocolate all over our mouths and hands. She looked at us each in the eye and showed us how to work a fork. She cut a small piece and placed it in her mouth; she was so lady-like. I tried to do the same but my fingers were covered with frosting. I looked towards Jose and Carlos and both their little mouths and lips had chocolate all over them; but why were they looking over my head in terror?

I slowly turned my chocolate stained face and saw my dad towering over me. He looked like he was ready to explode! I closed my eyes and waited for the strike, but nothing happened. I opened one eye slowly and saw an even bigger man standing behind dad. Tio Marko had grabbed my dad's arm before he could bring it down on my head. The giant looked squarely into my dad's eyes. The smiling giant had turned his brow into one just like dads. "Not in my house. Those kids are now part of my family and we don't hit our kids in my family! Understand?" His smile quickly came back and he wrapped his big arm around my dad's shoulders and they walked out together.

"Breathe," I heard Jenny say to me. I noticed I was scrunched up real tight in my chair, still waiting for the beatings to begin. "My mother and father never spank us," Jenny said.

"Well my father never spanks us either," I told Jenny. Carlos and Jose looked at me like I had just grown a horn out of my head. "He just beats us half to death; the other half he saves for tomorrow," I told her. I knew what was going to happen tonight. My dad would not be denied an opportunity like this. We had made a mess with the cake and then embarrassed him in front of his uncle; we were dead meat. My brothers and I did not finish our cake. We had plenty of room in our little bellies but now something else had filled it. The chocolate experience had been bittersweet: it tasted wonderful and I loved it, until my dad had come into the room. The room in our tummies that should have been filled with my first chocolate cake was now full of terror. I had a huge ball in my stomach called fear and hate. Jenny walked over and grabbed me by the hand and led me out of the room. "You boys go outside and play. We women are going to be busy cleaning your mess," she said.

For the rest of the afternoon our two families visited and caught up. My dad and his uncle talked about work and money. He would regularly hug my dad. It turned out my dad's dad and Marko were brothers. Unfortunately for both of them my grandfather had passed away a few years ago. Marko kept telling dad how much he favored his brother. My dad and his uncle had been sitting on the front porch talking as they watched the sunset behind the mountains in the west. Dad got up and started walking towards the truck. It was "Miller Time," I told Jimmy. I had learned that from T.V.

We were playing with this funny egg-shaped ball. Jimmy kept grabbing it with one arm and trying to run over me. He would occasionally use his other arm to shove me out of the way. When he got to the tree that he said marked the end zone he would throw the ball down as hard as he could. He had told me to throw him the ball and he would run it back and then I was to "tackle" him. I threw the ball as far as I could and it went over his head. I heard him say "wow" as he turned and chased the ball. I had been keeping an eye on dad and Marko. They were both leaning on the truck's hood. My dad walked around and opened the passenger side door. I knew what he was doing. He opened a white styro-foam icebox and grabbed a can of beer. I could see from here it was still wet and it was still probably cold. Marko put his huge hand on dad's shoulder and shook his head back and fourth. Dad regrettably put the can back. Then the lights went out.

Jimmy was fast and he had built up a good head of steam when he ran over me. By the time I got up he was dancing like a chicken and throwing the ball into the ground. I could hear Marko and my dad laughing. "What do they call this game?" I asked Jimmy.

"Boy, this man's game is called football." He had leaned into my face to tell me this. "Your turn," he said as he pointed down the yard and told me I was to run the ball back. I ran to the same place where he had stood and he threw the ball to me. It hit me right in the chest. I scrambled to pick it up while Jimmy charged towards me yelling all the way. I finally got the ball and started running towards him. In my mind I pretended my dad was behind me, chasing me, trying to kick me with his big boot. I hit Jimmy full stride and my shoulder hit him in the chest. He went down like a sack of poppas. I did not even break stride. I kept on running and started doing the same dance Jimmy had done earlier. When I looked back my dad and Marko were standing over Jimmy. My dad's eyes were burning and I could not meet his gaze. Marko then started laughing as Jimmy recovered. "How does it feel now?" Marko said. "You did the same thing to him earlier didn't you?" Jimmy tried to laugh through the pain. Soon I would be feeling more pain than anyone could imagine. "How long has Betito been playing football?" Marko asked my dad. "At least one hour," he replied. The sun was beginning to set and we were all getting ready for the night.

Tia Concha showed my mom to the guest room again and we all got ready for bed. Mom made us shower again while she and dad talked in the bedroom. I noticed a big bruise on my chest from where Jimmy had run over me. My brothers and I did not say a word as we washed. We got out of the shower and I saw dad looking outside between the curtains. The lights were slowly going out in the big house. He waited until the lights were out for awhile before he started. We were beaten one at a time. I always went first. He kept telling us if we screamed it would be worse. My body was numb. I wouldn't scream no matter how hard I was beaten. I knew if Marko saw what was going on he would do the same thing to my father. I considered yelling at the top of my lungs so I could wake the sleeping giant. I decided against it. What if he didn't hear me? Would it be worse for my brothers? I took the best my dad had to offer. I didn't cry or shed a tear. I felt like a rug having the dust beaten out of it. I just went with the direction of the punch or kick. It lasted for a few minutes; it might have been hours or days for all I knew. I can only imagine the terror my brothers must have felt as they watched what was happening to me and knowing they were next. We each got what he said we deserved. When he finished we were laying on the floor sobbing on the blankets my mom had laid out for us. My sides hurt from the kicks and the blows. I realized he had not touched my face. Usually I got at least one slap across the face or on the ears. This time all the hitting was done on my stomach, ribs, and rear end. My mother was lying on the bed and once again she did nothing. She just covered her face and cried. As we lay on the floor, my brothers sobbed until they fell asleep. I had too many experiences today to sleep so I just pretended. Too much had happened and sleep was impossible for now.

A new game had been introduced to me today that would draw me to it like a magnet. I already loved the game and had only played it for an hour. No wonder dad always turned the T.V. off when it came on. He had never let us watch the games on the television. If he caught us watching it, he would beat us. Now it was starting to make sense. Dad did not want us to have fun. I had also had my first taste of chocolate. It was almost as good as fried chicken. California was turning out to be a wonderful place. I really liked Marko's family and I wished I could be his son instead of the monster that was sitting in the dark, still breathing hard from the beatings he had just given us. I lay there thinking of all the things that had happened today. Then I heard my dad stand up and I tensed up once again. Surely he was not going to beat us again? I stopped breathing for a few seconds. Maybe if I pretended to be asleep a little harder he would not notice me. Then I heard the door open and close. The monster had left.

As I was slowly dozing off I dreamed of fairy tales like those of dragons and knights. George from the preschool had read stories like these and I loved how the hero always won the princess and would slay the evil monsters and dragons. I heard the door open and I imagined that the evil monster came back to his lair with his prize. The ice chest of beer had become a chest of gold. I fantasize that I ride up to the guest castle on my white steed and challenged the monster to come outside! I demanded the huge troglodyte meet me on the field of honor. I quickly remembered that cave dwelling trogs beat kids and have no honor. I dismount my white horse, unsheathe my mighty sword and head towards the door. With a mighty kick from my armored boot I shake the entire castle. "Come out you trog!" I yell. "Have you no honor!" I yell at the top of my lungs. I use the armored suit as a battering ram and break down the monster's door. I circle the huge beast with a raised sword. It also has a weapon in its huge hairy hands. I raise my battle sword higher to strike the demon. The huge sword strikes towards the villain's head quickly at first then begins to slow down, then slower, until finally it stops before I can damage one hair on its massive head. It has used its magic secret weapon on me. I hear a "pfft", it has opened the can of magic beer to put me to sleep again. It always happens before I can strike the monster dead.

Chapter 3
The Scarring

"Hurry up we're going to be late!" Jimmy yelled. I would never be late to my first day of school. He wasn't waiting on me. I was waiting on my brothers and mother. Today she was going to register us at the city elementary school. My Tia Concha was already at school ready to sign us up. She worked there as a teacher's aide. I had been dressed in Jimmy's hand-me-downs for an hour and had been waiting for everyone else. Mom was desperately trying to find something decent for my brothers to wear. She found the cleanest, oldest clothes and dressed Jose and Carlos and slicked back their hair with her fingers. Jose's hair was sticking straight up on the top of his head so mom licked her palm and then pressed his hair down. She had to do it a couple of times until his hair finally lay down. My dad was the one that had cut our hair so it wouldn't do any good to complain. After all the fuss was over she stepped back and looked at her little men. I remember her eyes shedding a tear, this was the first time we had registered at a real school. We were now officially going to begin our education. This was not a migrant school with volunteer teachers, this was the best California had to offer.

We walked to the school since it was only few blocks away. The scenery was so different from the bus drive to the migrant school in Texas. There was no loud school bus or groups of kids that could not speak English. This was a real school with kids who did not have to work in the fields. It was all foreign to me but I was sure I could adjust. As we walked we saw other kids making their way to school. Jimmy led the way and I walked next to him.

Poor Carlos and Jose had to walk to school holding mom's hand. Jimmy was waving to other kids along the way, and the sun shined through walnut trees that towered overhead. It was a beautiful morning, nothing short of perfect. The school house suddenly appeared as we turned right at the next block. I suddenly stopped and my jaw dropped. It just sprang up and took up everything I could see. My eyes struggled to take it all in. The school building was red brick and surrounded with trees. Children stood around the front of it, near two long skinny poles. Cars were dropping off children at another driveway to the side of one building. There was so much going on. Jimmy turned around and said, "Hurry up! What's the problem?" I suddenly realized I was frozen in my tracks.

I took a few running steps and caught up with Jimmy. He started telling me that he wanted me to be on his football team as he rubbed his chest. He said it still hurt a little bit, only when he laughed. I was going to get to play football with other kids! I had so much to look forward to. The road suddenly turned to concrete and we were walking on school property. Jimmy said he was to take us to the office and talk to his mom. We walked through a breezeway and it led to a big door marked "office." Jimmy grabbed the door knob with both hands and he motioned for me to walk through; I could feel my mom and brothers coming in behind me. Tia Concha was there and she was all smiles as she greeted us. She asked us to sit down while she got all the forms ready. Jimmy waved goodbye to us and then he hugged his mom and left the office. On his way out he told me he would be looking for me during recess. He would be setting everything up for the big game. I really didn't know what he was talking about. My Tia motioned for my mom to come around this long counter and take a chair. They talked and signed papers while my brothers and I sat in the front area of the office. Kids would walk in with notes that they handed to the grownups and sometimes a parent would walk in holding their child's hand. There was so much going on, it was all so exciting. I was ready to start but what was the holdup? A tall lady walked to where my mom and Tia were talking and they exchanged a few words. I noticed mom was talking in Spanish with everyone. The tall lady said that I would be going with her, and the other boys would meet their teachers shortly. The tall lady turned away from my mom with a big smile and then started walking towards me. I had been leaning forward so I could listen in on their conversation. I had heard her name was Mrs. Mendez.

Mrs. Mendez came around the counter and caught me stretching forward so I could eavesdrop on the grownups. She gave me a puzzled look so I quickly sat back in my chair and tried to look as innocent as I could. "Albert, are you ready to go to class?" I was shocked! I had never been called Albert. I had been always called Betito. I just looked up and nodded. I was not sure how to respond. Nodding was the easiest thing to do. She extended her hand and I reached out for it hesitantly, I had one eye on my teacher and the other on my mother. My mom waved at me and I felt better. I looked over at my brothers and waved goodbye to them. I felt like I was taking a step in the right direction for the life that lay ahead. Mrs. Mendez led me out the office door and back out to the front of the school and into the parking lot. I was scared for a minute because I thought she was going to send me back home. I was puzzled because all the kids were lined up in front of the two skinny poles. There were lots of kids, short ones, tall ones, Anglos and Hispanics. They were all in straight lines, one next to each other, in no particular order.

Mrs. Mendez took me to one line and placed me at the end of it. I noticed two grown-ups were hanging towel sized cloths on strings on the two poles. One towel was red, white, and blue. The other towel had a hairy dog looking thing on it. A very tall man walked in front of the lines and smiled at everyone. He winked at a few kids and teachers and turned to face the poles. The two adults pulled on ropes that ran up the side of the poles and the two towels began to rise. All the children then placed their right hands on the middle of their chest. As both towels were almost halfway up I heard the tall man say, "I pledge allegiance to the flag of the United States of America." I turned around and looked to see every child saying the same thing. I saw Jose and Carlos at the other end of the lines looking as confused as I was. Mrs. Mendez leaned down and placed my hand on my chest. She put her arm around my side as she whispered in my ear to follow along. I flinched in pain, she had pressed against the bruise I had gotten last night from the evil trog. She pulled back in surprise as I wiggled loose from her grip. By that time the entire schools kids were saying, "indivisible, with liberty and justice for all."

After the kids stopped talking the tall man welcomed everyone and the teachers led the children into the hallways that connected to classrooms. I looked up at Mrs. Mendez. She was tall for a Hispanic woman, I guess. I can only compare her to the women at the camps and my mom. She was also very pretty. Her hair was in a dark stylish bob. Her clothes were very clean and neat. She had on a skirt and matching top. I kept looking at her up and down. She had on shoes that I had never seen before. It was like she was perched up on little points. The women from the camp usually only wore canvas sneakers like me. I had never seen one in those things. They were dark but had a shiny finish to them. I would never see anyone wearing this to the fields. Not even the teachers at the migrant preschool wore anything like this. Mrs. Mendez must have realized I was frozen in place so she leaned down and asked me in Spanish: "Stas listo? (are you ready?)"

I looked up and said. "Si, but I do speak English." She smiled and asked me to follow her. She looked over my head and asked the entire class of about fifteen boys and girls to follow her. I followed my new teacher and behind me was my new student body. I realized I was at the front of the line again!

Mrs. Mendez took us to our classroom and everyone found their seat. After everyone was seated she looked around for an empty desk. She found one and slid it to the front of the class. I took my seat and looked around. The class smelled like old books and kids. It was so exciting. While I was busy looking over my classroom my teacher asked me to stand in front of the class and tell everyone my name and a little something about myself. She looked at me and said not to be scared as I made my move to the front. I whispered to her I was okay as I passed by her. I stood at the front of the class and looked over my new audience. I had done this before, in English and Spanish so I was a little confused. I looked over at my teacher and asked her what version she would like to hear. She said to use the short English story. I told everyone my name was Albert, and that I had come all the way from Texas. Someone in the back shouted, "Where's your horse and gun?" I looked at my teacher puzzled. She told the class that not everyone from Texas had a horse and gun. I told everyone I was not a cowboy and I could also speak Spanish. I was on a roll and I was going to let everyone know I could play football but my teacher said that was enough.

"We will begin by reading a book called "Curious George," said Mrs. Mendez. My eyes lit up with excitement. I knew this book! I raised my arm in anticipation. "Yes, Albert?" asked Mrs. Mendez.

"I know this story. Do you want me to help you read it?"

Mrs. Mendez looked at me very puzzled. She was very surprised that I knew the story and was offering to help. "Thank you Albert. I'll do it for know." I just smiled and nodded at her. She began to read the story and I was mouthing the words because I knew what was coming. I had also started telling the kids around me what was coming. The teacher had to tell me to hush. I felt a little embarrassed because I had to be told to be quiet. I sat on my hands and scrunched my lips. I would be quiet this time. She just didn't know I had so much to share.

The class continued on and the teacher did what teachers do. I sat in my desk and I spent the entire day just looking at what a real classroom looked like. I felt little eyes on me from all sides. It was at this point that I began to notice that I was the only Hispanic in the class. I was beginning to wonder where all the Mexicans were. I looked back at the kids exactly the same way they looked at me, curious and cautious. I had never been surrounded by so many Anglo kids in my life! They were all the same as I was, so why were they all staring at me? I rubbed the top of my head. Maybe my coconut was showing. I kept looking around and smiling back at the kids; whatever they saw in me was confusing. I was just a little kid like them. The only difference was that I was just a little darker than they were.

During lunch I was sitting down at the table and heard a kid say, "We've got a new wetback in class." First it was coconuts, now it was wetback. My head is hard and my back is wet. Those kids had it all wrong. They were also talking about how the Mexicans needed to stay out in the fields and their kids should be out there with them. They did not know that I had been out in the fields before and now it was time for me get out. I could not understand why I was supposed to stay out there. I wanted to get an education just like they were getting.

After lunch we went to recess. In the playground I began looking for Jimmy, but he found me first. "Come on, we've got to get you on the field quickly!" he told me. I ran to the open field next to the school and there were two groups of kids out there. They were facing each other. There were about eleven kids on each side of an imaginary line. We ran out there and everyone greeted Jimmy with yells to get the game going. I heard someone say, "Bring on your secret weapon!" Jimmy motioned to me and our side of the line made a tight circle when the biggest kid on our team yelled, "Huddle up!" Jimmy had to lead me along and he grabbed me by the shoulder and pushed me inside the huddle. The kid that was barking orders to everyone, then looked me in the eye and said, "I heard you're the fastest Mexican out here."

I looked around and Jimmy was the only other Mexican on the field, and I knew I was faster than him. He must be right, so I looked and the big boy and nodded.

"I need you to run down the field as fast as you can and I am going to throw you ball," he said with a mean look in face. He kind of scared me; he was as big as I was but he just looked mean. I nodded again. He reached over and grabbed the collar of my shirt and pulled me towards him and he said, "Look greaser, don't drop the ball!" He let me go and we each went to a predetermined spot on that imaginary line again. Jimmy positioned me at the end of it and whispered directions to me as he made little pictures for me on the palm of his hand with his fingers. Okay, now the pressure was on. I knew if I dropped the ball that big kid would whip me good. I had already gotten a beating the night before and I did not want another one in front of all these kids. Jimmy told me that when the big kid said "hut one," I was to run down the field as fast as I could and I would get the ball thrown to me. I looked in front of me and a little red headed boy was looking like he wanted to hurt me too. "Bring it on, Mexican!" he growled at me. Well, at least everyone knows my nationality.

"Set, hut one!" The big boy yelled. I took off running and the little red headed boy started chasing me. I was taking large strides like when I ran from my dad or chased Jose. I looked over my shoulder and the big boy threw the ball. I can still see that ball to this day, turning in a nice tight spiral in the clear California sky, silhouetted in the sun. Even though I had only played football the previous day, there was an intense desire to catch that ball. I don't know if it was because I had something to prove or I was falling in love with the sport. Maybe I just wanted to prove that my hands were not greasy, I don't remember. I was fixated on that ball and I could not take my eyes off it. If the pros could have seen me, they would have hired me on the spot. I caught the ball with both hands and held on to it like my dad holds on to a beer with his big hands. I held it so tight no one could have pried it away from me. I could feel and hear the red head chasing me, but his footsteps were getting farther and farther behind. I closed my eyes and ran faster and faster. Then I heard the footsteps behind me stop and the kids started yelling, and booing. I looked over my shoulder and the kids had started yelling at me to stop. I guess I had run far enough, a few kids were running around with both arms pointing skyward. I started dancing like a chicken and threw the ball into the ground like Jimmy had taught me. "Not bad for a Mexican," the red headed boy told me as he ran up to me. He did not look happy. I felt like a real football player and most importantly I felt like a normal kid. My side of the team started jumping all over and slapping me on the back. I was so excited I did not notice the pain it was causing from my bruises. We started heading back to class because someone said the bell was going to ring.

The rest of the class was uneventful; we read and learned how to do math. It was easy and I had no problems at all. Some of the White kids were struggling. I offered to help them and they gave me dirty looks. One kid called me a "dumb Mexican." Dumb? I was trying to help him because he was having problems. I was learning the ropes of the pecking order. The bigger kids had all the respect from the smaller kids. The smart kids did not get that much respect, and then came the Mexicans. I was one the biggest and smartest kids in the class so I thought I should be top dog. I was completely wrong. Hispanics were at the bottom of the list, until it came time to play football. Then I was important, everyone would want me on their team. When it came to other activities I had to wait to get selected or stand on the side and watch the White kids. If only there were more Mexican kids around. I could be a big shot with them. I decided to talk to Jimmy after school. He told me to wait by the flag poles and we would walk home together.

"Jimmy, what's a wetback?" I asked him as we walked towards his house.

He turned and looked at me in the eyes and then dropped his head. "Albert, that's what they call us. It means that you crossed the river and came to America illegally."

"I just ignore it when the kids call me that."

It looked like I had just taken the wind out of his sails. I had so many more questions. I wanted to know what river was he talking about and how I could "come" to America? I was born in Texas, and knew Texas was in America. Now I was getting confused. I figured I would find out the pieces to this puzzle a little at a time. Jimmy looked like someone had punched him in the stomach. We continued to walk home and we talked about the game. Jimmy told me they had never seen anyone outrun "little red." I didn't think he was that fast, but what did I know, I had only been a pro, if only for a day. Besides, they had never seen me run from dad. We neared the house and there was no activity around it. Our old truck was parked in the front but I could not see mom or dad anywhere. Jimmy said that we could watch T.V. until his mom came home. We watched some shows as Jimmy prepared a funny food I had never seen before. He took two slices of bread, and put this brown sticky stuff on one side and this red runny stuff on the other slice. He then slapped the two pieces together and handed them to me. "Eat up pro, we'll have dinner later when mom comes home." I looked at the stuff and sniffed it. "What's wrong, haven't you ever had peanut butter and jelly before?" he asked with a laugh. "I thought butter was yellow," I told him. I thought Jimmy was going to hit the floor laughing. When I took a bite it stuck to the roof of my mouth. I thought I was going to choke! Jimmy handed me a glass of cold milk and I took a big gulp of it. I was finally able to wash down the big bite I had taken. Jimmy was still giggling at me. "I can't believe you don't know what peanut butter and jelly is. Yesterday you had never seen fried chicken and chocolate cake. Where are you from?" He asked. "What do you get to eat for your birthday?"

"Jimmy, if it can't be wrapped in a tortilla, I have probably never seen it or ate it," I told him. "As far as my birthday, what's that got to do with chocolate cake?"

Jimmy led me out to the patio, and told me we needed to talk. He explained to me how every birthday he has a big party and gets presents, almost like Christmas. I must have had a look that gave away my ignorance. "You don't know what I'm talking about do you?"

I shook my head and he explained birthday parties and Christmas presents. I had never had either one. I suddenly felt very cheated and deprived. I figured I had at least six presents coming and a whole lot more for Christmas. Jimmy told me kids that are good get presents from Santa Claus. I had always been good and I wanted to talk to this Santa guy. I explained to Jimmy that my mother and father never had birthday parties or Christmas. He put his arm around my shoulders and I guess he thought I was going to cry. I wasn't going to cry, I was too ignorant to know what to cry for. No, I would not cry. I will never cry for what was never offered. About that time Tio Marko pulled up in his truck with mom and dad.

Mom walked towards me and gave me a big hug. I had so much to tell her. I told her I loved school and could not wait to go again tomorrow. She smiled and hugged me again. I suddenly winced in pain as she squeezed a little too hard. I was still very sore from the battle with the troglodyte last night. Mom looked at me kind of funny and lifted up my shirt. Along my side she saw black and blue marks. Jimmy saw them also in disbelief. "I'm sorry Albert, did I do that yesterday?" he asked.

"Yeah, you sure did." I lied, as I punched him gently on the arm. My mother knew I had lied also. She lowered her head and walked inside the house. Dad and Tio Marko stayed outside. In the Mexican culture men do not help prepare meals. That job belongs to the girls and women. Tia Concha was walking up with Jose and Carlos in each hand. They both had stars in their eyes. They were as excited as I was. Tia let go of their hands and they ran towards me.

"We heard you outran Little Red!" yelled Jose. I was all smiles and Jimmy just started laughing. "Let's get the football and practice," he said. He disappeared into the house and that gave me time to drop the bomb on my brothers.

"What! We're supposed to get cakes and toys!" Jose said as his lower jaw hit the floor.

"Yeah, Jimmy told me all about it," I said. My brothers and I all turned and looked at my dad at the same time. He looked back at us and we all quickly dropped our gaze as well as our voices.

"Are you sure?" Jose asked.

"Well, Jimmy told me that on birthdays and Christmas we are supposed to get toys and cake," I told them, trying to reinforce my point and sound a little more convincing. We all turned and looked at my dad at the same time again.

"Go ask dad if we will have Christmas this year," Jose told me.

"No way," it was early October and I wanted to live till December to see my seventh birthday. I might be a dumb Mexican but I was not stupid. Jimmy came out from the house and threw me the football. "Come on, let's get ready for tomorrow," he shouted as he ran into the yard. I hated to tell him that I would not be going to school the next day, we never went to school two days in a row. I would go along with his plan and get ready to face Little Red again.

We threw the ball back and forth, and Jose tried to keep me from catching it. That's when we found Jose could leap like a deer, and he was faster than me! He was always a skinny kid and I guess that's what made him fast. I was thick and tall, he was tall and skinny. The one year difference between us did not affect his height. We were both the same height, I just outweighed him.

Jimmy had this big grin on his face like he was planning something. He had the ball in his hands and called us both over. "Who's the fastest?" he asked. I pointed at Jose as he nodded. "Great, I have got a plan." He placed me way over to right and Jose way over to the left. "Hut one!" he yelled. He threw the ball at me then repeated the process over and over again. He would throw at me then Jose until were both tired. He was trying to throw the ball over our heads but we just kept running under it. I noticed Tio Marko and dad had stopped talking and had been watching us for quite a while.

"I bet you are proud of those boys, they are strong and fast," He said. My dad just nodded. "They are going to be good football players like my boys. In fact they play Friday night. Let's go watch them." Tio Marko slapped my dad lightly on the shoulder. Once again my dad just nodded. I knew we were not going anywhere. Fridays are payday and we have to find a "wet" town to buy beer. We played in the yard for about an hour. Carlos had taken a seat on the steps and was reading a book. He would look up from time to time. He had learned to read on the trip through the desert and now was hungering for more knowledge just like me. California was turning out to be a wonderful state, except for the scars.

"Come and eat!" Jenny stuck her head out the door and yelled at us. All the men made their way into the house.

Dinner was not as exciting as the day before. I dared not go near the grown-up table again. I sat at the kids table. Today we were eating food my mom had helped prepare. I knew this because there were beans again. Jimmy was eating them up with a fork in one hand and tortilla in the other. My brothers and I just looked at him like he was a nut. As soon as Jimmy and Jenny had said their prayer he just tore into them like we had done with the fried chicken. He said that his mom never made fresh beans and tortillas anymore. I told him to stop eating and watch me. I grabbed a tortilla, tore off a little piece and made a tiny scoop out of it. With the larger section I shoved beans into the little part and raised it to my mouth. I repeated the process several times so he could watch. Jenny called me a slob and kept on with her fork. Jimmy told me if we didn't use our forks we were going to get grounded.

"Grounded, what's that?" I asked. "Is that when Tio Marko throws you into the ground?" Jimmy and Jenny both froze and looked at me and my brothers. We all looked serious. Jimmy put his fork down and told Jenny we did not even know about birthdays and Christmas so how were we supposed to know about grounding.

Jenny looked at me and said, "Grounding is when you don't get to watch T.V. or play outside. It's what happens when you get in trouble."

My brothers and I looked at each other with a dumb look. "We've been grounded almost all our lives!" Jose said with his eyes looking pretty confused.

I looked at Jimmy and said, "We don't get grounded, just stomped into the ground." Jimmy thought we were joking and tore into his beans again. After dinner we played again in the front yard. The women had the responsibility to clean the kitchen and wash the dishes. The men all went outside to talk business.

We played football and dad and Tio Marko talked until dark. We made our way to the guest house and prepared for bed. It was so nice to have a bathroom inside as well as a shower. I loved the way the warm water washed over me. I was not used to hot water very often, this was a treat. I just stood underneath the spray and soaked it all in. Jose got tired of waiting and pushed me out of the way. What a life, sharing a private moment like a shower with two brothers. Since the water was starting to get cooler I got out of Jose's way so he and Carlos could finish. We got out and start toweling off. I got the smart idea of rolling up my towel and snapping Carlos on the rear end when he bent over to dry his feet. The loud "snap" was almost as loud as the yelp he gave as he leaped into the air. He was about to start crying when my mom poked her head in the bathroom and told us that our dad was coming and if he heard us fighting we would get a beating again. Carlos sucked in the pain of the towel snap and I had a look of fear. If dad heard Carlos crying we would all get a beating tonight.

Carlos was the toughest and strongest out of the three of us. I think it's because mom and dad treated us all the same even though we are not the same age. Dad did not take into consideration that Carlos was two years younger than me when he dealt out discipline or beatings. Those experiences along with being the baby brother toughened Carlos at an early age. He gritted his teeth and gave me a look that told me revenge was coming, but he never cried out loud. We both knew that dad was a lot more painful than that towel snap. We finished getting ready for bed together, we lay blankets on the floor of the little guest house as mom entered the bathroom. I bent over and adjusted a blanket when I felt a little foot connect with my rear end. I flew headfirst into my pillow just as the door to the outside opened and my dad stepped in. "Why are you still awake! Get in bed all of you now!" I know he did not see Carlos kick me in the butt; if he had his foot would have followed. I looked over and Carlos was grinning ear to ear. Perfect timing, he knew there was no way for me to respond. My brothers and I quickly crawled under the covers and closed our eyes, just as dad turned off the lights I opened one eye slightly and saw Carlos with a grin across his tiny mouth. He timed it perfect this time.

I began to dream as I dozed off. It was another day of wonderful experiences. I learned that I could play football and I was not a dumb Mexican. George from the preschool would be so proud. I could read and write as well as anyone in the fourth grade class. The fact that I was the only Hispanic did not mean a thing to me. I lay in the dark thinking of what the next day would bring. I was not expecting to go to school tomorrow but no one had said we weren't. I just did not want to get my hopes up. More than once I had my feelings of anticipation crushed. Hope was not worth it right now. I would roll and buckle with the blows of life and from my dad. The darkness surrounded me until I rolled over and faced in the direction of the bathroom. I could see light from the bottom of the door. I angled my head so I could see underneath it. It did not work. I wondered what mom and dad were doing in the bathroom at the same time? I could hear muffled voices behind the closed door. Oh well, at least no one had been hit and no one was crying. The slim blade of light grew fainter as I slipped to off sleep, then the light got brighter and brighter.

"The Fighting Falcons have been led by Albert Rodriguez all year!" the announcer tells the crowd. The lights from the stadium seem to illuminate the entire town. On the field of play I line up in the huddle. The quarterback tells everyone the play. "All right Rod, we need you to score! This is the last play, we gotta have a touchdown or we'll loose the entire season."

"You have to get past the biggest, meanest, nastiest linebacker in the league to score." The entire huddle looks across the line of scrimmage and sees the other team ready to go. The only thing about this defense is there is only one player. He does not have a number but he is huge! He is so big and mean, that he does not even wear a helmet. I look harder and I realize I know this person. Dad? That's my dad! He is standing there with his hands on his hips looking like he is getting ready to kill me with his eyes.

We break the huddle and line up in our offense. I am in the back of the line, my number has been called. The play calls for me to get the hand-off right up the middle. The quarterback calls out, "down, set!" He looks over the defense.

"It's just one person!" I yell out to him. He continues to scan the other side of the line. I just shake my head and look to where I am supposed to run. Carlos and Jose are blocking for me. My dad sees me eying the spot where my brothers are lined up next to each other. He laughs and I know he knows what the play is. He stands over them and readies himself for the play to start. I can see my brother's knees begin to tremble as my dad is standing over them. He's going to kill them both then get me, I know he is. "Hut one!" the quarterback yells; the play is set for three.

"I'm going to kill you!" I hear my dad yell. He is jumping back and forth near the line of scrimmage, like he is teasing my brothers for what they are about to get. Carlos and Jose's little legs are trembling even more now.

"Hut two!" The quarterback yells. I stand firm, I have my legs spread shoulder width apart. My back is bent and I have my hands on my knees. My helmet is on tight. My chin strap is cutting into my jaw. Sweat is rolling down my cheeks, my right foot twitches.

"This is going to be ugly. The defense of the Big Nasty has been whipping the Falcons for almost seven years now," the announcer tells the crowd. The crowd is made up of only White people. Both sides are full of them. One side is yelling for me to win, the other side is calling me names. "Greaser!" some yell out. "Wetback!" I hear someone else scream. I turn my head just slightly to look at the favorable side.

"Hut three!" the quarterback has started the play! I push off my right foot and spring forward. The ball is placed into my midsection and I keep moving forward, my momentum is propelling me so fast the people in the bleachers become a big blur. Their words are no longer audible. Jose and Carlos are flying through the air. My dad has grabbed each one by the back of the head and tossed them off to the side. Other players are trying to help and they meet the same fate. The Big Nasty is not slowing down as he heads directly for me. I plant my left foot and tear into the turf as I make a move to the right. I know the Big Nasty is not known for his speed; I'll run to the outside and he'll never catch me. I will my legs to pump harder and I reach speeds that my little body has never known. I spot bulbs flashing in the blur of the lights as I increase my speed down the sideline. I open my mouth to suck in air as my lungs begin to scream for more oxygen. My smooth stride is beginning to turn into a swimming motion as my muscles begin to give out. I can see the goal line! I can hear pounding footsteps behind me! I have to keep going! If I don't score my life is over! I can feel hot air on the back of my neck, and it feels like a huge bull is about to run me down, but I just can't move any faster! At the five yard line I dive for the score. I can feel my body falling and falling. My eyes are wide and I open my mouth to yell as I ready my body for the impact of the turf.

I feel a warm hand on the back of my neck that gently pushes me from side to side. "Betito, wake up you're dreaming again." The Big nasty has turned into Mom? "Go ahead and get ready to go to school," she says to me.

Jimmy and I walked to school again, and this time Jose was with us. All we talked about was our plays that we had been working on in the front yard. "We'll show them what we can do today!" Jimmy tells us. I am so excited I get to go to school for two consecutive days. We approached the school yard and Jimmy told us we needed to hang around the flag pole. I asked him to help me understand why we had to all stand there and repeat some allegiance to the flag thing. He just shook his head back and forth and began to tell me all he knew. Jose and I were two ignorant children being exposed to a new world in California. There was just so much to take in, so much to learn. While Jimmy was talking, other kids began to walk up and say hello. Not all were nice: I heard Little Red say something about me needing to be at work. Jimmy told me to ignore him. "He's just sore you whipped him in football yesterday. Not only that, he got beat by a wetback," Jimmy said just loud enough for the little red headed boy to hear. Jimmy gave Little Red a mean look as he walked by. "Wait till he gets beat by two Greasers today," Jimmy told us.

"What two Greasers?" I asked. Jimmy just laughed as he slapped me on the back. My bruises were healing fast and it did not hurt this time. As the sun began to rise higher in the California sky the teachers came out and began to line the children up in rows. Mrs. Mendez came to greet us. "Good morning," she told us. We all three looked up and squinted our eyes; we had to look up to see her face, and her back was to the sun. "Are you ready for another day of school, Albert?" she asked. I looked up with one eye squinted and just nodded. I was grinning from ear to ear. Life had changed so fast in two days I couldn't believe my luck. There were no muddy fields, migrant schools or tin—roofed camps. I really thought that at this point things were really going to change for the better. I was half right and half wrong.

While my brothers and I were at school my father was spending time with his uncle. Tio Marko had taken him to the orchards that he managed. Since he was the General Manager he was able to get my dad a job very easily. My dad's ability to speak English helped a lot. He was given a job as a supervisor for a group of workers that had the job of picking peaches and nectarines. My dad no longer had to pick the fruit like the other Mexicans. He would now stand around and supervise. He would also drive the workers to their worksite from time to time. His employees were made up of families of migrant workers. There were about five families that made up about thirty people. The families were no different from the migrants we worked with in Texas. There were mothers, fathers, and their children. The only difference was that these kids were not going to school like I was. I got to go with my dad to work on the weekends sometimes and I watched the families picking the fruit under the trees. My dad would drive this machine called a shaker. It was a tractor with a long hydraulic arm in the front. He would drive up to the tree and extend the arm. It had two grips that would wrap around the trunk of the tree and shake it vigorously. After the fruit had fallen his employees would surround the tree and fill their baskets like I used to. This time there was no mud or tomatoes for me. Dad worked for his uncle Marko for a week and used that money to rent a house about a mile and half away from Marko's home.

The house we rented was very old. It was a simple white home that sat on a road that lead out of town. It was surrounded by a huge field that had corn planted in it. It had two bedrooms and an indoor bathroom. We stayed with Marko's family for one week too long according to dad. I really wanted to stay longer. The giant man made me feel so safe, and around him I knew that dad was on his best behavior. I knew it must have been hard to go all week long being able to drink only in the evening when no one was watching. The strain was going to end however. We moved into the tiny house and things began to change.

I choose to remember the good things about our time in that house. I remember that it had two huge walnut trees. We also had almond and fig trees in the yard. The most striking thing I recall was that the house was not level. If you stood in the front yard and looked straight at it, it titled to the left. In the small living area of the house the floor sloped in one direction and you could not open the front door. I was happy with it though. You have to take the good with the bad. It was still nicer than the migrant apartment in Texas. I had actually lived in houses with dirt floors and outdoor plumbing so this was just fine for me. I was more concerned with school. At this point I had gone to school for an entire week. I was so excited that I wished at that time we could have stayed there forever. If I could have seen the future I would have wished for something else.

Chapter 4
Feeding the Addiction

"Ya no tomes!" (stop drinking) My mom yelled. My dad just looked at her and laughed. He popped the top off the can and leaned his head back as he poured the cold beer down his throat. He was already staggering as he walked through the kitchen. His steps were shaky and he had to grab the counter as he made his way to the stove. My mother had dinner cooking and it was almost ready to serve. We were going to have chicken with rice. There were also of course the famous beans and tortillas as a side dish. My dad grabbed the big spoon off the countertop that my mom had been using to stir the rice. He filled the spoon with hot steaming rice and tossed it into his mouth. His eyes grew huge, turned red and instantly began to water as his face went into convulsions. His mouth rejected the hot food and he sprayed rice all over the open pans of food. With his other hand he quickly took a drink of beer in order to put out the flame that was blistering his tongue.

My mother put both her hands on her face and lowered her head. She had hurried home from work to prepare dinner as fast as possible for her family. Now a drunk had just spit all over it. She had tears coming out of her eyes as she pulled her hands away from her face. Her hands then went from an open position to two clenched fists. She leapt towards my dad and began to beat him in the face and chest. He just brushed her away with one swing of his large arm. This caused her to fall backwards on her rear end. As she was getting up for the second attack she looked over her shoulder and saw her three sons standing in the doorway to the kitchen witnessing the entire event.

It would be one of many fights I would see in that little house. This one ended quickly. My mother walked towards us and grabbed our hands and we went outside. My brothers and I were led to a wooden picnic table Uncle Marko had given us. Mom sat us down and told us to stay there until she called for us. We could hear my dad yelling for my mother to come back inside and serve him his dinner. It was Friday evening and my dad had cashed his paycheck at a local store in town that afternoon. He had used the money to buy his beer. He had probably begun drinking during his lunch hour. By the time he left work he was already drunk, putting his new job on the line. My mom went back inside. She began to cater to him. She would practically spoon feed him until he was full. Sometimes he would pass out at the table and mom would drag him to bed. When she was too tired she would leave him wherever he lay. As soon as dad was asleep she brought out three plates of food for us. I had been looking forward to chicken and rice; instead we got leftovers from the day before with tortillas. Mom said that since dad had spit all over the food it was not good to eat anymore.

While mom was feeding the drunk in the house my brothers and I sat on the table and talked about school. We had gotten so used to seeing this drama play out we treated it like it was not happening. Jose and I talked about football games at school and Carlos kept asking when he would get to play. We told Carlos he was still too young. This evening I had managed to grab a book as mom took us outside. I took advantage of the situation and read to my brothers. This time I would read a chapter and then pass it to Jose so he could read the next chapter. Carlos was still not reading as well as we were but he enjoyed the stories we read together. He would sit on the table with both hands on his face and his eyes wide open. We must have read four or five books this way. Eventually Carlos would join us in the story telling. Jose was taking his turn reading when my mother opened the back door with the plates of food. I turned my head and looked in her direction. She had a red mark on one side of her face and her eyes were red and I could tell she had been crying.

"What are you reading this time?" Mom asked me.

"We're reading about this knight from long ago that rescues the princess from the bad guy mommy," I told her. She smiled and put our plates in front of us. We looked down at the cold leftovers and then at her. We knew this was the best she could do for now.

"I know mijos, tomorrow I will make you all a big meal of anything you want," she said.

"Can I have fried chicken?" I yelled.

Mom looked at me told me to keep it down. She was worried I would wake up our father. "Si mijo, you can have some pollo frito," she said as she rubbed the top of my coconut head. She knew I had fallen in love with fried chicken ever since I had it at Tio Marko's house. My mom sat with us at the table and thumbed through the book as we ate.

"Mommy, can I teach you to read?" I asked her.

"No mijo, it's getting late and I want you to finish eating," she said without lifting her head from the book. The story we had been reading had a lot of pictures in it. I knew mom couldn't read, but loved to look at the pictures of the books we brought home. I also knew she was trying to cover the bruise on her face.

There were going to be more bumps and bruises while we lived in our little house. My dad began to spend more and more time at work. Not because he was working late but because he was spending more time with the "mojados." These were men that had come over from Mexico illegally and worked for Tio Marko also. They had no intention of becoming American citizens. They would work for a while and take their money back to Mexico. Some of them would continuously mail their cash home and stay in the states. I had met a few of them when dad took me to work. I was scared of them and stayed in the truck when dad would go visit them. My dad's duties had been expanded to working with these men. He would put them to work clearing out wooded areas to expand the fruit trees or string a line of fence. After work dad would go to their shack and drink beer with them. They only spoke Spanish. They would sit around and tell jokes. I don't know what it is about Mexican men, but when they get together and drink beer at night they always start a fire. They will stand around it and talk for hours. I know this because dad would not come home until real late. There were a few times he did not come home. This of course started more problems.

Mom and dad would fight like cats and dogs. It became very apparent that it was not going to change. After a while we just accepted it as a normal part of life. Dad came home late, drunk and mean. We tried to hide from him as much as possible but sometimes he found us. He began to spend more time with his workers than with us. I did not mind at all. I would have just appreciated it if he could have been a lot quieter when he came home late on a school night. He kept us up with his yelling and cursing at my mother. He had to have his dinner no matter what time it was. I don't know why he bothered. He would just be throwing it up in the morning. There were days that I would be so tired that I would take a nap after lunch instead of playing football. My brothers and I made due as best we could. We continued to read and share stories when my parents fought. If it was too noisy inside we just went outdoors. The great thing about California is that the weather is always wonderful. The fighting inside kept us from watching television also. I really believe that had a lot to do with our reading comprehension.

The only safe house for my brothers and I was the school. I had such a hunger for school I would hang around the buildings and try and talk to the teachers as they walked to their cars. I just wanted someone to talk to me and listen to anything I had to say. We were supposed to go to Tio Marko's house after school and wait for my mom. She would pick us up and take us home. Our house was not that far away but it was still a long walk. As time passed my dad made us walk home from school. He did not want us at his uncle's house anymore. I think it was because we might tell him that he was drinking a lot. The walk home took about an hour in order to cover the mile and a half. People would offer us rides as we walked home, we would always say no. My mother had said there were strangers out to get us. I asked mom what was a stranger? She said strangers were evil men that would hurt us. I told her we had a stranger living in our home. She laughed it off but realized I was speaking the truth. Our dad had become the person she was most worried about. His addiction to alcohol was slowly but steadily going out of control. His need for beer increased my desire for education as a form of escape.

At the school I would check out books from the library and take them home to read. I was not able to do that at the migrant school in Texas. My reading comprehension had gone up over my grade level and my English had gotten to the point where I was losing my Mexican accent. I was still sent to special speech classes. I had problems with any word that stated with "sh." I would pronounce a "battle ship" like "battle chip." I was determined to overcome this challenge and eventually did. As the months moved forward I found myself becoming acclimated to being around White children. They were no different than other kids in the fourth grade. Since there were no other Hispanics other than Jimmy and his family the thought that I should be treated differently started to fade. I was just another boy who wanted to enjoy fourth grade. The other children got used to me playing football and Little Red finally accepted the fact I could outrun him. If I could pick out my favorite elementary school this would be on the top of the list. As summer turned into fall then winter, the atmosphere of the school began to change. Everyone was focusing on Christmas.

The Holiday season was totally foreign to my brothers and me, but we were attempting to adapt quickly. The school had a Thanksgiving party then a Christmas party. There was so much candy and food that I thought I was in heaven! At home nothing changed though. We did not have a tree, stockings, or presents. At school the class had put up a tree and our teacher had presents under it for everyone. I had asked mom why we weren't having Christmas. She had told us that only White people did that. I did not believe that for a minute. Our teacher had shown us pictures of kids celebrating Christmas in books and the kids were of every color. I saw a kid that was darker than me. I thought that was strange. Until that that point in my life I had never seen a Black person.

At school I was enjoying the holiday season for the first time, but I wished I could do the same at home. The last day of school before the Christmas break our teacher let us open our little presents. We each got a little illustrated book that you could carry in your pocket. I think mine had a story about Rudolph, some deer with a red shiny nose. It had pictures in it so it was pretty easy to read. My bothers also got simple gifts and I thought they were the only gifts we were going to have.

At home my mom and dad were not concerned with Christmas. Dad was too busy with his drinking friends and mom was too busy working and caring for us and her drunk husband, whenever he came home. The weekend before Christmas that changed quickly. Tio Marko drove into our driveway in his truck. He called my dad outside and talked to him rather sternly. He did not come inside but I could hear the conversation was going in one direction. I saw Marko pointing towards the house and then point down the road. I even saw him grab my dad by the shoulders and look directly into his face. I wish I could have heard what was being said, I was watching everything through the screen door. It was pretty easy to hear through the screen; it had big holes in it. Isn't it funny how as a kid you think that a screen door with holes is easier to hear through than a screen with no holes in it? Anyway, the conversation was definitely one-sided and my dad was on the receiving end. Things finally calmed down and Marko got in his truck and left. Dad came back in the house and he looked very upset. As he walked into the house I recognized the look on his face and quickly found my brothers and snuck out the back door.

The field behind our house had been plowed so we could not hide there. I told my brothers to follow me and we climbed up the big walnut tree in the back yard. Tio Marko had built us a small tree house in it when we had first moved into the house. It was a simple tree house with a floor and only one wall. My dad was supposed to have finished it but he never did. We climbed up and sat Indian style together and read our story book. To this day I cannot remember the title of any of the books we read in the tree house. I guess it's because I have blocked out so much of those days. I can remember climbing up the tree and hiding in the corn field but that's about it. The bad thing about denial is that it is not selective. I chose to forget those miserable days when dad was home and now I can't recall any of the books we read in the tree, or at the picnic table. We would sit up in that tree house and pretend we had climbed away from our current situation. Our life was a constant struggle, not for life or living, but just a struggle to enjoy life. We could not have imagined it getting any worse. We were wrong.

Dad continued to drink and spend more time with his workers. Nothing seemed to bother him. He came home later and later. I guess he figured if he came home late enough he could avoid fighting with mom. To appease my mother he did bring home our first

Christmas tree a few days before Christmas. It looked like he had pulled over on the side of the road and cut it an hour before he came home. My brothers and I looked at it and wondered what he wanted us to do with it. It did not look like the trees we had seen in school. We had no decorations, ornaments or tinsel. The tree did not even have a base so it would stay up. My mother looked at dad with eyes that told the whole story. Her brown eyes looked like she wanted to replant that scrawny tree somewhere on my dad. She then looked at us and quickly managed to get into the Christmas spirit. Mom told dad to get a bucket and put the tree in it. Dad trimmed the bottom of the tree high enough so it could sit in the bucket, then filled the bucket with dirt. It looked pretty tacky but it worked. Jose and I helped him with that chore while Carlos and mom popped popcorn. She then got thread and made strings of popcorn with needle and thread. We put the tree in the living area and we strung the popcorn around it.

We stood around it and just stared it. It was the first time we had celebrated Christmas in this manner. It was so heartwarming and special I thought I was going to cry. Mom held my hand and I held Jose's and he held Carlos's. The only thing missing was dad. He was in the kitchen opening the refrigerator and grabbing his Christmas drink. We looked at him as he walked into the living room and took a drink from the can. He walked over to the tree and pushed the aluminum pull tab through one of the branches. He looked at his work and just laughed. That I cannot forget, nor can I forget the laughing he did as he walked out of sight back into the kitchen and out the back door. He was headed back to his real family.

The day before Christmas Tio Marko pulled into our driveway in his pickup truck. We ran out and hugged him. We were not seeing much of him. I think he was upset with dad. Every time he came over he had gifts for us. I believed in Santa Claus when I saw him. Some of the gifts he gave us that year were hand me downs from Jimmy and other things he had probably purchased at garage sales. When he got out of the truck he threw the football at me and I caught it in stride as I ran towards him. He grabbed me as I got close to him and he picked me up off my feet. When he had me in the air he asked me to throw the ball to Jose, he had something else for me. I did what he said and Jose began running with the ball around the truck. Carlos was standing on the back door steps watching the whole thing. He looked puzzled but started walking towards Tio Marko slowly. The huge man reached into the back of his truck and pulled out a cardboard box. He handed it to me and I looked inside it. It was full of comic books! I had seen other kids in school with them. The skinny books had pictures of men and women with huge muscles and cool names. I had not read any because the kids would not share them with me. I had my mouth open wide as I gasped with excitement and immediately ran towards the picnic table with my present. He then reached into the back of the truck again and pulled out a football helmet and tossed it to Carlos. He motioned for him to come closer and whispered something into his ear. Carlos later told us that Tio Marko had told him that he wanted him to wear the helmet so he could play football with the big boys and not get hurt. Carlos quickly put the helmet on and started chasing Jose. He was growling loudly as he chased him. My mother was standing on the back door steps now watching the entire scene.

"Where's Beto?" Tio Marko asked.

"He's working." Mom said in a voice that did not have much confidence.

"Oh," Tio Marko said, in a low voice. If dad was working why was Tio Marko here? Something was not adding up. Marko turned and looked at us having fun with our first Christmas presents. He had his hands on his hips and grin on his face. That man had a heart as big as Texas. He yelled for us to come back to the truck. He had something else in the bed. He reached into it and pulled out a bicycle! He handed one to me and he pulled one out for Jose and then another one for Carlos. Carlos's had little bitty extra wheels with the back tire. We were so excited we jumped on them and began to ride them in the yard. I rode mine around the walnut tree and came to a skidding stop in front of mom. I looked at her and she had tears coming out of her eyes. She took steps toward Marko and broke down in a crying fit as they hugged. My brothers and I stopped pedaling and watched the scene. Marko played it off and I heard him say that he had got a great deal on them at a garage sale. I knew the football and helmet were Jimmy's, but the rest he had to have had bought somewhere. I did not know whether to ride the bike or read my comics. Marko waved at us and got in his truck and began to back out of our driveway. Carlos had on his helmet and was on his bike chasing Jose. Jose rode his bike and held the football at the same time. They looked so funny, as they chased each other around the trees in our yard. I put my bike against the house and carried my box up the tree house. I had to read about the heroes in my skinny books.

"Betito, come and eat!" My mom yelled. I wasn't hungry. I had been so involved in my comics I did not realized that it was starting to get dark. I must have been in that tree for hours. I had read about heroes that had the power of bats and spiders. Other heroes could shoot laser beams from their eyes and fly through the air. I was fascinated with these skinny books. I climbed down the tree with my box and tried to read and eat dinner at the same time but mom made me put them up. I started to eat fast so I could get back to comics and mom got mad. She told me that if I did not eat slower she would take the books from me. That was all she had to say. I slowed down and ate like a normal person. That is, as a normal person using a tortilla and not spoons or forks. My brothers watched me gobble down my food and laughed. I think that is what upset my mom. I smiled and continued to eat at a slower pace. Mom smiled back at us and she ate Christmas Eve dinner with us. Dad was nowhere to be seen. That was fine with my brothers and me; we knew what shape he would be in when he finally came home.

Dad came in late that night, drunk as usual. We had been up watching the television. We were keeping tabs on the news and the location of Santa Claus. The reporter stated that he had just left the western seaboard and was headed inland. Mom said that we since we had already gotten gifts he was only going to visit the poor kids. I asked mom if he would visit the poor kids at the migrant camp. Mom nodded as she headed toward the back door. She told us to turn off the T.V. and get to bed. Dad was making a racket as he came in. We knew the routine. We headed to our bedroom and prepared for bed. I closed the bedroom door and turned off the light. We listened to our parents in the dark. We were expecting the fight of the century. Dad had skipped out on our Christmas Eve dinner and spent it with his friends drinking. Our ears were straining to hear the blow by blow account, but nothing happened. We could hear dad sitting down to dinner and the banging of pots and pans. We were confused, what was happening? There was no screaming and yelling. Maybe dad had killed mom! Instead we heard the noise of a drunk having dinner and our mom waiting on him.

It was so quiet the noise was deafening. Our ears must not be working right. We could hear dad at the table and the footsteps of mom as she walked back and forth to the table. That meant she was heating up the tortillas for him. We lay in our beds and tried to pick out words from our parents but none were loud enough to hear. I was tempted to get out of bed and peek out of our bedroom but decided against it. We heard a chair fall over as dad got up from the table and mom's hastened steps went to him. We could make out the noises of them headed to the bedroom. Dad was being taken to bed. Christmas Eve had gone off without a fight. At the time I could not understand what had occurred, but now I can. Mom was trying her best to make our first celebration of Christmas as special as possible. If all she had to do was let dad have his way for one night she would do it. Mom gave us a special kind of present: a night of peace. We would sleep in a quiet home that night, one of a few we had during our stay there in that little broken down house.

I lay in bed and thought of all the poor kids that Santa would be visiting.

I wondered if the kids from the camp in Texas would be getting presents and if things would be different now that Santa knew we existed. If he did not know about us in Texas, maybe only kids in California experienced Christmas. It was all so confusing, all I knew was that I had a box full of comics under my bed and a bike parked outside. Things were really getting better now for us, I thought. I was laying flat on my back with my hands behind my head. My eyes were still wide open and sleep would be slow in coming. I decided to change my thoughts to the box of comics that was calling my name from under my bed. A smile hit my face when I thought of the heroes chasing bad guys. I had always considered myself a hero. Now I knew what a hero was supposed to look like. I giggled a bit. I sure would look funny in tights and a cape. But who would be my villain? Carlos and Jose weren't bad guys. I guess there was always dad. I could rely on him to be the one trying to destroy the world. The villains in the comic books are always out for world domination and conquest. My villain was only out to make life miserable for a few kids. I pictured myself flying through the air, the wind in my face and the villains running from me. Who would dare challenge me now? My eyes were slowly coming to a close but a smile stayed on my face. Villains beware.

"Stand aside villain!" Coconut Man yelled at the Evil Drunk. "Don't make me blast you with my super laser eye death rays!" Evil Drunk just laughed at the hero. He spit half digested food at him. The acidic content could rot metal or anything it came into contact with. Coconut Man leapt fifty feet into the air and hovered in a position that resembled a cross. The hero's costume never came close to being soiled. Our hero was too fast; he could dodge that filth all day. "I warned you Evil Drunk. Prepare to meet your match!" Coconut man yelled while he hovered into a firing position. He tilted his head an inch lower and tensed his lips on his muscular jaw. The area around his mouth was the only skin showing on his head. The rest was covered by a dark brown mask. He wore an amber covered visor that was beginning to glow with a white hot light. Instantly a bolt of light shot out from the visor and struck the Evil Drunk in the chest. The intense light silhouetted the hero against the blue sky. The rest of uniform was also dark brown. It made his massive arms and chest seem that much bigger. The only distinguishing marks on the uniform were two interlinked "C's" on his chest. We all knew what that stood for. Everyone loved the Coconut Man. He was all brown on the outside, but on the inside he was harnessing the power of a white star, a supernova of intense light. He could focus that energy on Evil Drunks anywhere in the galaxy. This particular drunk was trying to ruin Christmas.

Evil Drunk fell backwards in a blast of light and heat. The rays from Coconut Man could melt diamonds. Evil Drunk hit the ground like an iron beam. Innocent bystanders could feel the waves of heat radiating from the blast. Evil Drunk lay on his back, steam and vapor rising from his chest. The uniform he was wearing was made of denim. It was not tailored like that of the hero. His was dirty, filthy, and it reeked of alcohol and half digested food. The area of the white blast had charred the villain's shirt. It was burned in a perfect circle. That was the part that had "ED," on it.

The battle continued and Coconut Man would blast the bad guy over and over. Evil Drunk would fall but he would rise and shoot the foul matter out of his mouth towards the hero. I can still hear the noise of the Evil Drunk's throat as it contracted and forced vile fluid up into a stream. Over and over he did this but it never hit the hero. The scene of battle was starting to fade but the noise made by the villain was getting louder. Slowly I was waking from my sleep. I lay in my bed and the noise was still continuing. That was odd. I looked at my brothers in their bunk beds. They were still asleep. I got out of bed and followed the noise into the kitchen. I went to the back door and the noise was getting louder. It had a throaty echo to it now. In between the disgusting sounds I could hear a cough that I recognized. It was not that of Evil Drunk, just my dad. I slowly cracked the back door enough to look out and I saw him. He was bent over expelling last night's dinner. He must have had tequila with his other family. He was paying for it now. What a way to start Christmas day. I was ready for the holidays to get over with so I could get back to school.

Christmas day began like any other day for us. We did not have presents from mom and dad, but we did have our new bikes from Tio Marko. We were riding them as soon as my brothers woke up. While mom was fixing breakfast we were playing in the yard. Carlos had his helmet on and was once again chasing Jose who had the football. It was a like Christmas for any other child in America. That soon changed. Dad came out and saw us playing and he started yelling at us to come to him. "Where did you get those bikes?" He yelled. I could tell he was still hurting from the tequila. He had to hold his head as he waited for the answer.

"We got them from Tio Marko," I told him. His head must have started hurting more because he closed both his eyes as his mouth puckered like he had bit a sour candy. He went back inside and I could hear him yelling at mom. I did not tell dad about the other gifts we had gotten. I was scared he would take my comics away, so I had hidden the box under my bed. We continued to play outside while mom and dad had it out. Mom was cooking breakfast for us. We were going to have eggs, bacon and tortillas with beans.

Mom finally called us in to eat. Dad was not at the table as usual. We sat down to eat and started on the food. To this day that is still my favorite breakfast, next to menudo. As we were eating dad came in with a glass of something fizzy. He looked like a mess; his hair was matted and his face was pale. He told my mom we were going to take the bikes back to Tio Marko. My mom looked at him and told him to take them back by himself. I didn't worry about losing the bikes. Dad would not dare insult Tio Marko by returning the gifts. Tio Marko could take dad apart at the seams if he wanted.

Dad walked out of the kitchen with a scowl on his face. His mean stares were starting to have less of an effect on us now. The worst thing he could do was beat us anyway. We could take the best he dished out and survive.

As dad turned the corner of the kitchen and was out of sight I began to copy his facial features. I looked at Carlos and tried to look as threatening as dad. Carlos just laughed. Jose almost spit food everywhere when he saw me. Mom was even smiling as she watched us eat. Usually she would get upset if we played at the table, but today was going to be different. She told us that today we would be making tamales and that as soon as we finished breakfast, we would get started. I loved to eat tamales but making them was hard work. I would rather read my comics. Jose and Carlos told her they wanted to ride their bikes. All mom had to do was start walking out of the kitchen, saying she was going to get our dad. We quickly jumped out of the chairs and began preparing to make tamales. I said we could take whatever dad dished out, not that we enjoyed it. Besides, tamales would be the only thing we would actually be unwrapping today.

Jose and I sat at the table and cleaned the corn husks. When we bought them they still had the long stringy hair-like silk that hung out the end of the corn leaves. We had to pull them off one by one. Carlos would then take the husks and wash them in the sink and lay them on the kitchen counter to dry.

Mom had already made the "masa" and had it in a huge bowl. She made the masa by using ground corn meal and water to make a thick batter. We had to spread this on the corn husks. She would then add the meat that she had simmering in a huge pot. The meat was a combination of pork and beef. The pork came from a hog's head she had been boiling for hours. It used to look so funny, a snout and ears poking out of the top of a pot on the stove. I still remember scaring Carlos by telling him that dad had killed a Mexican worker that looked like a pig and put his head in the refrigerator. When Carlos opened the door to see it for himself he had burst into screams and yells. It took us an hour to calm him down. We had done this when dad wasn't home of course.

Now the head had meat falling off the bone. Mom ran the meat through a molino, (sausage grinder) and did the same with a beef roast. She would mix the meat together and then add chili and peppers. Once everything was ready the assembly line would begin. Carlos would hand a cleaned husk to Jose. He would smear masa on it and hand it to me. I would put a tablespoon of meat in it and fold it shut. I would hand it to mom who would place it into a pot she had layered with more corn husks. She had put a little bit of water in the pot so it would create the steam that finished cooking the tamales.

We worked on the tamales from ten in the morning till four in the evening. We had taken a short break for lunch and then started up again. Once the tamales were cooking in the huge pot they began to give a wonderful aroma. There is nothing better than tamales steaming in the pot. Mom let us go play while the steam did the rest. Even outside we could smell the tamales cooking. We were outside playing when I suddenly realized that dad's truck was still in the yard. He had been here all day. I guess he had been sleeping the entire time we had been working on the tamales. I wondered if tequila makes you sleep all day. I was kind of glad dad had slept Christmas day away. It meant that we did not have to see him while we worked and played. To make sure he slept more I called Jose and Carlos over to me and told them not to make any noise. I had them put their bikes away and I snuck back into the house. I slowly made my way into our bedroom. I grabbed my box of comics from under the bed and retraced my steps back outside. I then had my brothers climb up the tree house. I handed them each a comic book I thought they would enjoy. We sat there and each of us read comics until mom called us in for dinner. It was early evening and the sun was beginning to descend in the western horizon. I took my comics back from Carlos and Jose and we started down the tree.

We walked into the kitchen and froze when we saw dad at the table eating tamales. We stared at each other and then at mom. This was something we were not used to. I had my box of comics and was more frightened than my brothers. I did not want him to take them. I emboldened myself and kept on walking past dad and went straight to our room and put the box back under my bed. Dad kept un-wrapping tamales and eating them. He never said a thing about my box. When I returned from the bedroom I saw he had a big pile of corn husks in front of him. He must have eaten a dozen already. I was angry that we had worked all day to make them and dad had just helped himself to the first dozen. He had a can of coke in front of him and a small bowl of jalapenos. He loved to take a bite of anything and chase it with a bite of a green pepper. He would then wash it down with a can of coke. It was strange: he could drink beer all day, but when it came to eating he would never eat and drink beer at the same time. He always had to have his coke.

Mom put a plate of tamales on the table for each of us. There was a dozen on every plate. My brothers and I sat down uneasily at the table. I guess the closest resemblance is when a huge male lion is eating and the subordinate males ease up to the carcass. We did not know what to expect. We each gingerly un-wrapped the steaming cornhusks and used a fork to eat the tamales. We gave dad a curious glance as we ate. Mom was also staring at us, but didn't join us. The table only had four chairs. Dad leaned back after the last tamale and stretched. He put both arms behind his head and we flinched. I thought he was going to smack us. He just grinned as he stood up. We gave a sigh of relief as he walked away towards his bedroom. We heard a manly belch as he turned the corner. We giggled when we heard him but did not laugh out loud. Mom just shook her head as she turned her attention back to the tamales in the pot.

She took out all the tamales and let them cool in smaller pots. We would be putting them in the freezer and refrigerator. In a few weeks we would be sick of them. She put a few dozen in a big brown bag and then set it on the stove top. Dad had come back in the kitchen. He was dressed in his work clothes. He said something to my mom as he walked out the door. Mom's eyes glared at him as he walked out. We heard him turn on the truck and back out of the yard. I really thought mom was going to say something but she didn't. Our gift of peace was still being given. My mom stepped outside and then walked back inside. She handed me the bag of tamales and told me to quickly take them to Tio Marko's house. It was not dark yet and she had waited for this opportunity. She did not have anything to give Marko's family but a few dozen tamales. She kneeled down in front of me and asked me to be quick because she did not know what time dad would come back home. I wasn't worried because we knew he would be out all night. I was sure mom was just saying that to make me hurry.

I asked mom if Jose could come with me and she just nodded. Jose and I ran outside and hopped on our bikes. Mom handed me the bag and I placed it on my lap. I grimaced in pain; the bag was still too hot. Mom laughed and ran back in the house. She handed me a towel and told me to use it as a cushion for the hot bag.

Jose and I pedaled the bikes to the edge of the road and turned towards town directly towards Tio Marko's house. I kept the bag of tamales on my lap, this time cushioned by the towel. When we arrived at the destination it was dusk. Jose and I walked up the stairs with the steaming bag of food. It was now spotted with grease and beginning to tear. I knocked on the door and Jimmy answered. He was surprised to see me and quickly let me in. Tia Concha came and grabbed the bag and rushed it to the kitchen. Jimmy and Jenny were all smiles as they greeted us and led us into the living area.

I froze in my tracks as I came into view of their Christmas tree. It was magnificent. It had to be three or four times the size of the one we had. It made our tree look like a branch with popcorn on it. This one had glass globes and flickering lights all over it and on top was something that resembled a star. Jose began to walk around it. Underneath were presents that had not been opened. He looked so tiny standing next to the tree.

Tio Marko came into the room with arms outstretched and reached down and hugged me. He scooped me up in his powerful arms and swung me around as he yelled Merry Christmas. As he set me down he grabbed Jose and did the same thing. It was so weird being hugged by this father figure of a man. It felt strange and wonderful at the same time. I was thinking how lucky Jimmy was to have a parent like this. I wasn't jealous of the worldly things, just the fact that he felt love and warmth from his dad. I shared nothing like that with my father. I told Marko that mom had sent me with the tamales and we had to hurry and get back before it got dark. Marko walked to the window and looked outside, he pointed out that it was already dark.

"Where's your father?" Marko asked me. I told him that he was working. Marko gave me a look that resembled my father's mean stare. "Betito I did not tell your dad to work today, it's Christmas," he told me as he kneeled in front of me. He had his hands on my shoulders and was looking me in the eyes. "Please don't blame me for making your dad work today."

"I know he not working, he's spending time with the mojados," I told him. I may be young but I was not believing for minute that dad was working today.

Jose had come over and he was standing next to Marko. "How did you two get here?" he asked. I told him we had ridden the bicycles he had given us yesterday. Marko called Jimmy and told him to take us outside while he warmed up the truck. Jimmy led us outside and we waited for his dad to bring the truck around. Marko loaded our bikes in the back and then picked us up one by one and put is in the back with the bikes. He pulled out of the driveway and headed for our house.

Jimmy asked us if we liked the football and helmet. I smiled. I told him we really liked the bikes too. As we headed home I stood up in the back of the truck and faced in the direction that we were headed. I was standing behind the cab and the cool California air was blowing in my face. I asked Jose to hand me the towel I had used to protect me from the tamales so I could tie it around my neck. Jose and Jimmy began to laugh. Coconut Man had come to life. I stood in the back of that truck with my little chest poking out and my hands on my hips. "Look Jimmy I'm a superhero!" I yelled. The wind was whipping the towel around and my hair was flying around in my face. I looked down and Jose and Jimmy were on the bed of the truck laughing so hard Jimmy had tears coming out of his eyes. "What's so funny?" I asked.

"Coconut Man looks like he messed his cape!" Jimmy said in between his laughs. I took off the towel and saw that the tamales had leaked grease all over the towel. The stain was directly over my rear end. I started laughing. I took the towel and rolled it into a round cylinder and started hitting Jimmy and Jose on the head. It didn't hurt them but it made me feel better. "Laugh at Coconut Man, will you!" I shouted. In the cab Tio Marko looked back and saw us playing. He had a huge smile on his face.

Once we arrived at our home Tio Marko helped us out of the truck and we put the bikes away. It was dark now and getting cool. Mom had come outside and spoke with Marko. I saw he had his hands on his hips and was no longer smiling. I thought to myself the entire conversation was a waste and headed inside and went to my room. I pulled out a comic book and began to read. I heard Marko drive off and mom come back inside. She came into the bedroom and thanked me for delivering the bag. I smiled at her and returned to my skinny book. Jose walked into the room and asked me if he could read a comic. I nodded to him but never took my eyes away from the page. He climbed into his bunk and began to read. Carlos came in and reached into my box and grabbed a comic without asking and crawled into his bottom bunk. I was about to say something but I had just gotten to the good part of my story. The hero had the villain on the run. I loved this stuff! It was so addictive. This is how life should be: the hero always wins and the villain gets blasted into something called atoms.

Carlos asked, "What's a laser beam?"

Jose responded, "A laser beam is something that comes out hero's eyes and blasts bad guys." I had my mouth open but Jose had beaten me to the answer. He was always faster than me. Then it hit me. Both my brothers were reading and comprehending everything they read.

Tio Marko knew what we were going through. Short of calling the authorities he could only do so much. The box of comics he had purchased at a garage sale was much more than skinny books. They were a source of escape for us. In his mind he must have known we would read those pages and wander into another world where heroes win and villains don't. As I grew older I would continue to add comics to my collection. I would purchase them any way I could. I bought them at garage sales, flea markets or from other kids. I rarely bought them at retail. I could not afford the dime or quarter they cost. I once traded tamales in the school lunch room for a special comic book and went hungry that day, but I fed my mind for an entire week. The comic was a special edition the kid had already read. It was much more to me. It had the entire storyline in one edition. I didn't have to hope and pray I would stumble on the other comics for the entire story. This one had the entire series in one book. I would have paid a week's worth of lunches to get it.

Old Tio Marko knew what he was doing. As I grew older I even toyed with the idea of writing and drawing my own comic book. I had a hero and a villain I invented. I even got as far as two or three pages, but I never finished. I guess the fear of personal failure took over. I should have looked back at my strengths and not what others thought of me. I had read all the comics in the box by the time school started back up.

I was excited once school started back up because we no longer had to walk. My brothers and I now rode our bikes. The long walk became a short ride. We were still leaving at the same time for a while. Mom had told us to leave at a specific time so we continued to listen to her. We were arriving before the teachers with our new bikes. We took the football and played catch or read in the playground until the other kids arrived. Mrs. Mendez finally asked me why we were there so early. I told her that my mother had instructed us to leave when this hand was in between the six and seven and the little hand on the six. She laughed and said that would be perfect if we were walking but now that we had bikes we could leave later. She took me to a clock and showed me the new time we could leave. I thanked her for the information and went back to playing catch with Jose. The next day we were just as early. Mrs. Mendez asked why we were so early again and I told her we just loved school and didn't want to take a chance on being late. She gave me a puzzled look but accepted the answer. I went back to playing football with my brothers as Jimmy walked into the playground. We threw the football at him and he motioned us to come to him.

"Did you guys watch the football game last night?" he asked. We just looked at him and shook our heads. He knew the answer before he asked the question. He began to describe the action as we listened to him recall the events from last night's game. He looked at Carlos and you could see his mind beginning to work. He gave Carlos the ball and told him to squat down with the ball in front of him. Carlos gave him a funny look so Jimmy had to show him how to do it. Carlos got the picture and got into position. We had seen pictures of this in school. I instantly knew where I needed to be. I quickly got a few feet behind Jimmy in case he wanted to hand me the ball. Jose took his position on the far right side of us. Jimmy yelled to Jose to go deep on one. "Down, set, hut one!" Jose took off and Jimmy took the ball from Carlos. He stepped backwards a few feet and launched the ball towards Jose. He caught the ball and Jimmy started yelping and hollering. Jose spiked the ball as soon as he passed the walnut trees. We all knew that was the goal line.

"Well, well, what do we have here?" Little Red asked, stepping up. "Looks like the All American Wetback team to me." He walked by with a fake smile on his face.

I instantly ran up to him and got in his face. I would handle him like a hero. I stood directly in front of him with our noses almost touching, like I had seen in the comics. My chest was out and my arms were bent at the elbow ready to strike. I made a face like my dad as I looked into Little Red's eyes. He began to back pedal, and took a step backward as I took one forward. "I don't like what you said!" I told him in the deepest voice a nine year old could push out of his mouth. Red looked at me and continued to walk backward. His head was moving left to right. I did not release my gaze from his eyes. I felt my fists were clenched and ready to strike. This was no dream.

Little Red's back was against one of the walnut trees in the yard. I was now in his face and he had no where to go. I could see fear in his eyes. I felt power running through my body and I knew I could give him a beating like the ones I had gotten from my dad. The rage of nine years was slowly working its way out of me. I was ready to explode my misery and frustrations on this one individual. My left hand shot out and grabbed his shirt. My right hand raised and I picked out a target on his face. I would be crushing his nose. That was where the heroes in the comics always hit the bad guys. Before I could move my hand I felt something on my shoulder. Jimmy had come up behind me and put his hand on my right side. "Albert, he's not worth it," Jimmy said in a mild soothing voice. "You might get kicked out of school if you hit him."

That was all he had to say. I let the kid go and lowered my head. The poor boy had sweat on his brow. He took a step sideways and then another to get out of arm's reach. He then bolted as fast as he could. At that time, he could have outrun me or even Jose. "Wow, how did you do that?" Carlos yelled. I wasn't sure what had just happened but it felt pretty good. I could have easily hurt that kid. It felt better having the power to destroy and not using it. That was first time I stood up for myself and my brothers, but it wouldn't be the last.

Things were different now at school. The story of the showdown in the playground soon was being told in every classroom. Kids that never talked to me began to pick me for their teams. Jimmy and I were now "cool kids." Jose and Carlos were also walking around with their chins a little higher. It felt good to be on equal terms with the other kids. I could get used to this.

The school was small but it was a first step to being equal. I stayed in the yard after school and played football with my brothers and Jimmy. I was never in a hurry to get home. Other kids now joined us. Before the "incident" with Red no one ever came to play with the little Mexican boys. We played for an hour after school before we headed home, walking to our bikes a little taller a little bigger and ready for anything. The spring and early summer were going to be different now. They would not change at home, though. They were going to reach an all-new level of violence. The only sanctuary was our school and Tio Marko.

Chapter 5
On the Move Again

"Run mijos run!" My mom shouted at me and my brothers. We were running as fast as we could. We ran out the door, through the yard and entered the corn field next to house. As we entered the field we had to let go of each other's hands. The corn was now over six feet tall and it would be ready to harvest soon. We entered the rows and ran in the direction of town. Luckily the rows were planted in the same direction. It is very difficult to run against the rows. Jose was running in the same row as I was. He was already about ten feet in front of me. My mother and Carlos were in the rows next to me. It was as mild day in May. The sun was shining in sky and the golden strands poking out of the corn were beginning to turn a brownish color. The tassels on the tops of the plants also had a golden yellow to them. The sun in the western sky gave them a glow if you looked at them just right. We didn't have time to enjoy that right now. We were running for our lives at this moment. Mom and dad had just had a terrible fight. It all stemmed from his drinking, which was nothing new of course. Dad was staggering drunk and had hit mom in the face. She had a bruise on the side of her mouth and blood was visible on the corner of her lips. She had pushed dad away and he had fallen over a chair. We took that opportunity to leave the house. It would be a few minutes before he could get up. The only difference this time was that he was yelling and swearing he would kill us all. Dad had the tools to do it now. He had bought a few shotguns and kept them in the house. He and his Mexican workers used them to kill deer that came into the orchards at night.

The great thing about shotguns is that they are not made for shooting targets at long distances. For example, if you are shooting at a mother and three boys running away from you and they had a head start, you had no chance of hitting them. That is why I can't understand why dad was standing on the front porch shooting at us. We were way too far for him to hit us. I kept telling mom that, and she didn't believe me. She kept urging me to run and catch up with Jose. There was no way I could catch Jose. He was faster than me and he was not looking back. The row of corn began to take an upwards slope. We were getting closer to the end of the field and the land began to rise. At the end of the field we would be approaching a small road that marked the edge of town. We had run about a half a mile and at this point I could still make out our little house. I could also see my dad on the porch pointing a rifle at us. I could see the puff of smoke before I could hear the report of the shotgun. It is still in my mind today. At that distance the white and gray smoke spewed out from the barrel then the blast would hit my ears. At that range you could see the blast before you could hear it. It was like the whole event was happening in slow motion. I can still recall the corn leafs scratching my face and seeing the fear in my mother's eyes.

The ground slowly began to dip. That's when I heard the roar of the truck engine and the screeching of tires on the asphalt. My dad was driving up and down the road looking for us. He would be expecting us to come out at the end of the field of corn. He was driving his truck up and down the road to catch us. I could make out the truck as he drove it to the end of the field as fast as the truck would go. He would slam on the brakes and come to a screeching halt and then put the truck in reverse and go backwards and repeat the process as he looked into the corn. The rows were running parallel to the road. As I tried to look for my dad my mother pushed me down to the ground from behind. I hit the dirt in a swimming motion. I landed on my chest and bounced a few times. Jose was already on the ground in front of me. Since the land sloped where we were at, dad would not be able to see us until we stood up. Carlos was in a row a few feet away and he was on his belly also.

Mom was directly behind me. Stark terror had replaced fear and she was no longer crying. We could still hear the truck. Dad was still revving the truck as fast as it would go then slam on the brakes. I can imagine the skid marks he was leaving on road. We could hear and smell the rubber from the tires as he tortured the truck. I raised my head to try and catch a glimpse of the road and I felt a smack on my backside. My mother had slapped me so hard on my rear I thought I had been shot. Jose and Carlos's head snapped around and their eyes said the same thing. The noise of my mother's slap made them think the same thing. As soon as they saw my mom scolding me they once again began to scan the rows for any sign of my dad. Then there was silence. The truck engine turned off and we heard the door open and slam shut.

There are only two sounds a shotgun makes. One is the blast and the other is the cocking noise. Both are very distinctive and will send chills up and down your spine if you are not the one holding the gun. We had already heard the shooting noise now we were hearing the cocking sound. My dad was getting out of the truck and cocking the shotgun as he walked towards the corn. We could hear him getting closer. "Get out of the field now!" I heard him yell. His voice was that of an enraged man. The words were slurred but had a message. We could tell that the alcohol still had its grip on him. I raised my head an inch off the dirt and I could see my dad's head and shoulders from my position. "Get out now!" He yelled again. For a second I felt like he was looking right at me. He raised the rifle and put it to his shoulder. He lowered the barrel till it came horizontal to the corn. I felt like it was pointed directly at me. I closed my eyes and put my hands over my ears. I was preparing for one of the sounds a shotgun makes, the blast.

Click. I heard my dad yell in frustration and head back to the truck. I raised my head and saw him throw the gun into the cab. He staggered into the driver's seat and turned the motor on, put the truck in gear and spun it around in the direction of the house. He was smoking the tires, sending gravel into the air. He was headed home to get more shells for his gun. Once the truck was headed towards our house I felt my mom stand up and I did the same. She did not have to tell me again to run. I just had to follow Jose's lead. He was already ten yards ahead of me headed for Marko's house.

We arrived at Marko's house covered in sweat and panting for air. I fell on my back in his yard as did my brothers. Jenny came out and began yelling for her mother. Marko was not home. My mom went inside with Concha. Jimmy finally came outside and sat in the grass with us. We told him the story of what had just happened. At first he did not believe us. Then we saw the truck come around the corner. We all got up and took off running across the yard and into the house. Jimmy was not taking any chances. He ran to his mother and told her that my dad was outside. Concha walked outside with a look that was worse than my dad's meanest scowl. I saw a side of this matriarch that made me realize who really kept this family together. She had no fear of my dad or his gun. She marched straight out the door and to the driver's side of the truck and got in my dad's face. I was watching through the living room window. I couldn't hear a word that was being said but I could guess. I saw dad stick his head out and yell something at Concha. He was rewarded with a slap across the face. I winced in pain but felt no remorse for dad. I was thinking of all the heroines in my comics and who resembled Tia Concha. Dad looked toward the house and then at Concha. He called her something and put the truck in gear and spun the tires as he drove off. That was the first time I ever saw dad back down from a woman, or anyone else for that matter. Jimmy rounded up me and my brothers and took us to his room. We sat on his bed and he asked us to recant the story of the corn field again. He thought the whole this was exciting. I shook my head and disagreed. That is the most scared I have ever been.

During our stay with Marko's family we continued to attend school every day. I heard Marko and mom talking about what she should do. Marko had gone to our house and talked to dad a few times. I wish I could have been a fly on that wall. I hoped he had slapped him around like he had mom. Jimmy tried to keep us informed as much as possible but he did not know what was going on. Mom was being very quiet. She would go to work and come in to help Concha with dinner. Mom had actually learned to drive while we were in California. Dad had bought a little used car so she could drive to work in a nearby town. Marko and Concha had to go to the house to bring it back. Mom was still terrified from the events of the corn field. A few days into our stay with Marko, dad came by in the evening. Marko went out to meet him and they talked. He would not let dad out of the truck. They talked for a short while and then Marko came into the house and walked out with my mother. This went on a few days and I knew what it was leading to. I was hoping we could stay with Marko's family for at least eight or nine years. I was wrong as usual. Our stay turned into more of a visit.

Once we moved back in we could tell dad was making an effort to spend more time with us. He drank less and attempted to change. I did not like having him around. I liked it more when he was gone. It gave me an opportunity to read and spend time with my comics. Dad eventually found my box and tried to throw it away. Mom kept him from doing that. I think it was because he knew that Marko had given them to me. The fact that it was just comics could not have bothered him, it must have been that I was enjoying them and Marko had given them to me.

I climbed into my tree and escaped the world below. Mom and dad had settled into a quiet domestic life. All seemed well until about two months after we moved back in. Dad was walking out of the house after dinner. He had a shotgun in his hand. He told mom he was going to go deer hunting with his workers. He said something about deer ravaging the orchard and eating the buds and shoots. I was still frightened every time I saw the gun and made sure I had a quick escape route. I kept one eye on dad and the other on the door that led to the outside. Dad hugged mom as he walked out and told her not to wait up. She made a poor attempt at a hug and stared at the floor. I was angry, sad and confused all at the same time. We both knew it was inevitable.

When we came home the next day from school, dad was already home. It was Friday and this is when he usually cashed his check and came home late. When we came in the back door he was in the kitchen cooking something that smelled pretty good. He told us to sit down and eat; he had actually cooked dinner. We heard mom pulling into the yard as we sat down. Dad handed us each a plate of something that looked like carne asada. It smelled great and we just stared at it. Dad looked at us and was probably wondering what was wrong. I couldn't tell him we were in shock. Dad had never prepared dinner for us, much less serve us steak. Mom came into the kitchen and was also in shock. Dad had prepared a plate for her also. We decided it was okay and we began to eat. The meat had a funny taste to it and was kind of tough but we ate it anyway. Mom sat down and joined us as dad worked the kitchen. Dad said we were eating deer meat. I suddenly got a picture of reindeer and Santa's sled. Still, it wasn't bad and sure did beat our usual beans and tortillas. Mom was just happy she did not have to cook after a hard day of work. Dad said he had come in late in the morning with a deer carcass and had cut out the choice parts and put the rest in the freezer. He had slept most of the day and decided to cook us dinner. I had a suspicion we were being set up for something but I kept my mouth full of venison and did not say a word. Carlos and Jose were busy chewing their food and I guess they did not share my suspicion. As soon as we finished eating dad told mom he was going out again to hunt deer. Mom tried to talk him out of it.

Dad would not budge on the fact that he needed to spend the night out again with his friends. Mom was sure of where this was headed. While they were arguing my brothers and I went to our rooms and changed into our play clothes. We had a few hours of daylight left and we wanted to play. Mom and dad stayed in the kitchen and shouted at each other. I climbed into my tree house and watched my brothers wrestle each other. I did not care for the rough type of play. I would rather read and educate my brain. From my vantage point I could also listen better as my parents had it out. I saw dad come out of the house with his shotgun again and head towards his truck. Mom was right on his heels. He tossed the gun into the cab and climbed in. He was not drunk but acted like it. I had not seen him drinking and he did not smell like alcohol. But something was just not right about this whole thing.

Dad had backed into the road without looking because he was yelling at mom. Mom tried to warn dad, but he was not listening. He hit the oncoming car in the front passenger side bumper with a loud crashing sound. Both vehicles came to an instant stop after the collision. I just stayed in the tree and watched the entire event. Mom ran to the scene as fast as she could. Carlos and Jose were frozen in place. The noise had put them in a state of confusion. They probably thought the noise was from the shotgun. Then they saw mom running. By the time everyone settled down, the passengers of the car had come out and were reviewing the damage. I could see that the front end of the car was crushed, as was the bumper of the truck. The car had gotten the worse end of the deal. Dad was apologizing to the occupants as best he could. The driver was a tall white man dressed in nice clothes. The female occupant was standing off the road and talking to mom. I looked a little closer and was sure that the lady was a teacher at school. I did not know her name but she definitely worked at the school. Dad and the man exchanged a few words and dad even helped him restart the car. After everything had settled down the couple slowly drove off and dad pulled the truck back into the yard.

The accident was definitely dad's fault. He was slightly drunk and had backed into the road at a high rate of speed without looking. At that time I did not know how such matters were handled. I guess dad would have to pay for the damage he had done to car. I did not know where the money would come from. We definitely didn't have the resources to pay for a major repair on that couple's car, much less dad's truck. I stayed in the tree as mom and dad talked about what to do. Dad said something about getting money from the Mexicans that worked for him. Mom was furious; she did not know that dad had been lending them money. I thought she was going to hit dad. Instead she turned around and went into the house. Dad got into mom's little car and drove away. This time he looked both ways. I found out later he had gone to his Mexican workers and tried to collect money he was owed. Unfortunately some of them did not want to pay. Dad got into a fight with a few of them and beat one mojado pretty bad. His friends told dad they would be getting even. The following week was going to be very bad, and would cause more changes in our life.

Dad came home the next morning with a handful of cash. Mom was glad to see the money but was mad that he had let the Mexicans borrow it. I saw them counting it. Dad then told mom about the fight he had gotten into trying to collect it. I guess that made him think mom would think more of him as a provider.

That Monday morning mom and dad went to work and we went to school as usual. When we came home there was a car parked on the opposite side of the house. There was no reason for the car to be there. The only thing on the other side of the road from our house was another field. As we rode our bikes by we saw four Mexican men in the car, I recognized them as the mojados from the orchards where dad worked. I felt a chill as our eyes met. As soon as we got into the yard I made Carlos and Jose get into the house and I locked the doors. I even dug into dad's closet to see if I could find the shotgun. I could not find it. We did not have a telephone at that time. I wished Tio Marko was here.

We kept peeking out the window and watched the car the men were in. I was ready to use a butcher knife Jose had brought me if I needed to. As we were watching the street mom's car came into view. She slowly pulled into the yard and looked at the car curiously. I ran to the back door and unlocked it for mom.

Mom came into the house quickly, I had the door open for her and she quickly locked the door behind her. I told her about the men on the other side of the street. She went to the window and looked out. The driver of the car was staring directly at us. Mom and I were peering out the living room window and I knew he saw us. His face was dark and his eyes were narrow. His hair was black and long. His face was unshaven and his lips were dark. The eyes gave everything away. The eyes are a window to the soul, I once heard someone say. If that was true I did not want to see this man's soul. Maybe the darkness of his face was caused by bruises my dad had left on him.

Maybe they were natural, I will never know. The dark man kept his gaze on our window as the car slowly pulled away. My mom and I kept our faces glued to the window as we watched the car pull away. Carlos and Jose kept pulling on my clothes so they could get a look but I kept pushing them away. Once the car was gone I handed the butcher knife to mom. She took it with a surprised look and her eyes became misty. She knelt down and hugged me for taking up for my brothers. I wish she could have seen me handle Little Red. Mom took the knife and walked back to the kitchen with it. My brothers and I followed her and we sat at the table and watched her get ready to prepare dinner.

We were sitting at the table when dad drove in from work. He walked in the back door and mom began to fill him in on what had happened. He looked furious and was about to go back out when mom grabbed him and began to cry as she told him that the men were here when my brothers and I got home from school. She then pointed to the butcher knife she had purposely left on the counter. Dad stared at the knife, then at me. I was scared of my dad but the dark man in car terrified me. Dad kept his gaze on me and I had to lower my head. My dad walked out of the kitchen and into his bedroom. He returned to the kitchen with a pistol. I had never seen it before. It was small but looked deadly. It resembled something out of a western movie dad would watch on television sometimes. He told mom to follow him outside and told us to stay put. They walked out into the field that once held corn. It was wide open now since the corn had been harvested. We watched mom and dad from the kitchen window as they practiced with the gun. Dad had set up a tin can and they were shooting at it. I still recall that they never even came close to hitting it. We could see dirt fly up all around it, but they never hit it.

Mom and dad came in talking about what they should do. Dad said something about getting more guns and possibly teaching me how to use them. Mom was not going with that idea. Then I heard mom talk about her family. My brothers and I ate a dinner of leftovers that evening and we went out to play. We eventually made our way to the tin can mom and dad had been shooting at. I saw that the closest they came was about ten feet to it. No wonder dad used a shotgun.

We played in the yard until dusk that evening. We began to play a new game after what we had experienced. We made little pistols with our fingers. We ran around mom's car and dad's bent-up truck and pretended to shoot at each other. We pretended we were better shots than our parents and we took turns getting shot. We even got into fights and wrestling skirmishes when one of us did not agree that they had been hit or did not die fast enough. It was one of the first times we played with pretend guns. Before that we did not really understand the concept of shooting at each other. We were beginning to learn a new type of violence now. In our minds no one really gets hurt from being shot with a loaded finger, they only pretend to be hit and fall on the ground.

That evening, as we went to bed, there was a strange mood in the house. Jose and Carlos sensed it too.

"Betito what's going to happen if the dark man comes back?" Carlos asked me. It was dark and he was in his bunk bed. I could tell from his voice he was worried and not able to sleep.

I told him, "don't worry Coconut Man will save you." I was rewarded with a small laugh and that helped him relax and I could sense him and Jose drift off to sleep. Coconut Man didn't exist but the dark man did. I was old enough to understand that. I did not really know what was going to happen but I had a feeling something was about to. I lay in bed and thought about all the possible things that could unfold. I thought about mom and dad calling the police and having the bad guys arrested. What about having a shoot-out with the bad guys? My brothers and I could help. No, that wasn't a good idea either. I kept dreaming of ideas, which made me sleepy. I was at the point of mental exhaustion when sleep finally came. I was so tired I did not dream that night.

In the morning when my mother woke us I noticed she was not dressed for work. Dad was still home also. Things were really getting strange. She helped us prepare for school and told us she would be driving us and we would not need our bikes. I usually looked forward to the bike ride to school but we seldom got to ride in mom's car so I was not bothered by this change in our schedule. I did remind mom that we were going to be late because we were not leaving at the time she had designated. She assured me we would be on time and continued working in the kitchen. I saw a pile of potatoes and eggs and began to worry. She had made a large pile of tortillas that morning and handed us a tacito of scrambled eggs and bacon for breakfast. We ate them at the table with a glass of milk as we continued to watch mom.

Dad was outside tinkering with the truck and was making a racket. It sounded like he was hitting something with hammer. I walked to the door and peeked out and saw that he was attempting to pound the rear bumper back into shape. He was working on the truck as we pulled out and headed for school. Mom did not let us take the football with us like we normally did. At the rate we were going we would not have time to play anyway. We never left this late.

On the way to school mom told us not to say anything about her and dad not working today. I wondered who she thought I would tell. Mom dropped us off at the front of the school and told us she would pick us up at the same location in the afternoon.

In class we continued to learn about reading and writing. The math was hard for me and I talked to the teacher about getting special help. Fractions were really giving me problems. Mrs. Mendez had helped me along but she was spending too much time with me and neglecting the other kids. She told me I could get more attention if she sent me to the "special ed" class. It made me wonder who Ed was and why he was special.

That evening mom picked us up at school. This of course cut into our football games we usually played with the other kids. She was exactly where she dropped us off earlier in the day. When we pulled into the driveway dad's truck had changed. It now had the familiar camper shell back on it. The rear bumper was bent back into shape. It needed smoothing and painting but it looked a lot better than it did in the morning. The site of the camper gave me bad memories of the trip across the desert. As we were getting out of the car I asked mom why the camper was back on the truck. She ignored my question and took us inside the house. She had dinner ready for us. It was boiled eggs and potatoes with tortillas. Things were getting worse by the minute. The house looked different. I noticed some items that had been there this morning were gone now. Pots and pans that mom had out on the counters were gone and so was the table and chairs. Mom said we could take our food outside and eat on the picnic table if we wanted. My brothers and I walked outside and sat on the table. Mom had given us our meal on paper towels instead of plates. I was really starting to worry now. When we finally sat at the wooden table I noticed a small trailer parked behind the house. I walked towards it as I ate my potato burrito. I had given my eggs to Jose because I hated boiled eggs. I walked around the trailer and looked inside it since the back doors were wide open. In it were the contents of our house. I saw our bunk beds, television and mom and dads bed. What was going on?

I stood there chewing my potato taco and I felt someone coming up behind me. I turned and there was dad. He had a box in his hands: it was my comics. My collection had grown and I probably had over fifty books in the box. He handed me the box and asked me if I wanted to put it in the trailer or the truck so I could have something to read tomorrow. I was in shock! Dad was asking me for my opinion and was concerned about my reading. I bit into the burrito and held in my mouth as I took the box with both hands. I must have looked like the village idiot: I had a big burrito in my mouth, a box of comics in my hands and a look of disbelief in my eyes. Carlos and Jose had witnessed the entire event, but waited till dad went back inside before they approached me. They were asking me questions as if I had all the answers. I was not able to answer anything they asked. I could only guess that we were leaving town in a hurry. At the time I did not think I would be spending one more night in our little house and that was okay with me. I did not mind; there were no good memories there anyway.

Mom and dad had cleaned out the house while we were at school. They did it pretty quickly because there was not much to load into the trailer and truck. We did have more than we did when we came over from Texas. Dad pulled the truck around to the back of the house and hooked up the trailer. Mom loaded food into her little car. We were ready to go.

Mom came up to me and my brothers as we finished our tacitos. She asked who wanted to ride with dad and who wanted to ride with her. To me that was a stupid question. I told her I would ride with her and Jose and Carlos could ride in the back seat. She pointed out that her back seat had boxes in it and did not have room for passengers. I lowered my head and turned towards my brothers. I told them they could both sit with mom and I would ride with dad. If anyone was going to face the wrath of my father it would not be my brothers. I walked over to his truck and crawled into the back of the camper. I found my box of comics and placed it in the cab of the truck. At least I would have something to read. Dad told us to get into the car and truck as he did a final walk-through of the house.

I got into the truck with a long face. I really did not like being away from my brothers for a long period of time. I also did not like being with my dad for a long period of time. It was starting to get dark and I guess dad was planning to use the cover of darkness to get away from his mojados and the people he had backed into. Well, at least things could only get better wherever we were going. As we were loading into our vehicles I noticed we were still wearing the same clothes we had gone to school in.

We pulled out of the yard with our headlights on. The beams cast a gloom and eerie glow on the area where we had played for over a year. I could see the bare areas of dirt where I had tackled Jose and Carlos on Saturday afternoons. There was another spot where I had fallen off my bike when Carlos hit me with the football.

I had to assume that my parents were doing the right thing for us. My mind wandered to Tio Marko and his family. I would miss them terribly. Jimmy would be wondering where we were at in the morning. His football was in the truck camper as was the helmet Carlos wore. As the truck left, my body racked from side to side. I grabbed the door to steady myself. I thought for a second about jumping out of the truck and running for Marko's house. I decided against it. The corn that had concealed my family months ago was gone now and there was no place to hide. I felt a lump in my throat as the truck pointed in the opposite direction on the road we took to school. I put my left hand on the side of my face so dad would not see the tears that were forming in my eyes. The house had bad memories but the school had nothing but good ones, as did Marko's family. I wondered if Carlos and Jose were feeling the same things. I could not look through the truck to see if mom's car was behind us. I looked at the rearview mirror and tried to look at the right angle till I caught sight of the lights from mom's cars. There it was; my mother and brothers were directly behind us. It was difficult to see at times, to keep the car in view of the mirror, because of the trailer. I secretly feared mom would get lost and I would be stuck with dad. I guess my dad noticed my uneasiness and kept quiet for a while.

The cab of the truck was dark except for the instrument panel. There was not enough light for me to read, so I sat and looked into the night. I had not said a word to my dad since we had left the house. I wonder now if this bothered him, how can you have a child that is frightened to even speak to his own father? At that time I did not care, I just wanted out of the truck. How could I escape? A voice in the dark softly said, "Why don't you go to sleep?" I looked at the dark figure that was my dad and I noticed he was handing me a blanket. I took it from him and wrapped myself in it. I tried to get as comfortable as possible, but at the same time staying as far away from dad. I finally found a comfortable position as I leaned against the passenger door. "Lock the door so you don't fall out." I reached over and pushed the locking button down and the mechanism locked the door. Now I really felt trapped. I had my head against the glass and I continued to look at the lights on the road. I thought of the rides in the migrant bus back in Texas. I was feeling some of the same thoughts again. I still felt there was more to life than this. I knew the vehicle to a better life was not this old truck.

Staring out at the darkness was making my eyes heavy. We were now out of site from any city. The only lights were those of other cars as they passed us or came towards us on the road. My eyes were getting heavier and heavier. Sometimes my dad would hit a bump in the road and my eyes would open wide. I would look in the rear view mirror to make sure mom was still behind us. I could only guess the small headlights following us were hers.

Total darkness hit my eyes then bright lights enveloped the office. I was sitting in a chair with wheels on it. I was surrounded by a beautiful wooden desk. There were pens, papers and folders neatly organized in front of me. I had a phone at one corner of desk. The door to my office was open. I had an overhead view of all this like I was hovering over the entire scene.

This has been a dream that I have had ever since I can remember. I am wearing a stiff, white, starched shirt and a red tie. It matches with the suit pants that are tailored perfectly for me. I don't have on canvas sneakers but instead my feet have black leather Italian-style dress shoes. They have a silver buckle on the side. The buckle matches with the belt wrapped around my waist. My hair is short and clipped neatly around my ears. I have no beard or mustache. I look like I stepped out of an executive clothing catalogue. In my dream I always see myself at this desk. I am signing papers and calling people. The strange thing is that the phone never rings, I am only calling out. There is a coat rack in the corner of the office. My suit coat is hanging there as well as a trench coat. On the floor is an umbrella.

This dream has been with me as a child, through my teenage years. I guess I took the advice of George at the migrant preschool. When I dreamed, I dreamed big. I have always wanted to wear a suit to work, have a nice office and I am the person giving orders, not taking them. I continue to make calls and give orders, not in a controlling manner, but in a manner where other people respect my advice and solutions. As I put down the phone I see a huge gold ring on my right hand. It has a shiny stone imbedded in a star. Around the star is the name of something I can't make out. Later in life I realized that it was a graduation ring from college.

The truck had stopped and I felt my dad exiting the vehicle. I awoke to bright lights and the smell of gasoline. Dad was pumping gas into the truck.

I could see mom's car parked behind us. She would probably be refueling also. I waited until my thoughts were fully recovered and the dream was gone before I freed myself from the blanket. I had wrapped myself like a cocoon. I unlocked the door and stepped out and walked slowly toward mom's car. I was still groggy from sleeping. I noticed Carlos and Jose were asleep. One was in the front seat and the other in the back, surrounded by boxes. Mom sat behind the wheel and she looked tired. Her eyes were wide and had dark spots underneath them. I walked around to her side of the car and she smiled at me as I walked to her. She asked me if I was hungry. I shook my head. I knew she would hand me a burrito of boiled eggs. I was hungry, but not that hungry. I knew I would be getting my fill of potatoes tomorrow. At this point I didn't know if it was late evening or early morning. My dad moved the truck up enough so my mom could fill up her car with gas. She motioned for me to move and she pulled up next to the pump. Dad came over and began to fuel her car. He looked at me and asked me if I was hungry. Once again I shook my head and walked back to the truck. I could see mom and dad talking as he filled her car. When dad finished he motioned for me to come to him. How did he know I was watching him? He asked me to go with him into the store to pay for the gas. He sent me to the bathroom while he walked around in the store. When I came out he tossed me a bag of corn chips and a candy bar with a soda. I had a confused look on my face that quickly turned into a smile. This was strange, but I was hungry. Dad paid the clerk for the gas and snacks and we headed back to the truck.

Dad and I were headed down the road again with mom trailing behind us. I had opened the bag of chips and was making crunching sounds with every bite. Dad looked at me and said, "The boiled egg burritos are pretty bad aren't they?"

I looked over to him and nodded. "They make Jose smell pretty bad too," I said. He laughed and started chewing on corn nuts he had purchased at the gas station. We continued down the road a few miles then I asked him, "Where are we going?"

Dad kept his gaze on the road and responded. "We're going to Palm Springs to stay with your uncle Barry. He's your mom's brother."

I nodded my head like I knew who he was. I had never met him. "What's Palm Springs like?" I asked.

Dad looked forward and continued to chew the corn nuts. You could only see his face when a car's headlights illuminated the cab of the truck. He looked powerful again as the bright lights created shadows on his face. He took a minute to answer then he finally said, "Palm Springs is where a lot of rich people live. It is also a desert. You'll like it." That was enough to confuse anybody. We were headed to the desert where rich people lived? Why would anyone want to live in the desert? I finished off the chips and started in on the candy bar. I bit into it and savored the taste of the chocolate. I don't think dad had ever bought me a candy bar before. I looked at dad again and began to wonder what was causing the change. I suddenly realized he had not had a beer since the incident with the wreck and the mojados. I wonder if his real family being threatened had forced my dad to change. Whatever the reason, this was a better dad than the one I had a few days ago. I was beginning to feel better about the move now. Where ever Palm Springs was, we were headed there in the dark. Things were definitely changing again.

Chapter 6
Adios to Agriculture

"Wake up Betito!" Were the first words I heard in Palm Springs, California. We had finally arrived. I was expecting a longer drive, but this was alright. I did not enjoy driving through deserts at night and I had not slept very much. The sugar and caffeine from the candy bar and cola had kept me awake for hours. I sat in the truck with my dad but had not said more than a few words to him, watching the headlights as they grew brighter and brighter on the road in front of me. I was fascinated how they would start out as a pinpoint of light in the distance then eclipse in front of the truck. Watching the lights had finally put me sleep, only to be awakened a few hours later in the early morning hours before sunrise. We had definitely arrived, but where I was not sure. Everything was dark. My mind was still foggy with sleep and my vision was blurred. I saw a man and woman hugging my mother and father. I vaguely remembered their faces from somewhere in the past. I stayed in the truck and watched the scene from the cab under the comfort of my blanket. I kept one eye on mom and kept the other one closed. I had heard somewhere that you could sleep with one eye closed. I was trying that right now and it wasn't working. The open eye would slowly try to join the other one that was attempting to sleep.

My one half-asleep eye caught mom motioning for me to come to her. I unwrapped myself from the blanket and made my way to her. Mom and dad introduced me to my uncle Barry and aunt Ester. They were both about the same age as my mom and dad. You could see the resemblance between Barry and my mother. I learned that Barry was about two years older than mom. Ester was exactly the same age as mom.

Both made comments on how big I had gotten. I guess I was bigger, but I could not know what they had compared me to. I could still not recall where I had seen them before. Uncle Barry bent down and offered me a handshake. I took his hand and shook it. He squeezed my hand hard. I squeezed it back as hard as a nine year old could muster. He grinned and rubbed the top of my little coconut head. He mentioned something to my dad about how strong I was. Give me a football and I'll also show you how fast I am too, I thought to myself. Aunt Ester had my mother follow her into their house while dad and Uncle Barry talked.

The house that we walked into was nice and roomy. It had a thick carpet on the floor and large couches. The television that was the focus of the room was huge. I had never seen one that big. The couches were plush and inviting. I still felt very groggy and I felt that if I stopped moving I would fall asleep wherever I stood. On one couch there was a pile of blankets and pillows. My aunt pointed to them and my mom grabbed a pillow and blanket and told me to curl up on the couch and go to sleep. I eagerly grabbed the blanket and pillow and headed to the biggest of the sofas. I curled up in the fetal position and sleep started to come back to me. Just at the point of dozing off I heard someone walk into the room. I opened one eye and saw my dad carrying Jose into the living room. Mom was right behind him. She placed a pillow on the other end of the couch I was on and dad placed him in the makeshift sleeping spot. Mom covered him with the blanket. They both walked out and returned with Carlos. They placed him on the sofa opposite from the one Jose and I shared. Mom covered him with a blanket and she and dad started walking out. I raised my head and reminded them about Jose's bedwetting problem. Mom smiled and walked over to Jose and woke him up. They walked through the living room and disappeared.

As I tried to sleep I watched Carlos and Jose curl into their makeshift beds on the couches. The entire event was so strange and I couldn't make out why. The situation was so strange it was keeping me from going to sleep. What was so strange? Leaving our home without telling anyone? No, we had done that in Florida. Arriving in the dark to a strange home? No, we had already done that too. Then it hit me. When I saw dad carrying Jose and Carlos it was the first time I had ever seen my dad hold any of us. I thought that was strange. Tio Marko was always hugging Jenny and Jimmy. I had even heard him tell them that he loved them. I had never heard dad tell us that. Tio Marko had hugged me more than my dad had in my entire life. I wondered if being carried to bed counted for a hug? If it did I had been cheated again. Now that the mystery had been solved I took a final look around the unfamiliar surrounding and adjusted myself on the couch. It was really quite comfortable. I would not have any problems sleeping tonight. I decided to sleep with both eyes closed this time.

Sleep came quickly once I closed my eyes. The couch was warm and soft. The blankets and pillows smelled so different from what I was used to. Mom would wash all our clothes and blankets and make them smell so fresh. She would then dry everything on a clothes line. That gave everything a natural clean scent. Our blankets were so crisp when she changed our sheets and pillow cases. These were nice too, but they did not have a scent of freshness like my mom's. Somehow my body did not care. Sleep beckoned me, or maybe it was my dreams calling me. I drifted into deep sleep and from far away someone was calling me. It was a voice coming from a bank of fog. I could barely make out my name, but there it was again. "Betito, Betitio come here," the voice called. I curled tighter into my pillow and blanket but the voice kept summoning me.

"Here I am, here I am," I said softly. I did not know who was calling me from the fog so I had to be careful. "Who are you?" I asked the fog. Then a light began to make the fog glow and I could make out a figure with and outstretched hand. The figure was that of a large person. As big as he was I was not frightened or scared. For some reason I felt safe. The figure began to step out of the mist of the fog and suddenly it became clearer. It was Tio Marko. He had his hand outstretched and was motioning me to come to him. I felt like I was walking in slow motion to him. There were wisps of fog that looked like mini tornadoes around me. With every step the fog swirled around my legs. The closer I got to Marko, the brighter the lights became. It seemed like hours passed until I reached him. Suddenly there I was, in front of the gentle giant. He was looking down at me and his smile had faded. No longer did he wear the face of a happy man. His face was long and said. "Betito, why did you leave me?" he asked. I did not know how to answer him. Seeing him so sad made me want to cry.

I looked at Marko and tears filled my eyes. "I didn't want to go, really I didn't!" I told him as I wiped my eyes with my sleeves. I lowered my head. I could not bear seeing his face. I had let this man down. I did not even tell him good bye. He had been so good to me and my brothers and we did not even make an attempt to thank him.

"Sit down," Marko told me. Suddenly we were in his house and he motioned to a chair next to his. "Do you still have the box I gave you?" he asked. I nodded to him, even though I still could not bear to look at him. "Good, promise me you will keep reading them." I raised my head and looked at him. He was leaning forward in his chair and looking at me closely. "Promise me you will keep reading them!" he said a little louder.

"I promise, I promise!" I said to him. Suddenly my eyes once again filled with tears. I came out of my chair and hugged him. "I'm so sorry! I wanted to say good bye to you I really did, but dad wouldn't stop!" Marko put his huge hand over my lips and cut my rambling off.

He finally smiled and his eyes went soft. "I know," he said softly. That was all he had to say. I knew he understood. The huge man wrapped his arms around me and hugged me. I felt so warm and comforted. Now I knew everything was okay. All I had to do now was keep my promise.

The light began to return. I could make out voices of kids and adults. I could also make out the pinging sounds of spoons hitting bowls. "Hurry up or you will miss the bus," I heard a voice say.

"I don't want to go to school," I heard a child's voice protest. That's blasphemy, I thought to myself. I slowly opened my eyes and let them adjust to the brightness. I could see Carlos across the room from me. He was still wrapped up on the couch. He had his entire head poking out from the blanket. His black hair was poking straight up and he looked funny. I raised my head up and saw Jose covered by a blanket also.

"Hello," a little girl said. I almost jumped out of my skin! I was not fully awake and this girl had scared me half to death. She was standing directly behind me where I could not see her. I didn't think highly of girls at this point of my life but felt very embarrassed that one had scared me.

I regained my composure and looked straight up at her, "hi yourself!" I said to her in a deep voice. I was trying to look as mean as I could.

She started to laugh. "I scared you didn't I?" She said in a girl's giggly voice.

"No you didn't!" I told her in defiance.

"Then why is your hair sticking straight up?" she said in a laughing voice as she walked away. Now I really didn't like girls. I started rubbing the top of my head and I could feel that my hair was poking straight up. I rubbed my hair in an attempt to get it to lie down. I tried this four or five times and I could feel it was not working.

I sat up and surveyed the people that had so rudely awakened me. There was the antagonizing girl that I knew I would not like. She was about my age at first glance. She was thin with brown curly hair and dark eyes. She was way too perky for me. She was standing at the bar that separated the living area from the kitchen. She was doing some type of cheerleading move while another girl watched. The other girl had straight black hair and dark eyes. She was probably the same age as Jose. She was sitting at the table and had a white bowl in front of her. Across from her a boy that appeared to be younger than Carlos was eating something out of a white bowl. A box of cereal was on the table and the boy reached across the table for it to refill his bowl. I was about to stand up when the future cheerleader leapt into the air and kicked her legs out and pointed a hand at the ceiling. She let out a "Go team!" as she hit the height of her leap. At that precise moment I closed my eyes and hit the apex of my headache.

"God, I think I died and landed in something worse than a migrant camp," I thought to myself. I was really beginning to hate this girl. I walked over to the kitchen table and the girl had one leg bent behind her and one arm cocked at the elbow and the other pointing straight up. The girl at the table was clapping her hands in approval. She held that position for a few seconds like she was waiting for someone to give her a score. My cousin Nancy would eventually become a cheerleader for a large high school someday. This morning she was just annoying.

"You look like a chicken," I told her as I walked by her. Nancy stuck her tongue out at me and I pretended I did not see her.

"Betito! I'm going to tell your father what you told her!" I heard my mom say. She had walked into the kitchen unannounced.

Great, maybe he can put me out of my misery, I thought to myself. I realize now why I disliked cheerleaders. I had no problems with mornings. I enjoyed rising early and starting my day. I did have a problem with a cheerleader sharing the same room with me in the morning. Mom walked over to Jose and Carlos and woke them, then led us all to the bathroom. She had put out our toothbrushes and a change of clothes. Our aunt had set out towels and soap for a shower. I looked at my brothers and saw that we all really needed a good long shower with a lot of soap. We had not showered since the day before yesterday. All that time in a vehicle had put a little odor on us. My brothers and I had hair that was poking straight up as well as a look that said, "Please, wash me."

Mom closed the door to the bathroom and we began the task of washing up. I jumped in the shower first while my brothers brushed their teeth. We had this routine down. When I came out of the shower Jose was ready for his turn. I then began brushing my teeth. Since Carlos was the youngest he had to wait till last. My bothers and I said very little in the bathroom. I think we were still in shock over our move the night before. It's not that we had been uprooted from one location to another, we had done that before. I guess it's because we thought life was finally getting "normal" for us. Dad had cut down on his drinking, we had been going to school everyday and we had even enjoyed our first Christmas. The new unknown was now just outside the bathroom door. We did not know these people. All I did know was that there was a screaming cheerleader in the kitchen of this strange house. So far I was not impressed with Palm Springs.

After our showers we changed and found our mom in the kitchen, she had bowls of cereal waiting for us. We all sat at the table and ate while mom and my aunt talked a few feet away. I was eating very slowly. I wanted to hear every word they said. It is hard to eavesdrop while chewing crunchy food like corn flakes. I strained to pick out key words mom and Aunt Ester were talking about, and made out something about a job, and yes, school. There it was. The most important thing to me: when were we going to school? I heard my aunt say that dad and Uncle Barry had already left to go find a job. They had left very early in the morning and would not return till late in the evening. That was fine with me. I kept leaning in the direction of the conversation and it was getting harder to hear anything. Jose was chewing with his mouth open. He had a habit of doing that. The crunching sound was very annoying. Carlos sat across from me silently enjoying his bowl of cereal.

I gave Jose a mean look in hopes of getting him to close his mouth. It did not work. He returned my glance and kept right on chewing. "Chew with your mouth closed!" I said sternly. Jose leaned forward and proceeded to chew with his mouth open wider. A piece of corn flake fell out of his mouth and he picked it up and threw it back in. "Mom!" I yelled across the kitchen. My complaint fell on deaf ears. My mother was too busy discussing things like jobs and houses with my aunt to listen to me. I would get Jose later. I finished my bowl of cereal and skipped on seconds. Jose and Carlos were both on their second bowl. I stepped away form the table and took my bowl to the sink. As I walked by mom and my aunt I asked, "Where's the kids, are they in school?"

My aunt looked at me and said, "Yes, today is Friday and they will be in school all day."

"When are we going to school?"

"You will go to school on Monday," My aunt said. I was about to continue our conversation when my mom reached over to where I was standing and placed her hand on the back of my neck. She nudged me out of the kitchen with a slight pressure from her hand. I was about to ask another question but the pressure had increased to the point where my head was leaning forward and I thought I would fall. I got the message. I walked out of the kitchen and back to the table. I would have to talk to my brothers. I guess adults weren't ready to talk about education with me.

I walked back into the living room and sat on the couch. I looked around at my new surroundings and wondered what tomorrow would bring. I couldn't wait to go to school in this new town. I sank into the couch and leaned back into its cushions. I put my hands behind my back and looked into the future as far as I could. A smile came to face and I thought about football games to come. I pictured myself running for touchdowns, catching passes and spiking the ball. Wow, wait till they see me.

"Betito, come help me!" I got up from the couch and followed my mom's voice. It was coming from outside. My brothers followed me out as we tracked down mom. She was standing next to the truck and she had the camper door open. My aunt Ester was with her and she was pointing in the direction of an old house. I walked over to mom and she started walking towards the house and she asked me to follow. We walked through a sandy field. I thought we were going to unload the truck but instead we were walking to our new home. The house was surrounded by a sand-covered field with a few trees in it. It was a white wooden framed house. It needed a paint job really bad. It had cracks in the paint and it was peeling in some areas. We walked around the front of the house and entered through the front door. The door also needed paint. It creaked as Aunt Ester pushed it open. My brothers and I stayed outside while the mom and Ester walked through the interior. We walked around the outside and explored the new surroundings we would call home for the next year. The yard had no grass.

Palm Springs in 1974 was a desert unless it was being irrigated. There was no water falling on this yard. It was bare dirt and sand. A few bushes served as a lawn. At the edge of the "lawn" was a plantation of orange trees. They were tall and very green. It had ditches running in between the trees where water was pumped in to keep the trees thriving. I didn't care about the house; that was up to my mom. I had lived in worse. I couldn't wait to explore the groves of orange trees. If this was going to be home I would make the best of it.

That afternoon mom pulled the truck close to the house and we began to unload our belongings. The inside of the house was as bad as the outside, but it had four walls and a roof. It had two bedrooms and it was about the same size as the house we had left a day ago. We helped mom as best we could and saved the heavier things for dad and Uncle Barry. It only took us few hours before we had the truck and trailer empty. I stood outside in the dirt yard and looked over the house. It had our possessions in it but it did not feel like a home. I still felt like something was missing. This dilapidated house was not in my dreams. A star football player or a successful executive would not have a home like this. I wanted a house like Tio Marko's. It had to be big and wide. I wanted rooms for each of my brothers. I was growing tired of having to share a room. As much as I loved them it did not mean I wanted to share a bedroom with them. Instead of bunk beds I wanted my own bed with fresh sheets like they advertised on the television. I wanted toys that nine-year-old boys should have. Instead I had another old house with no grass in the front yard. I had lived in worse of course, but this did not really feel like an upgrade. At least we were through unloading. When you don't have much to move, unloading is very easy. My daydream was broken by the sound of our truck engine coming to life.

Mom drove the truck back to her brother's house. Both Carlos and Jose were in the truck so I began to walk towards to our neighbor's house. I was going to be within walking distance of Uncle Barry's and Aunt Ester's house. I guess that made us neighbors. I took my time walking, not in a hurry to eat lunch. We would not have power in the little house until Monday, and hopefully I would be in school when someone came out to take care of grown up things like electricity and gas.

The short walk seemed to take hours. My head was hung low and my brow was heavy. I was homesick for the small house we had left behind in the dark. I especially missed Jimmy and Tio Marko. I missed school most of all. It had taken so long to feel accepted by all the kids. It took lots of football games and touchdowns to prove a little Mexican boy was no different than the White kids. I had read the same books and made A's just like the smart Anglo boys and girls in the class. I felt like I would have to start all over again. I looked forward to the playground and the classroom at the school we were headed to, but regretted leaving the other school. It felt like I had deserted my friends. By the time I raised my head I was in my uncle's yard. His house was brick and actually had nice green grass in the yard. In the dark I had not noticed this, now it stood out like a sore thumb. I looked back at our house. There was a definite contrast in the colors. The brown dirt and the green grass only enhanced how bad our house looked.

"Betito, come and eat!" I heard my mom yell. I walked in the house before she could call for me again. I did not want to take a chance on her telling my dad I was not minding her. I headed to the table where Jose and Carlos were seated. They each had a sandwich and potato chips on a paper plate. We rarely had this kind of food at our last home so it was a nice change of pace. I thanked God we did not have to eat the tacos of boiled eggs and potatoes any more. I sat in the same chair where I had eaten cereal earlier that morning and began to eat. My mom and aunt were back at the same place again in the kitchen talking about woman stuff. This was getting very boring. I asked mom if I could take my plate outside. She nodded and I walked outside carrying a can of soda and my plate. I looked for a shady spot in the yard and put my lunch on the grass. I ran to the truck and grabbed my box of comics out of the front and headed back to my food. By the time I got there Jose was sitting in my spot. I really wanted to be alone but I guess Jose wanted the opposite. I knew that he was as scared as I was of going to a new school. I sat next to him and he scooted over a bit. We both had our back to the shade tree. I handed him a comic and grabbed one for me. We sat there and chewed our food without saying a word. We both finished our food and looked at each other, knowing what the other was thinking.

"Want some more?" Jose asked.

"Sure," I said. I handed Jose my paper plate and he headed back into the house. The sandwiches were pretty plain but the chips were good. I put the comic back and reached into the box and pulled out the first one I touched. Alright, the Avengers! My favorite; I had actually read this one several times. I stared at the cover and something clicked in my head. I looked at the art work on the front page. Could I draw this? I bet I could. Jose came back and handed me a plate with another sandwich on it. He had one also with a huge pile of chips. "Did mom give you that many chips?" I asked him.

"Nope," he said with a mouthful of chips. "I took them when she wasn't looking." This child must have a tapeworm, I thought to myself. I shook my head and continued to read my comic and started on my second sandwich. I was on my third page when Jose ripped a very loud burp. I turned my head and he had a look of pride.

"I bet you were proud of that one," I told him. Jose nodded and kept reading his comic.

We sat under the tree with my box of comics for hours. I think mom was just happy to have us out of her way so she could talk with Aunt Ester. I raised my head when I heard a car come down the driveway. The only reason a car would turn on the driveway was to get to our uncle's house or the junky little house. The car belonged to my uncle. My dad was in the front seat with him. I lowered my head back to the book. I really did not care he was back. In my mind he was responsible for uprooting my life. We could have stayed in the nice quiet town with the nice school if wasn't for him. It made me feel good to ignore him. I heard the car pull into the driveway and the car doors open and close. I kept on reading and soon hit the last page. My rear end was hurting so I changed positions and lay on my stomach. I pulled out another comic and started in on the first page. Spiderman, good choice I thought. Jose had gotten up and walked back into the house. I decided to stay in the yard and enjoy the shade a while longer. I did not care what was going on in the house. I should have though.

Jose came back out and my dad was behind him. I did not think anything about it until they both got closer. I knew something was wrong. Dad was walking with heavy steps behind Jose and I knew what that meant. They came closer and Jose came to stop, only for a second. Dad never broke stride. His right boot went from a step to a kick that resembled a football player kicking a football for the extra point. Jose went flying by me head first. What was going on? I was sure we had not done anything wrong. My dad ordered me to get up and start walking towards the old house. I jumped to my feet just in time to meet the same fate that had sent Jose face-first into the sand and dirt. I felt dad's boot connect with my tail bone, sending a sharp pain up my spine. Jose was already on his feet and running towards our new home. I hit the ground and bounced up and followed him. I had my hand on my rear in an attempt to protect myself. "Move your hand now!" I heard my dad yell. I did not do what he said and I felt his boot connect with my hand. I felt my finger ignite with pain. I swore he had just broken all my fingers. The kick pushed me forward but I did not fall. Jose was faster so he stayed far enough not to get another kick. We were both herded to the front door of the old house.

"Steal food!" my dad yelled. He could yell at the top of his lungs and no one would hear. The windows and doors were closed in this old shack. His heavy boot connected with my side and I was flung against the wall. Jose joined me against the same wall when dad caught him, and threw him like a rag doll. At least he was not kicked like I was. "If you ever call your cousin a chicken or steal food again I will beat you both again!" my dad yelled at us. The beating continued for a few bruising seconds that felt like hours. I waited for the shock to wear off and the numbness to set in. It was always the same, shock then numbness. I can best describe it as an outer body experience. I felt like I was hovering over the entire event. I no longer felt pain. Instead I began to think of why I was being kicked and punched. I recalled the "chicken" event but not the part about stealing food. Then I recalled Jose coming out earlier with the huge pile of chips. That was it! We were mercilessly being beaten for calling my cousin a chicken and Jose coming out with the big pile of chips! At least I knew why dad was so angered. My spirit seemed to hover over us until dad tired and he walked out of the house. We lay there for a few minutes and continued to cry. I heard the front door close and the screen door slam shut.

I waited for a few minutes and I continued to sob. I came to a crouching position and crawled to the closest window. I looked out and saw dad as he walked back to the brick house. The coast was clear so I looked down at Jose and tried to comfort him as best as I could. My toughness helped him a little and he slowly began to stop crying. In between sobs he asked me, "How do you keep from crying?" I told him I had learned it in a comic book and would help him by sharing it with him later. We both tried to sit on our rears but the kicks still smarted. We tried to lie on our stomachs but the kicks to the ribs hurt too. The least painful thing to do was stand. We stood there in the empty living room and talked while the sun began to set. We were too scared to leave. I asked him who had told dad what we had done. Jose looked at me and told me he had overheard mom and dad talking. Well, that was that. I could no longer even count on my mom for protection. From that point forward Jose and I began to grow closer together. We bonded because of adversity. When you cannot turn to your own mother and father you have to find someone. We knew we were on our own now, so we talked about how to get even with our parents, slowly we began to joke and cut up. I had managed to get Jose's mind off what had happened earlier. He had a short-term memory and recovered quickly. I on the other hand I did not.

I got over what had just happened but would not forget. We were both laughing about something Jose had said when we heard the front door creak open. We both froze. Our memories had not had time to forget the beating we had just received about an hour ago. We stood there expecting the worst. We listened to footsteps coming through the house. I relaxed my body, recognizing Carlos's footsteps. He had come to tell us to come to the brick house. He said it was time for dinner and dad had made it clear if we came crying it would be worse for both Jose and I. I laughed out loud and headed for the other house with Carlos and Jose following me. Carlos kept asking about why dad had taken us away. I told him not to worry about it. We walked into the living room of my uncle's house and his family was at the table having dinner. The kids were sitting at the coffee table with paper plates and plastic forks. My mother rose from the table and handed us each a plate of food. We took it to where the other kids were and joined them. I looked up and caught a stare from my father. I knew that look. It meant if I stepped out of line it would be a long night.

I sat next to Nancy and asked her about school. She was not in the mood to talk. In fact it looked like she had just received a whipping also. Her eyes were red and swollen. She did not have much to say. I looked at her sister Bonnie for an answer and it came. "She did not make the tryout for cheerleader," she said. I looked at Nancy and another tear came down her face. She stood up and headed for her room crying louder now. My dad stood up and started heading towards me. My Aunt Ester stopped him and told him it had nothing to do with me. Dad did not look convinced but bought the story any way. Bonnie looked at me and asked me, "What's your dad's problem?" I shrugged my shoulders and kept eating. Bonnie began to tell me how good Nancy had done in the tryouts and had lost anyway. She told me how Nancy had been the only Mexican girl to try out. I thought that was not a big deal. Evidently it was. Bonnie continued to tell me how the judges were made up of all the sixth graders at the school. A few of the other girls trying out had told the students how embarrassing it would be to have a "wetback" girl cheering for the team. As Bonnie continued the story I felt like I understood her situation. I recalled the football games at the last school. I told Bonnie of being called an "All American Wetback." She shook her head in disgust. She had no need, want or desire to be a cheerleader, but the way she described her sister, it sounded like Nancy had potential.

Nancy slowly got over her losing the cheerleading position. To help her feel better, her parents took her and my brothers out for pizza the next day.

I had never eaten pizza before. I guess it had to be good because Uncle Barry's kids were so excited over it. We piled into mom's car and she followed Aunt Ester with her kids. When we arrived at the restaurant we were seated at a long table. We were served soft drinks by a young man who kept coming around and asking if everything was alright. I sat there and took in the surroundings. I had never been to a sit down place to eat. We could never afford it, and plus there was dad. He did not like to go out in public much. He liked staying at home and drinking. In fact, that was where he was now. He and Uncle Barry had stayed home to drink beer.

I was next to mom, and Aunt Ester sat across from us. Nancy was at the head of the table, milking this cheerleader bit all the way. Mom and Ester were talking about mom's new job. She was going to clean rooms at a hotel with Ester, and dad had secured a job as a security guard. Mom was very excited. I heard her tell Ester how she was going to enjoy working indoors for a change. She was not excited about dad's hours. He would work from 11:00pm to 7:00am. I sat there and soaked up the conversation between mom and Ester. I had my elbows on the table and my hands cupped my face, until the pizza arrived then I sat upright to get a better look.

The person waiting our table had two additional people help bring three huge, round shaped, flat plates with something on them. Each person had a big plate that they put in the middle of the table. It smelled great! It looked like a huge tortilla with all kinds of stuff on it. All the pizzas were still steaming hot. I looked down the table and Jose and Carlos were in awe. Their little mouths were open and their eyes were trying to take it all in. It was overwhelming. The sights, the smells, it was almost too much. My aunt Ester took a funny-shaped knife and lifted a triangle out of the first pizza. It had trails of cheese falling off it. I leaned over and asked mom what it was. She told me it was cheese, and that Nancy would get the first slice because of the bad day she had Friday. I thought about the whole milking thing again but never took my eyes off the pizzas.

Nancy took the slice and blew on it to cool it down. Aunt Ester told mom to dig in and she began to put slices on my plate. I must have looked like I had not eaten in years. My mouth was watering as mom put a big slice on my plate. I took the plate and set it in front of me. The smell was wonderful but not familiar. It had these red circles on top and I guess it was white cheese with a red sauce underneath it all. I did not know how to eat this thing. I looked over and copied Nancy, using both hands to take a big bite of the steaming pizza. "Make sure it cools before you eat it," I heard Aunt Ester say a little too late. In a scene that resembled my dad in the kitchen, my eyes watered and the roof of my mouth began to blister. I threw the slice down and grabbed for my soda.

"The cheese is hot you dummy!" Nancy told me. Still, it tasted great. I grabbed the slice of pizza again and blew on it just like I had seen Nancy do. This worked better. My brothers and I had been exposed to pizza and Monday we would be facing something totally different and worse: racism.

Chapter 7
Burnt Potato Chip

On Monday we had to wake up earlier than usual. We were still living in our uncle's house. Today would be the last day we would spend the night there. We had six kids preparing for school and four adults preparing for work. With only two bathrooms it was a challenge. Mom and dad had been up for a while when they woke my brothers and me. Mom quickly rushed us into the guest bathroom and prepared us for school. Our clothes were nice this time, as nice as I knew they could be. I would wear a pair of jeans and a striped pullover shirt. Both were worn but had no holes. Once I was ready I went back to the couch where I had slept and folded my blanket into a nice square shape. I also did the same to my brothers' blankets. With that done I sat on the couch and waited for everyone else to finish getting ready for their day.

I still remember sitting at the kitchen table eating cereal with my brothers and cousins. I was excited yet scared. If what I had heard about Nancy's cheerleading tryouts were true, what could I expect? I shrugged those thoughts off and continued to eat my bowl of corn flakes. I looked up and Jose was once again eating with his mouth open. He was making sure the two girls could see him. I smiled and returned to my bowl. I would have manners and eat with my mouth closed. I read the back of the cereal box to practice my reading skills. I had very little time to read my comics this weekend and needed to brush up so I could impress my new teachers.

After breakfast my aunt and mother came in and lead us to the car. My cousins usually rode a bus to school but since we had to register today we all were going in together.

I kept looking out the window as we drove to school. There were was a large contrast in this land. Sand dunes that ended in deep rich green grass made for a strange landscape. It was evident where irrigation started and stopped. There were also large buildings that were new to me. In the agricultural areas that I was used to, there were never any sky scrapers or large office complexes. I kept my face pressed against the glass and ignored the rest of people in the car. My thoughts were not on childish games that were going on inside but of views into the future. I was once again feeling like I did not belong. I had felt that ever since we had arrived at my uncle's house.

My aunt led my brothers and me to the registration office as my cousins waved goodbye and went to their classrooms. We sat in the waiting area as mom tried her hardest to fill out the documents necessary to gain us access to public education. At one point I was called in to translate to the secretary. I tried my best but there are some words that just do not mix well in the Mexican language. It took over an hour but soon all the forms were complete. My mother and aunt left us and we waited for our teachers. I had waved at my mother but she had turned away and did not see my wave. I guess she was also in a hurry to get to her job. Maybe she wanted to make a good first impression.

One by one my brothers were taken away to their classes and soon I was the only one left. This place did not feel the same as the school I had left last week. It was larger, colder and I had yet to see one Hispanic child. I sat in the waiting area wondering how I would fit in. I had my hands in my face and my elbows resting on my knees. I was not smiling when an office assistant called me to her. She handed me a slip of paper and asked me if I could read it. I looked at it and then at her. I wanted to say, "I am Hispanic, not a second grader." Instead all I said was, "Yes ma'am." That was all my little voice could put out at that moment. The slip had only stated that I was supposed to report to room 512. I saw that it meant fifth grade, room 12. I saw a name too, Mrs. Banks.

"Welcome Alberto," Mrs. Banks told the classroom. I smiled as I stood in front of the class. "Alberto is new to our class and he will be sitting next to James." Mrs. Banks pointed to an empty desk in the back of the class. I smiled and walked towards my new seat. I took the straightest path and made no eye contact with any of the kids. From the front of the class I could see I was the only Hispanic in this classroom. There were about 20 kids in the room, all wearing nice clothes. "If you open up your desk, you will find an English book so you can follow along," Mrs. Banks told me as I sat down. I lifted the top of the desk and searched for the book. The boy next to me asked, "Do you need help?" I looked at him and shook my head. I found the book and closed the top of my desk. I guess that boy next to me also thought I could not read.

"Please turn to page eighty eight and Alberto will start reading on the second paragraph," Mrs. Banks told the class. I found the page and began to read. It was some story about Robin Hood. I had read this before so I started reading and tried my best not to mess up. I had read about two paragraphs when the teacher asked me to stop. She called on another student. That boy ended up being the one that had asked me for help. He read as best he could but struggled. After he read two paragraphs I leaned over and asked him if he needed help. The boy gave me a scowl. I smiled and followed along. The teacher randomly called on kids to read and for the most part everyone did well. A few struggled more than others but I sure did feel a lot better about my abilities now. I felt confident I could fit in. As we read a bell went off and the all the kids rose from their desks and headed out the door. I walked to Mrs. Banks and she informed me it was the bell that marked a fifteen minute break. We were to go to the bathrooms and stretch our legs. She selected James, the boy that sat in front of me, to show me where the boy's room was located. I followed him but he did not speak to me. I tried to ask him a few questions but he just ignored me. I gave up asking him anything and followed him into the bathroom.

I found a space in the long "trough" urinal and began to relieve myself. I heard someone say out loud, "Mexican piss!" All the sudden all the boys that were next to me zipped up and ran out of the boy's room. I stood at the urinal all alone and confused. I looked around and a boy came out of one of the stalls. He looked just as confused as I was. "What was that all about?" I asked him. He lifted up both arms in confusion as he walked to the sink to wash his hands. I used the sink next to him and washed my hands. He told me his name was Johnny. I recognized him as the boy that had asked me if I needed help looking for my English book. We both walked out of the restroom and found about fifteen boys and girls standing in front of the door giggling. They pointed at me and started laughing.

A girl stepped out of the crowd and said, "Is it true Mexican pee smells real bad?"

I kept walking past her and said, "Go in there and check for your self." I felt uncomfortable but kept walking. The hairs on the back of my neck stood on edge. I forced myself not to look back and keep walking, feeling like an antelope when it is hunted by a cheetah. It has to look forward and not waste time looking back. I followed my steps back to room 512. I could hear footsteps behind me. I could tell there were a lot kids behind me. I began to feel sweat on my brow and could not believe my first day of school was starting out so bad.

The door to our classroom was open and I walked inside. Then I felt a blow in the middle of my back. I fell forward and fell on my chest. I hit the floor and bounced up like a rubber ball. I spun around and both hands came up ready for action. My face had become wrinkled and I scanned the group of kids behind me. Everyone looked innocent. No one was going to step up to face me. I felt like a superhero with no one to fight.

"Alberto!" Mrs. Banks said. "What is the meaning of this?" she asked me. I told her someone had hit me in the back and had knocked me down.

"He just fell like a big dumb Mexican," James said. Mrs. Banks gave him a stern look and he kept walking to his desk with a touch of guilt in his step. I saw what I needed to. I would not turn my back on him again. I also knew I could not count on my teacher for help. At my last school something like this would not have been tolerated. Here the guilty party was not even addressed. I walked to my desk and when I came to where James was sitting I gave him my meanest look possible. I had to sit behind him so I had to get by him. I enlarged my field of view and saw that he was going to slide his foot out to trip me as I walked by. He stuck his foot out and I was ready for him. I stepped down as heavy as I could with the heel of my foot on top of the part of shoe that covered the toes. He gave out a yelp.

"What is going on back there?" Mrs. Banks asked.

"I accidentally stepped on James's foot. That's all," I said loud enough for her to hear me. I smiled my biggest smile possible then I sat down.

"Spic, I'll get you," he said under his breath. Spic? What was that? I had never heard that word before. The way he had used it must mean it's bad. I blew it off and listened to the teacher. She instructed us to get our math books out, and gave us an assignment. She then walked out of the classroom. I leaned over to Johnny and asked him what a spic was.

"It's a dirty Mexican, Alberto," he said. "I'm surprised you've never heard that word before."

"Well I've never known a spic before, that might explain it," I told him. I was hurt and stung. I had been called a lot of things but never this. I looked myself over. I had on my cleanest oldest clothes, so what was the problem. I had been called a wetback, coconut and now spic. It seemed it would never stop. I leaned over to Johnny and said, "Hey Johnny, please call me Albert." He smiled and nodded his head.

James turned around in his desk and said, "And I'll call you burnt potato chip." Once again I was baffled. What in the world was a burnt potato chip? Johnny was laughing as quietly as he could. I leaned over and asked what James was talking about.

He said, "A burnt potato chip is when you open a bag of chips and you have all white chips, except one that's burned and black. That's you." So that was it. I was the one burned chip in the bag of all white ones. I had learned how to make fun of Mexicans in two different ways in less than five minutes. I felt enraged, furious and powerless all in one second.

I wanted to get out of my chair and really hurt James. Then I remembered the incident at the old school when Little Red had made fun of my brothers and Jimmy, while we were playing football. I knew beating this kid was not the answer. I tried to ignore the whole thing but it was not easy. The teacher was still out of the class when James said out loud, "I smell something burning, you know like a burnt potato chip!"

I felt my head turn red and flushed. My temper was boiling over. I could not ignore this boy any more. I started to rise out of my chair when the door opened and Mrs. Banks walked back into the classroom. All the kids were giggling under their breaths. She looked around and everyone stopped. I was the only one in the class not smiling. She looked right at me. She must have noticed my face was red and I was angry, but she pretended like she did not notice and went to her desk and sat down. How could she pretend nothing was happening? I was too hurt to go to her so I decided to pretend nothing had happened. I felt like Superman with a kryptonite dagger though my heart. I was nothing to these kids, but they were ganging up on me for no other reason than I was a Mexican. I thought to myself, maybe things will change when they get to know me.

I continued to hope for change the rest of the day. I ended up eating lunch with the class but no one spoke to me. I ate in a group but alone. No one dared speak to the "burnt chip." James was very popular in the class and carried all the weight. I ate in silence. I felt very sad and rejected but inside I knew there would be better times. I also knew this was not going to be the only time I would be chastised for being Mexican. Halfway through lunch I lifted my chin and decided I would not let these kids ruin my day or life. I finished the meal and turned in my tray and went outside. I walked a little taller, a little straighter in my step. All the heroes in my comics were different, and so was I. So why should I let these people bring me down? I walked outside into the California sunshine with a smile on my face. I would be my own hero.

I walked around the playground and let the sun hit my face. If I was a "burnt potato chip," I would just have to get a little more toasty. I watched as the kids came out of the lunch room and began to play in the yard. I knew better than to go try and talk to any of them so I continued my walk on the edge of the playground. I reached a chain linked fence that marked the edge of the school property. I saw a Mexican boy leaning against the fence watching the kids play. I decided to walk over to him and see if he would be willing to talk to me. As I approached him I noticed he was wearing baggy tan pants and a solid white tee shirt. He had on funny canvas sneakers that had no shoe laces. As I got closer I noticed his hair was very short. It was cut down to the scalp. He looked at me as funny as I was looking at him, but he did not move from his leaning position against the fence. When I got within ten feet of him he quit leaning against the fence and stood in a slouchy position and put both his hands in pockets. He looked nothing like my cousins back in my old school. I stopped a few feet in front of him and decided to go ahead and say hi.

He introduced himself in Spanish as Miguel. We shook hands in confusion. I went for a regular shake and he grabbed my hand in a funny position I did not recognize. I gave him a puzzled look and he just grinned. He started speaking in Spanish and he told me he was in sixth grade. I told him I was in fifth grade, but in English. The conversation was not easy. He kept speaking in Spanish and I kept answering in English. Miguel finally asked me why I would not speak Spanish to him. I told him I preferred English because we were in school. I also told him I spoke Spanish at home but by speaking English in school it would help me get better grades. Miguel put his hands back in his pockets and leaned back against the fence. He grinned again, nodded his head in the way Hispanics do, up instead of down.

I have noticed Anglos nod by lowering their heads a few inches. Hispanics raise their heads in the opposite direction. Miguel did this and said, "You're a coconut, aren't you?"

I looked at Miguel and I lowered my gaze to the ground. I then put my hands in my pocket. Without looking up I told him, "What in the world is a coconut?" I felt so stupid by asking this, but I had no idea what it meant. Miguel was about to answer but the bell rang. He began to walk away and I followed next to him. He kept his hands in his pockets. His walk was funny in his baggy trousers. I looked over at him and his slouched pants made him look shorter than me even though he was taller. I was about to ask him what a coconut was but he stepped in the opposite direction and headed off to his class. As he walked away I noticed he had a red bandana in his back pocket. I thought how strange that was. Why hadn't mom and dad given me one? I also wondered if I should be dressed like him instead of looking like the White kids. I kept walking in the direction of my class and thinking of how I was not fitting in when I heard the pounding of footsteps behind me. I had completely forgotten about turning my back on James.

I hit the playground dirt in a cloud of dust. Since my hands were in my pocket I was not able to catch my fall and I landed on my chin. By the time I was able to push myself off the ground I felt kicks to my rear and ribs. For a moment I thought I was back home and getting another whipping. I quickly regrouped and remembered that I was still at school. Besides, these kicks were nothing like what I was used to. The feet kicking me were much smaller and covered in sneakers. To protect myself I let myself fall back on the ground and I started to roll away from the kicks. Instantly the kicks stopped and I heard the assailants run away. I felt like I had just been run over by a heard of cattle. I looked up and saw it was not cows but a herd of fifth graders.

I started to get to my feet when I heard a voice say, "Hurry up or you will be late!" It was Johnny, the boy that sat next to me in class. I rose and dusted myself off as best as I could. I was covered in dust and I had a tear in my shirt. Mom was going to be mad now. Johnny and I entered the class and I instantly made eye contact with James. He was smiling so big it made me sick to my stomach. He was leaning back in his desk and his hands were behind his neck. Both his legs were spread wide open as he sat in his desk. I felt like running over to him and beating him like a super hero beats a villain.

"Alberto, please sit down!" Mrs. Banks said in a loud voice. I thought to myself, is this woman not going to ask me what happened? I walked to my seat and this time James put his feet out of reach. I sat in my desk and I guess my demeanor gave something away. "Alberto, what's wrong?" Mrs. Banks asked. She sounded like she was mad at me for getting trampled.

"Mrs. Banks, please call me Albert," I told her. "I think it will be easier for all of us. My name is Albert. Not burnt potato chip." The whole class went silent. Then it erupted in laughter. I was the only one not laughing. I even noticed the teacher trying to keep from giggling.

She stood up and the class quickly went silent. She came out from behind her desk and stood in front of it. "Albert, I don't know what you are talking about, but you will not disturb my class again. Do you understand?"

"Yes ma'am," I responded. She walked back around her desk and sat down. She told everyone she was going to read a story. She pulled out a book and began to read about a boy that lived in a giant peach. It was a story I had never heard so I listened attentively.

I paid attention to the story but kept one eye on the back of James' head. There were so many things I wanted to do to his head but the story kept calling me back. I was so enthralled with the story that it made me forget about being trampled for a little while. I put my elbows on my desk and cupped my face with my hands. I could picture this huge peach sailing through the sky with a boy and the huge insects. Just as the story was getting good the teacher closed the book. I was in shock. How could she cut us off? It was just getting good! The way she had read the book to the class was hypnotizing. She had put emotion into the story. She had actually put different voices in for each character. I was so captivated by the way she did that. She may have let me get run over and trampled, but she introduced me to acting and story telling.

The day wound down to the late afternoon. By the time the last bell rang the kids were ready to call it a day. They all were worn down and needed to go home. I followed the kids to the bus stop where I was supposed to meet Nancy and my other cousins. I saw them standing in line close to the fence where I had met Miguel. I scanned the playground and I spotted my brothers walking towards me. I also kept turning around and making sure James and his gang was not close by. A real super hero would not be surprised twice in one day by the same trick. I stood in line with my chest out and my hands clenched in tiny fists. I had my feet slightly spread apart and my chin pointing out. I pictured myself standing in preparation for another attack. It never came. Instead my cousin Nancy walked up and said, "What's wrong? You look so goofy."

I did not answer her. Petty woman, doesn't she know who I am? I was scanning my surroundings looking for bad guys. In my mind I thought to myself, "I'll protect this weak female!"

My cousin was no weakling. She slapped me on the chest. "Wake up! Here comes our bus." She grabbed my hand and pulled me into the bus when the doors opened. She dragged me all the way to the back of the bus and she hopped into the last seat. I sat against the window and she sat against the aisle. Now I was being dragged around by a girl. This day had gotten worse and worse by the minute.

I sat in the bus looking out the window. I watched kids loading into buses up and down the street. Teachers were shouting orders at children and bus drivers were doing their best to keep order. I could tell the mob mentality had kicked in with all the kids. All of them could not be supervised. In our bus boys were running up and down the aisle hitting girls and being silly. It was a bit beneath me. I had no urge to chase girls or act foolish. I sat in the bus with my head against the glass dreaming of something better. I was once again in comic book land where heroes win and villains don't. Sometimes I wished I could stay in this fantasy land all day. In my world no one hurt me and no one cared if I was little too dark or a little to light. I had seen in my comics that there were heroes with darker skin than myself. I had never actually seen anyone darker than Hispanics except on television. I moved my head away from the window and looked down at my sneaker. My shoe lace was undone so I bent over in my seat to tie my laces. The timing could not have been better.

A boy walked to the back of the bus and saw that a Mexican girl was in the seat that he wanted. "Get out of my seat!" he told her. He was standing far enough away where he could not see me bent over in the seat.

I did not know my cousin that well, but in the short time I knew her I was pretty sure she was not going to move for anyone. Nancy stood up and looked the boy in the face. "No!" she shouted at him. The boy was about to push her when I stood up. At nine I was bigger than most the boys in my age group. I stood a full head above this one and my shoulders were much wider.

I don't think that scared him as much as my dark eyes and brow. I reached my full height and looked the boy in the face. I instantly recognized him as one of the boys that had trampled over me and also as one of the culprits from the bathroom. The boy had both hands in front of him as if he was ready to push Nancy. His eyes became a bit wider when he realized he was instantly outnumbered. He was lucky; Nancy would have really hurt this boy more than I could.

I stepped in front of Nancy so I could get closer to the boy. Nancy moved out of my way. She leaned against the window so she could give me more room, or get a better view of the drama that was about to unfold. I came out from behind the seat and got right in the boy's face. The boy lowered his hands and put them in his pocket and lowered his head. "You're scared of a burnt potato chip?" I asked him. Since his head was down I was able to see if the bus driver had come in yet. Nope. This was going to be good. The back six seats of the bus got quiet. "I asked you a question!" I had raised my voice a little louder, but not loud enough to get too much attention. The rest of the kids were still doing their own thing. The boy did not answer but he did take a step back. I reached out and grabbed his shirt and pulled him closer. "What's wrong?" I asked him. "Oh I forgot, you had told me that Mexicans smell bad." That got the attention of a few Mexican boys that were watching the action in the back of the bus. "Look at me!" I shouted in his face. He slowly raised his head and looked at me. I made the meanest face I could and put my face less than half an inch from his face. "Where is your gang now?" I asked him in the deepest voice I could. In my mind I was once again the hero ready to strike down an evil villain. I pictured myself as the comic book character that was made of stone. He was hard as a rock on the outside but still had feelings and sensitive on the inside.

I looked at this pathetic boy who had tears welling up in his eyes. His face was flush and he was beginning to get a runny nose. "What have I ever done to you?" I asked him in a throaty growl. "I asked you a question!"

"Nothing," he responded.

I wanted to hit this boy so bad but he was so helpless. I reached out and grabbed him by the shoulders and pulled him closely. I heard him whimper as if he was going to begin blubbering. I put my face on the side of his head and whispered in his ear. "If you ever come near me or my cousin, I will destroy you." He nodded his head and I shook his shoulders once for good measure. I released my grip and he started backing away. He took about four steps backward and fell on his rear end. One of the Mexican boys had stuck his foot out and tripped him. The boy quickly turned around in his seat and faced the front. The boy on the floor looked up and the Mexican boy lifted both arms and scrunched his head into his shoulders. "I don't know what happened," I heard him say. The White boy lifted himself off the floor and made his way to the front of the bus.

"What did you tell him?" Nancy asked me. I told her what I had whispered in his ear and she laughed. "You are so weird."

I thought how silly that had sounded. I smiled and sat back in the bus seat. It might have been silly but it always worked in the comics. I laughed a bit and the bus finally began to roll. As the landscape began to change to desert the quality of the housing diminished as did the amount of White kids getting off the bus. By the time we reached our destination there were no Anglo kids in the bus. At our stop I exited the bus with Nancy and looked back. There were only five kids left and they were all Mexican. I guessed all the Hispanics lived farther out of town. I let the observation pass and I left the bus with my cousin. We walked towards her house as my mother had instructed. She would not be home till later. I looked at Nancy and asked her about Miguel. They were in the same grade so I hoped they would know each other. "He's a Pachuco," she said. I was confused. At this point I thought you were either Mexican or White. She explained that Miguel belonged to a gang and was already doing drugs. Nancy continued to educate me about drugs, gangs and how Mexicans were broken up into little groups. I was totally confused. If he was in the bad part of Mexican culture, where was I? She told me I was probably a coconut.

I froze in my tracks. She stopped and turned around. "What's the problem?" she asked. I had a wide eyed look on my face. "Albert there's nothing wrong with that," she said. She said she was called the same thing by other Mexicans. She explained she was called "White girl" and coconut just like me. She said she took it as compliment. She was planning on going to college someday. She did not want to live in a broken down house and have ten kids like some of our other relatives. She talked about how she wanted to marry a man someday that was smart and made lots of money. Nancy was a very pretty girl. She would grow up to be a beautiful young lady and fulfill her dream. She eventually married a man she met in college. That man was also a "coconut."

I talked more about our struggles and things we had in common. She told me that she really enjoyed how I had handled the boy on the bus. She explained that I was man enough to face him but never really hit him. I quickly changed the topic of the conversation and continued to discuss how we had so much in common. I really didn't like girls but I saw this as a chance to learn about myself and the direction I wanted to go. We chatted until we entered her house. She went to her room to change and I sat in the living room and turned on the television. I scanned the channels until I found what I was looking for. The cartoons were on and my favorite show was on. The Fantastic Four were chasing bad guys. I watched as The Thing clobbered the villain. The Thing was made of stone but all human on the inside. He was just like me. I had grown a hard shell on the outside but on the inside I was just a normal nine year old boy. I watched how The Thing stood and positioned himself to look even bigger than he was. I stood and attempted to duplicate his posture. "It's clobbering time!" I yelled.

"You're weird." Nancy said behind me. Yeah, today was not a good day at all.

Chapter 8
Revenge Is Mine

I used to love school, but now I hated it. I was getting beat up, pushed around and no one would do anything about it. I was feeling trapped. My teacher would not do anything about it. I had told her I was being harassed and picked on. The only thing she did was to move my chair closer to the front of the room. I now had to sit on the front row because I was considered the trouble maker. The only good thing that came out of the move was that now I was able to get work done without being bothered by the bully in my class. I still kept an eye out for James but it was when I was on the playground that the troubles began. That morning it seemed like something bad was going to happen and it did.

My mother noticed I had lost all my excitement for school but I would not give her a reason. I was scared she would also blame me just like my teacher had. I was no longer up before the alarm and getting ready an hour before my brothers awoke. I probably looked like I was moving in slow motion now in my preparation for school. I was getting dressed and noticed my jeans had scrapes on the knees. It was from the last time James and his friends had trampled over me in the school yard. I was so tired of having to watch my back. They were not tough enough to come at me directly. They always got me when my back was turned. As I dressed I noticed my shirt sleeve had a tear in it. Mom had whipped me for coming home with torn clothes. We could not afford a new shirt so she had stitched it up as best she could. I continued dressing and headed to the kitchen.

Mom was preparing breakfast for us again. Dad had just come in from working the night shift as a security guard. He was sitting at the table eating a tacito. His eyes showed the stress of teaching his body to stay awake when it should be sleeping. He would go to bed as soon as my brothers and I left and go to work as we were coming home. I kind of liked this arrangement even though I was pretty sure he didn't. I ate my breakfast standing up as I kept one eye on the road that led to our bus stop. I would leave as soon as I saw Nancy head out. My brothers would follow me when I left. I was growing up and my brothers were starting to follow me more and more. I finished my tacito and was about to ask for another when my dad rose from the table. I noticed the revolver around his waist.

I found it so ironic that someone would pay my dad to wear a gun. My mind went back to the cornfield incident where he had shot at us. I instantly felt chills up and down my spine. I changed my mind and headed out the door. My brothers were still eating and started to get up to follow me. One look from my dad and they sat back down. "Finish your breakfast," he told them in Spanish. "And where are you going?" he asked me.

I never looked up at him but said, "I thought I saw Nancy coming out of her house." He told me to sit at the table till my brothers finished eating and then we could go. He walked past me and headed to his room. I looked at my brothers and told them to hurry up. I did this quietly enough so dad would not hear me. They took bigger bites of their food and we all headed out the door. As we walked to the bus stop Nancy and Bonnie came out and joined us.

The ride to school was quiet enough but something in the back of my mind told me something was going to happen. The road noise from the bus was lulling my mind to my comics. I thought about Spiderman and how his spider sense warned him of danger. I wished I had something like that. It sure would help when I was being ganged up on. I started to daydream about having powers like Spiderman. I could picture myself leaping into the air and shooting webs. If I could be like him I would never let anyone pick on me again.

"Get up!" Nancy said to me. I realized we were at school and needed to get out of the bus.

I walked to my class without any problems. James and his friends never bothered me this early in the day; it was always after lunch or after school. I walked to my class and entered it without incident. I sat there and waited for the other students to come in so the teacher could call roll. I sat in my desk and looked directly at my teacher. She never acknowledged me. She smiled at the other kids and even told them good morning. I thought about greeting her in Spanish just for kicks, but decided against it.

I cannot remember what we studied that day in class. My only recollections were from the lunch room and the playground. I sat with all the kids in a group but was totally ignored as usual. I ate in silence as the other children laughed and joked about me. "I didn't know Mexicans ate American food," I heard James say.

"Pizza is not American food, stupid," I told him. I made a mean face and looked directly at him. He was sitting about three spaces down from me and he knew he was safe. He responded by using his spoon to shoot some peas at me. I brushed the food off my shirt and noticed a green spot. Mom would probably beat me for that. I wanted to shoot some food back at him but knew I would be the one to get in trouble, not him. Besides, I was hungry so I finished my plate and headed out of the cafeteria.

I liked to finish eating quickly so I could get out before James and his friends. This way I could keep an eye on them. I watched from a distance as he and his friends came out and began to walk around the playground. I kept far enough away from them so they could not see me. I noticed they were starting to walk towards the fence area where the buses picked us up. The group was about ten boys. They followed James as he walked directly to a Mexican boy that was leaning against the fence minding his own business as usual. It was Miguel. As they walked towards him I knew what was about to happen. I didn't need to be Spiderman to see this drama unfold. I was far enough away to see what was happening but not close enough to hear it. I saw James walk up to Miguel and call him something then push him to the ground. He stepped back and the other boys began to kick Miguel as he rolled on the ground. I instantly felt warm all over and then my head became hot with rage.

I remembered reading the Hulk comics. I loved the way Bruce Banner became the monster when he was angered. I felt the same way at that instant. Miguel had not done a thing to anyone. He just happened to be Brown. I walked towards the group of boys that was beating Miguel. James had moved to the back of the gang and was not participating. He was yelling instructions to the group. "Whip that Mexican Greaser!" I heard him yell. He stood at the back and was making punching and kicking movements. He was really enjoying watching the boys beat Miguel. I walked up behind him with both fists closed and ready for action. I was not going to take this any more. I came within striking distance and tapped him on the shoulder with my left hand. I had never seen a super hero hit anyone from behind. When James turned his head I used my entire body to punch with my right hand. I brought all the frustration I had in me down on this poor boy.

I felt my hand connect below his right eye. He hit the dirt with the back of his shoulders and covered his face. For a minute the world went silent. The boys had turned and saw me standing over James like a giant green monster. Both my hands were clenched in fists and I was looking for another target. Then the sounds came back. James began screaming at the top of his lungs. He had drawn his hands away from his face and saw the blood. I looked down and saw the tear in his flesh before I saw it bleed. He had a cut below his eye. It was right on his cheek bone. I saw it turn white then instantly go red with blood. James had blood running through his hands and fingers and was looking at me with great fear. Suddenly it did not feel very good to be a big tough super hero. I had rescued Miguel, but at what price? I looked down at James and then raised my head towards the other boys.

James's gang took off running. Miguel was getting up and James continued to scream. Miguel took one look at James and he took off running. I was frozen to that spot on the ground where I had decided to strike back. There was no turning back now. I knew James was going to die and I was going to jail for the rest of my life. I just stood there and stared at the blood on James's hand, clothes and now the ground. I heard footsteps coming behind me and I turned to see a teacher I did not know running to assist James. I moved out of the way as this lady began to help him. She put her hand directly on the cut and lifted him off the ground and took him away. She ran with him in her arms and I decided to run in the opposite direction.

I ran to the boy's bathroom and hid in a stall. I lowered the toilet seat and stood on it. If I stood straight up I could see over the stall door. I stood there for what seemed hours even though it was probably only thirty minutes or so. I had locked the stall door so no one could come in. I heard boys come in to use the bathroom and they were talking about some Mexican boy whipping James and his whole gang. I could hear them as they used the trough and talk about the "wetback" that had killed James. I felt powerful for an instant then sick to my stomach as I thought back to the cut on James's face. I could see the white and pink flesh turn bright red as the blood had began to flow. I heard the bathroom empty again and I sat down on the toilet to collect my thoughts. I was planning on how to escape from school and head home when the door opened again. I quickly stood on the toilet seat again. I heard a man call my name but I did not respond.

"Albert, you have to ride the bus home anyway. Come on out." He was right. Unless I wanted to steal a car as well as murder someone I had no choice. I responded to the voice and came out of the stall.

A man with a white shirt and tie greeted me at the bathroom door in Spanish. The sun was at his back and I could not see him very well. I closed one eye to get a better look and told him I could speak English very well. I heard him laugh and I came out of the bathroom. I was terrified at what was going to happen next. I knew this man was a police officer and he was taking me away for life. As we started to walk down the hallway he extended his hand and he asked me to hold it. I took his hand and walked with him. I looked up at him and asked, "Am I going to jail?"

The man looked down at me and said, "No son, I just want to talk to you." I thought that was odd, a White man calling me son. He led me to his office and a secretary looked at me with a scowl. I ignored her gaze and followed the man into the office. I recognized the letters on his door and realized he was the principal. He pointed to a chair in front of his desk and he asked me to sit down as he walked around and sat behind the big desk.

"Albert, why did you hit that boy?" he asked. I looked at him squarely in the eyes and began to tell him of all the reasons I had for striking James. I began with the trampling I was receiving almost daily, the racist remarks and the beatings other Mexican boys were getting in the school yard. I can still remember talking to this man without being scared. I told him everything I could and I never shed a tear. I did not feel any guilt for what I had done. The man had both of his hands clasped together in front of his face as he listened to me. He let me speak and never interrupted me or asked any other questions. When I finished he looked at me and smiled. I was in shock. I had expected a policeman to walk in and cuff me at any second. The only thing he said was, "Okay." He stood up and asked me to follow him.

"Albert your bus leaves in a few minutes so you have to hurry," he said.

Those were the last words I ever had with the principal. I was never disciplined or talked to again about the fight I had with James. The teacher in my class was transferred out and a new teacher took her place. She was very nice to me. At the time I wondered what was going on. Disciplining me would not have fixed anything. It took action from the principal to go to the source of the problem. I expected the worst and the best happened. I am sorry today for striking that boy and I do not believe violence serves any purpose. However there are cases where self-defense is needed.

I reached my bus, and walked to the back where my cousin was waiting for me. The news had traveled fast. "We thought you were going to jail!" Nancy said. I told her everything was okay and that I would not fight anybody again for a long time. While we were talking I looked up and saw that every Mexican kid in the bus was standing around us and trying to listen to our conversation. The seats around us that usually held only two children now had four or five.

"Did you kill James?" one boy asked in Spanish. "No!" I yelled back to him. "Leave me alone!" I told them all. I did not feel guilty about hitting the boy, but I did not want to talk about it either. I just wanted to be left alone. The sight of the cut on the boys face was troubling me. Maybe it brought back some of the beatings I had gotten. I never remembered any blood, but sometimes your soul bleeds and not your body. The bus driver had to eventually come to the rear of the bus and tell every one to sit down.

The ride home was quiet. I kept looking out the window and Nancy did not ask me any questions. I was in fifth grade and ten years old and should not have to be hitting kids in the eye to protect myself. I wondered how many kids James and his little gang had beaten up and gotten away with it? I hoped this would change things and he would leave people in peace. The bus finally stopped at our road. Nancy and I walked out of the bus and toward her house. We walked in silence and I was glad she didn't ask me any questions. I still thought a police car was going to pull up at any second and take me away. As we neared her house I decided I would go to my house instead of hers. I looked at her and said, "Promise me you won't tell your parents about the fight." She just nodded her head and kept walking. I was scared that I would get a beating if my parents found out I was fighting at school.

I waved goodbye to Nancy and walked through the dry field to our old house. Dad was still home and he should be getting ready to head to work. At least he would be too busy to notice me. My brothers had arrived on an earlier bus and were probably at Nancy's house watching television. I just did not feel like being around people right now. I walked to the front of the house and caught a glimpse of something in the house. Dad was not getting ready for work. He was sitting on the couch without a shirt on and drinking beer. I was beginning to wonder what was going on. It was almost five in the afternoon and I knew he started at seven. Mom would be coming home soon and she usually fixed dinner for us and dad before he went to work. I knew there was going to be a fight when mom came home and saw him drunk.

I decided to walk back to my uncle's house. My brothers were much more fun to deal with than my dad. Maybe he wasn't drunk at all and was just having a beer before work. I really didn't care. It had become mom's problem anyways. My brothers and I tried to stay away from home as much as possible. If dad would let us, we would spend the night at Nancy's house. Her dad did not drink or treat his kids bad. In fact he was a great uncle to be around. In the evening we would go over and he would teach us how to box. I guess that's where I learned to throw a mean right jab. He actually had big red gloves. I will never forget when he put the gloves on Nancy and me, so I could box with her. I felt strange fighting a girl, until Nancy hit me in the nose. Then it got serious. Her dad stopped us before anybody got hurt. He wanted his daughters to be able to take care of themselves, and they sure could.

We ended up staying at Nancy's house past seven that evening. Her mom had us fixed sandwiches for dinner. Afterwards we played in the yard until we heard mom call us in.

We all froze when we saw dad's truck. He had not gone to work. We knew to be on our best behavior as we walked in the house. Mom was in the kitchen fixing dinner. I walked over to her and I saw her face. I could tell she had been crying. Without turning her head she asked if we were still hungry. My brothers said yes but I said no. After all that had happened today I was not very hungry.

While my brothers ate I went into the room all three of us shared. I reached under my bed and dragged out the box of comics. I reached into the box and pulled out a comic and hopped into bed. I was almost through when mom poked her head in the room and told me to get ready for bed. Time must have flown. I did not realize it was that late. I headed to the bathroom to shower before my brothers could get in there. As my mom entered her room I could see my dad sleeping on their bed. I guess he was not feeling well and would not be going to work after all. I washed up and headed back to bed. I liked to read until my brothers came to bed. It gave me some quiet time before they came into the room. I picked up my comic book and finished reading it. I pulled the box back out and looked for the other comics that went with it.

In this comic Iron Man was the hero. He was covered in metal and could not be hurt. I had probably read this comic five or six times. I still enjoyed it. As I continued to read Carlos came in and grabbed a comic and climbed into his bunk bed. Jose followed shortly and soon all three of us were reading. I was almost to the end when mom came by and turned the lights off. I let the comic hit the floor and rolled over on my side and started to fall asleep. It slowly got dark and then it became as white as the sun.

I was laying flat on my back and my metal mask had a tear below the slit that let me see out of it. James was standing over me with both fists clenched. He was also a lot bigger and had huge muscles. I looked myself over to make sure I was not hurt anywhere else. I saw I was covered in a metal suit that showed off my muscular body. Maybe this dream was pitting me against him on equal terms. He was White and I could not tell what I was. We were going to fight because he was bad, and I guess I was good. It was not a fight against a Brown and White. It was good against evil.

I raised myself off the ground and I began to circle James. Underneath my mask I knew I was smiling. This is what I had been waiting for. I would have my revenge on everything James had done to me. My hands tensed underneath the metal gloves as I prepared to deal with this evil villain. James leapt towards me and I caught him in mid air. I raised him over my head like super heroes do in comics and slammed him to the ground. I looked down and saw the enemy flat on his back. His arms were outstretched and his face showed pain. I immediately jumped on him and sat on his chest. One hand shot out and grabbed him around the neck. I raised my other arm and prepared to strike. My teeth were gritted tightly as I knew what I had to do. I could feel sweat building under my mask. I had to do this, I had to hit him. I looked down and the dream faded. I could once again see James as he looked in the playground.

His face was pale and his eyes were wide open. On the corner of his cheek below his eye was that huge cut again. Then in slow motion it began to bleed, slowly at first then the blood came in waves. I stood up and started backing away from him as he continued to bleed. I looked down and my metal gloved hands were covered in blood. I raised both hands to my mask for a better look and yes, it was blood. I kept walking backwards and slipped in something wet and slippery. In my dream the floor was covered with James' blood. It was everywhere. The ground was so wet I could not stand up. My arms and legs could not get a grip on anything and I went into a swimming motion as I tried to stand. I felt blood entering my mask and choking me as I tried to get away. My hands reached up to the mask to try and pull it off but it was stuck. Then someone helped me.

"Albert, wake up!" yelled Carlos. "You'll wake dad up." I woke up with my chest soaking as well as my pillow and sheet. I was scared to turn the light on, but I knew it was not blood. Carlos crawled back into bed and I lay there for some time. I felt so bad about hitting James. At first I had felt good, now I was not so sure. It did not matter what they had done to me. I just did not like what I had done. The heroes in my comics made it look so easy, why was it so hard in real life? Sometime during the night I fell back asleep and did not think of blood or violence anymore.

The new teacher was much younger than Mrs. Banks. James was also no longer in my class. It made my day a lot nicer not having to watch my back. The remarks in the lunch room also stopped. I quit hearing the name calling and laughing behind my back. Things were getting enjoyable at school and I was beginning to look forward to liking school once again. The days went by and fifth grade was getting easier and easier. The days turned into weeks and I thought we would end up staying in the little house a lot longer. I was wrong.

Dad continued to miss work or go to work with alcohol on his breath. I guess his boss at work did not like the idea of someone who drank carrying a gun. One week we were surprised to find him home day after day. This time he was not even trying to go to work. I figured out he had lost his job. Mom and dad began to fight and the roller coaster ride started again. Later on dad went out to find work, without the help of my uncle. I think there was some friction since my uncle had stuck his neck out to find work for him the first time. Dad spent about two weeks without any luck and I think he used this time to catch up on his sleep. Mom would go to work, we would go to school and dad would sleep off the prior night's beer. It may have been a great vacation for him but it was not for mom. It got to the point where I would take a few comics or anything else I could read into the orchards around the house. I would fix a little bed of grass under a tree and read until mom called me in or it got dark. I hated being in our house listening to my parents fight.

I was managing to keep good grades in school even though I had so much going wrong at home. I kept remembering what George at the migrant preschool had told me many years before. "Dream, but when you dream, dream big." In my darkest hours, I kept that thought in my mind. I would have something nicer in my life. All this pain and loneliness was just preparation for something else. I don't know how I did it some days. I guess someone was watching over me. My brothers and I shed many tears in those days. California was both cruel and kind. Now we would be moving again.

We came home from school one day and we knew the drill. Dad had a trailer backed up to the door of the old house and mom was loading her car. "Here we go again," I thought to myself. I wondered where we would be going next. I walked towards mom and she asked me to help load the trailer and the truck. I knew that meant I would have to help my dad. I entered the house and it was already empty. I looked in my room and it was cleaned out. I guess he and mom had already loaded everything. My mind went to the thought of eating boiled eggs and potatoes again. I could feel my stomach contracting and getting gassy. I walked back outside and mom was closing the door on her car. I asked her, "Where are we going?"

"Texas." She replied.

Chapter 9
Back To Texas

The drive back to Texas was not as bad as the drive to California. My brothers and I did not have to ride in the back of a pickup truck. We took turns driving with mom in her car or with dad in his truck. Both vehicles were loaded down with our meager belongings. None of us wanted to drive with dad. It was not that he was being mean, but it was just that there were bad memories that he was carrying with him. My brothers and I secretly fought with each other to see who would have to ride in the truck with him. I usually lost because I was the oldest. Carlos and Jose would beg me to let them ride with mom. I felt like the sacrificial lamb and would get in the truck with dad and endure the silence for hours at a time.

The road looked the same as it had a few years ago. Cactus and desert plants dotted the landscape as we drove through the countryside of Arizona and New Mexico. When I rode with dad I buried my head in my comics and tried not to look at him. He drove with his eyes scanning the road and never said much. Every now and then he would ask me to hand him a box of cigarettes from the glove compartment of the truck. I loved the way they smelled when he initially lit them, but once lit they choked me. Dad kept the window of the truck rolled down since it had no air conditioner. The dry desert wind blowing through the cab kept the smoke out and made me very sleepy. Dad kept a big bottle of Coke in a cup holder. I knew the heat had to make him drowsy also, although he never showed it. He kept his gaze facing east and the highway seemed to go on forever.

The funny thing about the road through the desert is the mirages. I would look down the road and swear there were puddles everywhere. I would wait till we came over a hill and the water would vanish. I could also see the heat rising from the road. I wanted to ask my dad what caused the disappearing puddles on the road, but I never did. One look at him told me he was not in the mood to talk. He had that same dark menacing look on his face he had been wearing ever since he lost his job with the security guard company. I just sat back in seat and watched the puddles vanish as we got closer to them.

When I rode with mom I asked her where in Texas we were going. She talked about dad's brother that lived near San Antonio. I asked mom about San Antonio and what it was like there. She told me stories about the Alamo and how all of the southwest used to be part of Mexico hundreds of years ago. I sat back in the car seat and listened to mom talk about the history of the Mexican people. I enjoyed listening to these stories.

The history of the Mexican people is slowly dying away. No one is recording them and the story tellers are slowly fading away. I realize that now and wish I would have written some of them down. At ten years old, that thought was not on my mind, it was on what the future would bring in Texas. We had been moving almost every two years now. We had no roots and everything we owned was in two old vehicles. I longed for a "normal" home like that of my cousins. I thought back to Tio Marko and his family and my cousin Nancy and her father. How had they ended up so fortunate and my brothers and I so unlucky? Those two families had it so good and here I was in the middle of the desert again. Well, at least we weren't in our underwear in the back of a camper. I looked in the backseat of the car and Jose was asleep, the desert air had gotten to him. I was feeling drowsy also. I stuck my head out the window of mom's car and let the dry wind hit my face. Instead I got something else. A big green grasshopper hit me in the mouth! I had green and yellow grasshopper goop all over my mouth and face. Mom laughed at me and handed me a rag. She poured soda on it to moisten it and I used it to clean my face. The laughter woke up Jose and he began to laugh also. I had bug parts hanging from my mouth and lips. I looked in the rear view mirror and saw I had pieces of the bug in my teeth. What a day this was going to be.

I stayed in mom's car for the rest of the day and we followed close behind dad's truck. Carlos was stuck with dad this time. I kept looking back at the sunset. Since we were driving east the sunset was at our backs. The colors of the desert sunset are beautiful. There are red, yellow and orange colors that give the entire landscape a glow that is incredible. Even at that early age I appreciated the beauty of it all. As dusk was beginning to fall we stopped at a rest area on the side of the road. Mom made us dinner from an ice chest she had put together for us. She prepared sandwiches of cold cuts she had bought before we left. The ice had long since melted but it was still cool and a nice change of pace from the boiled eggs and potatoes I was expecting. We even got a can of soda each. My brothers and I each had a few sandwiches with potato chips. Jose thought it would be funny to burp loudly from the sodas. He looked at dad watching us and changed his mind. While we ate mom brought out blankets and I helped clear the concrete picnic table for our bed. Mom and dad would each sleep in their vehicles tonight. We slept under the stars.

The nights in the desert are cool but not cold. The sky is so clear the stars seem to explode with brilliance. I stayed awake as long as I could to stare at them. I had seen pictures of the Big Dipper and the Little Dipper and I looked for them in the sky. I don't know if I ever found them. I was just amazed at how the stars lit up the night in the desert. I wondered why the stars were not as bright in California, and if the they would be as bright in Texas. The star gazing eventually put me to sleep and the night turned into dawn. The sun was rising in the direction we were heading. Mom helped me put the blankets away and then I helped her make more sandwiches for breakfast. As I ate my food I looked around and could not find my dad. I asked mom where he was and she just shrugged her shoulders. I guess mom was still upset with dad. He eventually appeared as he walked in from the desert. Dad loved walking in the wilderness. I guess it was a calming thing to him. He walked into the picnic area and grabbed a can of Coke from the ice chest and headed for his truck. He did not have to say a word.

I sat in the truck and stared out into the empty space of western Texas. The land has a beauty about it in the morning light, and an orange and yellow glow to it as we drove eastward into the sun. Slowly but surely the land started to change. The desert began to give way to scrub brush and mesquite trees. There were more and more houses along the highway and these turned into small towns, then cities. I asked dad where were we headed in Texas and he did not say a word in response. I already new we were going to San

Antonio but I wanted to hear it from him. It was an attempt by me to start a conversation. I hated sitting and not being able to talk for hours at a time. We drove through the morning and around noon we stopped at a gas station in a small town to fuel our vehicles.

Mom stepped out of her car and came to the truck and asked me if I was hungry. I nodded and she then walked around and began talking to dad. He reached into his wallet and gave mom some money and she disappeared into the store. After dad fueled the truck he did the same with mom's car and went into the store as mom was coming out. She moved the car under a large tree for shade and called me over. She had a bag of sodas and chips for us. She opened the ice chest in the trunk of the car and began to make sandwiches for us. The cold soda was refreshing and the sandwiches were cool from being in the ice chest. My brothers and I sat under the tree while mom sat in the car. She had made a sandwich for dad also and had it ready for him wrapped in a paper towel.

We saw dad walk out of the store with another bag and wondered what it was. I was hoping he had bought us candy bars or cookies. He got into the truck and drove to where we were parked. He got out and walked to where my mother was. I noticed he had a can of beer in his hand about the same time mom did. Mom extended the sandwich to dad and he ignored the gesture. She did not say anything to dad. I heard them talk about how close we were to our destination. Dad turned around walked to a pay phone in the store parking lot and made a phone call. I guess he was calling his brother to let him know how we were progressing. While that was going on I got up from under the tree and climbed into the back seat of mom's car and stretched out. I was not going to get stuck with dad again. I knew my brothers tricks now.

We drove for another two hours and pulled into another gas station. There a man that resembled my dad stepped out of a big fancy car. The car was very long and looked new. The man that stepped out of it was slender and very clean cut. He wore denim jeans and a tee shirt with something printed on the front and back. I could not make out what was on the front of it but the back had airplanes on it. I asked mom about it and she said he was in the air force. At the time I had no idea what that was but it was my first exposure to the military. As a fifth grader I had no concept of the air force, but I liked the picture of the jets on the back of my uncle's shirt. Dad got out of the truck and he shook hands with his brother. My mom said his name was Nathan as he turned and waved at my mom.

Dad got back in his truck and he motioned my mom to follow him. Dad followed Uncle Nathan as we turned into a nice residential neighborhood. I was totally shocked. There was no agriculture or industry of any kind in this area. All the houses were brick and had nice manicured lawns. I stuck my head out of the window to get a better look around and a motion caught my eye. I looked up and saw two sleek objects flying through the air above us. I gasped in astonishment as two fighter jets from the air base flew by. I yelled and waved at Carlos in mom's car and he poked his head out to get a better view. We must have looked like two dogs with our heads sticking out of the car and truck with our mouths hanging wide open. The jets moved out of sight and we put our heads back in the car as mom continued to follow dad to my uncle's house.

We arrived at Uncle Nathan's house and I instantly felt overwhelmed. He had a new car and a new truck in the drive way. The house was also new. It was all brick and the lawn was like something out of a picture. All around the houses were all the same. Everything looked so clean. Across the street a man was mowing the lawn. I was used to having a dirt or rock driveway and a shack for a house. I guess that my uncle had done better for himself than my dad had. My uncle asked us to follow him into the house and we followed him almost apprehensively. This was the nicest house I had ever been in. The front door had a glass door in front of it. I had never seen that before. I followed mom and dad into the house and I felt like I was entering a palace. I could feel my brothers following behind me. I felt someone tap me on my shoulder and I turned my head. Carlos asked me, "Why are you walking on your tip toes?"

I looked down at my feet and saw I was walking on my toes. I ignored the question and turned my head back to the front. I forced myself to walk normally. I was scared to be in this beautiful home and was frightened I would somehow get it dirty.

Uncle Nathan's wife was at the formal dining table setting plates and glasses. She smiled and put down a glass and walked over and hugged my mom and dad. She was a pretty lady with well kept hair and makeup on her face. I stared at her and realized the stark contrast between her and my mother. Mom had her hair pulled straight back and I can never recall my mom painting her face. My aunt wore a nice dress and high heeled shoes, while my mom had on a pair of faded jeans and a white tee shirt. Mom and dad both shared that shirt. I don't believe my uncle and aunt shared their clothes. I awoke from my observations when my aunt asked me for my name. I knew she already knew the answer but I humored her just the same. I gave her my name and age and she smiled and did the same thing with my brothers. I had already moved my gaze to the food on the table anyway.

My uncle motioned to my dad that the "kiddy" table was in the kitchen. Dad followed Nathan into the kitchen and I saw that they had another table that was already set up with paper plates and plastic cups. On the middle of the table was a plate full of hamburger and hot dog buns. Nathan told my dad that we could start eating as soon as he brought in the meat. He also told dad that the grownups would be having steaks. I looked down at the "kiddy" table and thanked God we weren't going to eat anything out of an ice chest again. Carlos and Jose were jockeying for a chair when our aunt came in and asked us if we wanted to go to the bathroom to wash our hands. We all shook our heads in unison and began to sit. She asked us again and this time she really emphasized that we needed to wash our hands. I remembered the teachers at the preschool always made us wash before we ate so I nodded my head and motioned for my brothers to follow. We all followed my aunt and she led us to the bathroom. She pointed out a hand towel and a bar of soap.

I stood back and waited while Carlos and Jose lathered up their little hands and rinsed them in the white sink. While they dried their hands I decided to investigate what was in the cabinets above the toilet and sink. I had my head in the cabinet when I felt a sharp pain on the back of my head and then my forehead met the shelf. My dad had come into the bathroom and caught me snooping. Carlos and Jose were too busy chatting to warn me of his presence. I thought I had broken my head as it bounced off the cabinet. I fell backwards and almost fell into the tub. Tears filled my eyes and then dried instantly. I knew better than to show pain. My dad looked at me with steel cold eyes and I knew that I would really get it if I broke down and cried. "Wash your hands and get into the kitchen!" My dad growled. He turned and left as quickly as he had appeared. Carlos and Jose helped me off the floor and I looked at myself in mirror. I had a straight line bruise across my forehead. It was red and looked like someone had taken a red marker and drew a line to mark where it hurt the most. I ignored the pain and washed my hands.

Carlos and Jose tried to apologize for not warning me and I told them it was not their fault as we walked back to kitchen. My aunt saw my bruise and quickly went over to me and began to show me more attention than I had ever had. I told her I had slipped on water and hit my head. My mom came over and she began to show concern and my dad pretended like nothing had happened. It was all too familiar. No one cared, or could do anything anyway. I acted strong and let mom and my aunt know I was okay. Out of the corner of my eye I could feel the heat of my dad watching. To help change the subject I asked my aunt if the hamburgers were almost ready. She smiled as she and my mom began to get lunch ready. Mom asked us to sit at the table and wait for the food.

We ate quietly and kept an eye out for dad. Carlos and Jose agreed that we needed to watch out for each other a little bit better. If we didn't cover for each other, who would? Even after we finished eating we stayed at the table. We could hear the grown-ups talking at the "big people" table. I did not want to take the chance of getting hit again so we just sat and talked. "Do you think we'll spend the night here?" asked Jose.

"I don't know," I replied. We sat at the "kiddy" table and talked about school and what we could expect the next day. I did what I could to comfort my brothers even though I was probably lying to them.

I told Carlos and Jose how people in Texas liked Mexicans like us a lot better than they did in California. Carlos laughed and asked me if I was going to crack any heads like I had done at the last school. I laughed and shook my head. "We won't have to fight here at all, things will be better," I said. If I only knew that I was making things up as I went along. People in Texas were not much different than those in California. All people have a preconceived idea of people that are different than them. People also do not like people that are supposed to be the same, but are not. I was finding that out quickly and would see it again soon enough. I was doing my best to convince my brothers how everything would be better when my aunt Carmen came into the kitchen. She asked us if we were full and we all nodded. She then asked us to go outside and play while she and mom cleaned the table.

As my brothers and I walked outside and we saw my uncle and dad each having a beer. We looked at each other and knew it would be a long night. We walked into the back yard and were amazed at how green the grass was and how everything was so neat. My aunt and uncle had no children so there were no toys to play with. We walked around the backyard along the chain linked fence. We glanced into the neighbor's yards and saw piles of toys that their kids had. We stood at the fence in amazement: how could a family have so many toys in the back yard? There was a swing set and a sand box full on red trucks and yellow bulldozers. The construction trucks were so big I could see the Tonka logo on the side. My brothers and I had never owned a Tonka toy. I had heard they were the best. We stared for a while into the yard until we heard our dad call us "babosos." That means people that stare too much.

We continued to walk around the yard and looked into other people's yards. My dad had gone back inside. Carlos and Jose asked me more questions about Texas and I continued to make things up as I went along. I told them everything they wanted to hear. I told them there were more Mexicans here so I should not have to fight anymore and that mom and dad would each get good jobs and we would have lots of money. "Do you think we'll get a Tonka truck and a sand box?" asked Jose.

"Sure!" I tried to sound as convincing as I could. We walked and talked and did not notice that the sun was beginning to set in the San Antonio suburb. Our mom called us in and led us to the bathroom. This time I would not be a Curious George. The knot on my head still hurt as a reminder to be a little smarter.

My mother and aunt fixed us places to sleep in the living room. We were getting too big to share a couch so I made Carlos and Jose sleep on the floor. The blankets and pillows had a clean spring smell to them and they were very soft. I curled into a ball on the big couch and closed my eyes. All of my fears and worries seemed to vanish. Everything was quiet in the dark living room. The long drive and good food had helped us fall asleep fast. I did not fight the inviting darkness and sleep; I embraced it. This was the only place where I was in charge and ruled in my dream world. Villains and mean people knew not to challenge me here. Everyone respected me for my ability and intelligence. All was dark in my world, then the blue sky came alive. With a thunderous roar the fighter jets passed overhead. I had my head raised and was amazed at their speed and agility and my mouth was open with awe. Then a hand pushed my shoulder.

"Move it soldier!" A big man yelled at me. I fell forward and that's when I heard the bombs blast and felt the hot wind of war hit my face. "Don't you want to live?" the big man asked me. He had fallen next to me and lifted his head to see ahead of him. He ducked his head and rolled over on his back, raising his rifle to check the action and ammunition. "Ya got enough ammo son?" he asked me. I nodded and copied his actions. We were both on our backs and our rifles were ready. "Ya ever been shot at before, boy?" he asked. I nodded and recalled the corn field in California. "Good, because this time you get to shoot back!" The big man rose and took off running and shooting at the same time. I quickly jumped to my feet and did the same thing. All of the sudden I realized I had been on this battleground before. The corn leaves hitting my face and smell of corn pollen were unmistakable. I stopped running and shooting and saw what we were attacking. It was the little house in California. I was a soldier fighting the enemy that was in the house.

I began to run again. I wanted to shoot the enemy that had shot at me. Overhead the jets flew again. I hit the ground in between the corn and heard the bombs go off. I could smell the gun powder mix with fire and earth. I rose again and started shooting my gun in the direction of the little house. I could feel the grip of the rifle getting warmer and warmer from every bullet that was fired. The heat was making me sweat. I hit the ground again and rolled on my back to reload. It came to me I had not seen what I was shooting at. I rolled on my stomach and launched myself in the direction of the house again. I finally came to high vantage point again and saw my target. My dad was standing on the front porch with his shotgun. He was bare from the waste up and had no shoes on. He was firing into the corn as he had before. I now knew who the enemy was. Then I saw a form in the window of the house shooting at me also. I recognized that face. He had a cut over his eye that was bleeding. I froze as the figure and dad both pointed their guns at me.

I felt the pressure on my shoulder and I knew I had been hit. "Shut up!" a voice said. I recognized the voice. It was Jose. "You're dreaming again!" He had hit me on the shoulder to wake me. I fought to uncover myself and realized I had wrapped the blankets over my head. "You woke me up," Jose complained. I rolled over and pretended not to hear him. I wanted to tell him my dream but decided against it. I am sure this was the first dream I had about being in a war environment but not the last. I have reoccurring visions in my sleep of battle fields and conflicts in which I am dressed in military wear. I can see myself shooting at the enemy but that specific dream at my aunt and uncle's house was the only time I saw what I was shooting at. I discuss them with my wife and it leads me to believe I still have much forgiving to do. However, forgetting is not an option I have mastered. Sleep came back to me and my battles faded into darkness again.

Morning came and my mother asked me how I slept. I couldn't tell her so I just smiled and helped her fold the blankets. I checked my shoulder just in case: nothing. My mom woke my brothers and led us to the bathroom. We washed up and then had breakfast at the "kiddy" table again. I looked around and my dad was not to be seen. I listened in on my mom and aunt to find out what was going on. I heard them talk about dad and my uncle going to look for a job. My aunt said that her husband was on vacation for a few weeks. I had no idea what a vacation was. I had heard the word but had never had one. I also heard her call the vacation a "leave." She stated it was a military word.

My brothers and I finished our cereal and cleaned our table and put the dishes in the sink. I watched as my aunt came by and opened the door to something under her counter and put the dishes away. I walked over to her and asked her if she wanted me to wash the dishes before she put them away. She smiled and said that this was an automatic dish washing machine. I had never heard of this and stared at it or a few seconds. I wondered how that machine cleaned the beans off the frying pans. I turned and walked back to my brothers to tell them. No more soaking the frying pan to get the grease off!

I found my brothers at the front door staring outside. They were watching a mother walk two children down the sidewalk. I walked up behind them and saw the image that still stays with me to this day. The mother had two children, a girl about my age and a boy about the same age as Carlos. The girl had hair the color of the sun. It fell on her shoulders and it resembled a golden waterfall. The mother walked her children in front of my uncle's house and girl looked in the direction of the front door. My brothers and I froze. We knew she could see us through the glass. She smiled and waved. I can still recall her smile. It lit up her face and for a second a breeze caught her hair. Strands of it fluttered around her face as she continued to walk by. Her mother turned and smiled also. It was evident where the little girl had gotten her looks from. My brothers and I must have looked like three monkeys behind a cage. We did not wave back. We just stood there transfixed on the little girl. We all turned and looked at each other at the same time.

"Wow, did you see that?" Carlos asked.

"See what?" I responded. I turned and walked away. I was way to cool to talk about girls. I walked to my aunt and asked her where the school was. She told me it was just a few blocks away and most of the kids walked to school. I thanked her and walked back to the front door. My brothers were still watching the flow of kids down the sidewalk. I stood with them until my mom and aunt came to us and told us to follow them. We began to walk down the road with other kids and head towards the school. I stared at the children that walked around us. Some had their parents and others were alone. I kept my eyes open in search of a certain little golden haired girl in a blue turtle neck sweater. I could not find her.

Chapter 10
New Kid In School

I knew the routine. I had gotten pretty good at it. I stood at the front of the class and told everyone my name and a little about myself. This time it was not as easy. I had found the blonde haired girl with the waterfall of sunshine on her shoulders. I tried to speak but my voice cracked and made no sense at all. As I tried to tell the fifth graders about myself I fumbled with my words and all the kids laughed, except for one girl with an empty desk next to hers. The teacher eventually put an end to my struggles and told the class I was a new student that struggled with English and everyone was supposed to help me. She then guided me by my shoulders and led me to the seat I was praying to get. I wanted to let her know I spoke English just fine but I was scared she would move me from the seat I had my eyes on. I played along and almost tripped when she showed me my seat for the remainder of fifth grade.

I sat next to the girl who had stolen my heart from the second I saw her. I looked at her and smiled. She smiled back and lowered her eyes in a shy girl kind of way. I did the same and felt my face become warm and my ears got quite hot. I knew when my ears did that they turned red. I cupped my hands on my ears to hide my embarrassment. I knew she would see my ears and laugh at me. I lowered my elbows and rested my head in my hands as I turned my attention to the teacher. I watched her walk back and forth in front of the class as she began her lesson. I never heard a word she said. All my attention was focused at the girl sitting to my right. I faced forward and my eyes strained to catch a better view of her.

It was the first time I remember being interested in girls. I do not recall noticing them before the girl in fifth grade. Later that day I found out her name was Debbie. I liked the way her name sounded when I called it out. I silently repeated it over and over in my mind while I sat next to her. I found myself looking for excuses to look in her direction just to take in her site. It was during one of these glances that I noticed a Mexican boy on the other side of the class. While I was watching Debbie, he had been watching me. I looked past Debbie's blond hair and focused on the boy that was looking directly at me.

Rudy was about my height but much skinnier. His face was darker and his hair longer. His clothes were nicer than mine, but then again everyone had nicer clothes than me. Rudy and I stared at each other. I was thinking that maybe he was after Debbie. He had been in this school first so maybe I was intruding. I didn't care. I would look at this girl as much as I wanted. Rudy obviously didn't know about what I had done to James in California. I turned my face to the front of the class and listened to the teacher's lesson for a few minutes and then back to the right. There was Rudy again, staring right back at me. This time I noticed he was not looking at Debbie.

The class went on and on. I tried to pay attention but it was hard. I felt like reaching over and touching her hair, but of course I did not. I sat on my hands instead. The teacher talked for what seemed like days before she told us to get in line for a bathroom break. All the kids stood up and walked towards the door. I felt lost. I looked at the class and wondered what I should do. I spotted Debbie waving at me to get in line in front of her. I smiled and jumped in line in front of her. That drew attention from Rudy. He called out to the teacher and told her I was cutting in line. She smiled and said it was okay, that would be my place in the line from now on. I turned and gave Rudy a smart smile. It did not go over well with him. He raised a fist at me and snarled his face. I turned around and ignored his threat. Rudy had no idea who he was dealing with.

Our class walked to the bathrooms in line and Debbie started talking to me. I was so excited that I tried to walk backwards so I could face her. The teacher told me to turn around because I almost fell. I turned and the teacher walked by me and touched my shoulder. She leaned over and quietly asked me to behave. I gave her a smile and nodded my head. When she got to the front of the line she raised her hands and the line stopped directly in front of the bathrooms. She counted five boys and five girls at a time to go into the bathroom. I would end up with Rudy. The boys and I headed into the bathroom and I decided to go into a stall. When I entered the stall I quickly turned towards the door instead of the toilet. I had a feeling Rudy would start something and I was right.

Rudy opened the door and did not expect me to be standing there waiting for him. I caught him by surprise and he almost fell over backwards. "What do you want?" I asked him firmly in my best mean voice.

"I don't want anything," he said in a cracking voice.

"Good!" I told him as I turned and finished my business in the stall. I washed my hands and walked outside to get back in line. I was lucky to get behind Debbie this time. I smiled and looked in front of me. I made a conscious effort not to look down. I felt a little ashamed to look at a girl's rear end. I had heard it was a very bad thing to do so I kept my eyes fixed on the top of her head. We were almost to the front door of class when I took a little peek and looked down.

The rest of the morning class was much like the first part. The teacher talked and I looked towards the front and then at Debbie. Rudy still stared at me and I still ignored the stare. Soon, the teacher asked everyone to line up again and prepare for lunch. I fell into place again in front of Debbie and realized how hungry I was. Lunch was timed just right at this school. I walked in line to the cafeteria and turned to look back at every opportunity. The teacher had to tell me to turn around a few times. I didn't care. I had found the first girl I can ever recall having a crush on. We walked through the serving line and nice Mexican ladies filled my plate as we filed by. They smiled at me and one even said hello in Spanish. I responded to her greeting in the same way. I looked over my shoulder and Debbie looked puzzled. With our plates full we headed to the lunch room table area where I tried to find a space for me and Debbie to sit. I spotted two seats next to each other and Debbie and I sat down and started to eat our lunch. During our meal I struggled with my words. Thankfully she helped me along.

"How do you say hello in Spanish?" Debbie asked me. I swallowed a bite of my sandwich and tried to respond. She giggled as I tried to force down the big bite I had taken. I chewed a little faster and smiled at the same time. By this time a few boys and girls sitting next to us were getting into the conversation with us. "Hola." I finally got the word out. I then began to explain that you also used the time of day as a greeting and started to teach Debbie how to say good morning and good afternoon. Debbie listened and she tried to mouth words I had taught her. I noticed a few of the kids were doing the same thing. As they practiced the greetings I finished my lunch. A boy named Brian leaned over from the opposite side of the table and asked me, "How do you say stupid in wetback?" I leaned across the table and motioned for him to come closer so I could give the answer and he complied. I looked from side to side just to be funny and said in a low voice, "Brian." The table broke out in laughter as the kids heard my answer. Even Brian cracked a grin. The teacher came over and ushered out the kids that had completed their lunch.

Debbie and I walked towards the end of the kitchen where you turned your plates in. I was greeted once again by Mexican women working the dishwashers and processing the leftovers. Debbie smiled at the lady that took her plate and said, "Hola." The lady smiled back at her and said, "Buenos dias." Debbie waved and we walked out together and headed towards the playground. She told me the rules about lunchtime and how we had about fifteen minutes before a bell would ring that would let us know to go back to class. As we walked she told me that she wanted to go talk to her girlfriends. I walked over to a group of boys throwing a football and decide I would check out the competition. I watched as Brian threw the football at Rudy as he ran down the field. I knew they were no match for me. I continued to eye Brian and Rudy and I quickly had a grin across my face.

One of the boys from the team Brian and Rudy were playing against asked me if I wanted to play. I nodded and quickly ran into the huddle. The dark headed boy told me that they could not stop Brian and Rudy from scoring on them. I told the boy I could score against them at any time. I kneeled and drew a play on the dirt. I told him I would run straight down the field and all he had to do was throw the ball in front of me as far as he could. I would take care of the rest. We lined up and I looked at Rudy across from me. I gave him what I call my "Rodriguez" look. It is a combination of scowl and a dark stare. Rudy looked surprised and the ball was snapped as he tried to figure out what I was up to. I took off running as fast as I could and Rudy still had not moved. I ran down the field and looked back as the dark haired boy heaved the ball as hard as he could. It all looked so familiar: the sky, the sun, clouds and the ball falling easily into my outstretched hands. It was like California all over again.

I ran into the imaginary end zone and turned to see Rudy finally coming in to challenge me. "Hola," I said to him. He stopped directly in front of me and gave me his dirty look.

Brian ran over to me and slapped the ball out of my hands. "Wetback!" he yelled at me.

"Brian!" I yelled back at him. At that point a few of the kids started laughing. Yup, just like California. There would always be a James or a Brian wherever I went. I heard Brian call my name but I kept on walking. I even closed my eyes as I walked. I did not want to repeat the scene that still tortured me. The tearing of flesh above James' eye was still vividly fresh in my mind. I heard footsteps running towards me so I turned and saw Brian running at me with both fists clenched. I stopped and prepared myself, I however did not raise my hands. Brian's fist hit me directly in the middle of my chest. I fell back and landed on my rear end. Rudy ran over and started calling me names. How odd, here was a Mexican boy helping this other boy who had been calling me wetback.

I stood up and dusted myself off and turned and walked away again. I did not want to fight today. It was my first day in a school in Texas and I did not want to start it in this manner. I felt two hands push me in the back and this time I fell forwards on my chest. I picked myself up and saw Rudy standing in front of me grinning. It was he who had pushed me in the back. I looked at him and said, "At least Brian hit me in the front." I turned around and walked away again. I closed my eyes and felt tears welling up. I just did not want to fight. Why me? What had I done? I felt my fists clench and a small tear escaped my closed eyes.

"Sissy!" I heard Brian call out. He had managed to walk next to me and saw my weakness leak out. He then pushed me on the shoulder and I stumbled to the right. Rudy was on the opposite side and he pushed me back towards Brian. I braced myself for another push and then the bell rang.

Class was quieter now. I sat in my desk and never heard another word the teacher said for the rest of the day. Even Debbie had lost her golden shine. I had expected a different response here in Texas. I had expected different treatment from other Mexican kids like Rudy. I guess I was wrong. I sat there with my head hung low and I felt sorrow creeping its way up my throat. I closed my eyes and forced my throat to swallow the huge ball of misery and pain that I was holding in. Wherever I went someone was trying to hurt me mentally or physically. I wanted to cry but I knew I couldn't. Brian and Rudy had already seen me shed a tear, and that would not happen again. I wished I had someone to talk to, someone like Tio Marko, in California. He would know what to say to make it better. I thought about talking to my dad, but I just shrugged that off. Suddenly all the kids around me started to rise up out of their chairs. I felt a small hand on my shoulder. It was Debbie. She said, "Its break time, we're going to the bathrooms."

We lined up once again to go the bathrooms and I caught Brian and Rudy eying me and talking in a low voice. I knew what was going to happen. I was going to be beaten again if I did not do something. I thought about telling the teacher but decided against it. I was already a sissy, no need being a snitch also. I decided to handle it with my fists. I had done it before, I could do it again. The line moved ahead and the boys and girls each entered their bathrooms. I entered and found Rudy and Brian standing inside waiting on me. I knew I had to act fast and quick. I thought how The Hulk or The Thing would handle this. I reacted without thinking or flinching. Brian called me a wetback as I entered. I did not even hesitate. Before he got another word out I punched him directly in the nose. Rudy's mouth opened in shock and I punched him in the middle of the stomach. Brian's eyes instantly watered and he lost sight of me. He was bigger so I had to deal with him first. Rudy was a sidekick. He did not have to courage to face me directly. With Brian unable to see I kicked his feet out from beneath him and he fell on his back. I started to kick him as hard as I could. First in the ribs then in the back, I kicked as hard as I could. He started to plead with me to stop so I did. I looked around and the other boys were just standing there watching me. I guess Brian was the class bully and had always had his way. No one tried to help him, not even Rudy. He was on his knees holding his belly. I stepped over Brian and walked to the urinal. I unzipped my pants and took care of my business. I made my face show no emotion, this time there were no tears from me. I washed my hands and walked out the door. As I walked out another boy walked in and the line moved on. I walked back to class and sat down at my desk. No one could have guessed the drama that had just played out in the boy's room.

No one told the teacher what had happened. I don't know if it was because no one liked Brian or Rudy, or they were scared of me. I never told anyone about what I had done to those boys. It was either me or them. I had been beaten so many times I was tired of it. There was no sense in bragging about it anyway. It was just something that happened and I handled it the best way I could. I had learned to act quickly and decisively from reading my comic books, and watching my dad. The heroes in the books always acted with precision and no emotion. My dad was the same way. He never showed emotion when he beat us; it was just something that had to be done. No point in wasting emotion. I was now learning from the best and the worst. To me the best were the figures in the comics and the worst was my dad. The only difference in what had happened today was that when Brian pleaded with me to stop, I did. The heroes never beat someone to death, they stopped also. My dad, that's another story.

After school I walked back to my aunt and uncle's house. I looked for Debbie so I could walk with her but I could not find her. I spotted Rudy and Brian but they avoided my stare. I left the school grounds and spotted my brothers waiting for me. We greeted each other and started walking together. They asked me about my first day and I said nothing about the bathroom incident. They told me about what they had gone through. It was nothing like my first day. It seemed that I was always the one that was getting into fights or trouble. I didn't look for it but it somehow found me. The three of us walked to our uncle's house and stared at the houses and how beautiful they looked. This was our first look at suburban America. We had always lived in the country and were not used to brick house subdivisions. I was praying inside that we would have a house like these. The majority of them had chain linked fences in the back where kids were playing or a family pet was kept. That was totally foreign to us. The thought of having a private backyard with toys and swings just did not exist. We continued to walk and I kept dreaming of what our house would look like.

When we arrived at our relative's house dad's truck was there as well as mom's car. We walked up to the front door and froze. We weren't sure whether we should ring the bell or walk in. My brothers and I stared at each other. They were looking at me to make the decision on how we would enter the house. I made my choice and rang the bell. Shortly the door opened and it was my aunt. She ushered us in and led us to the kitchen table. There was a pile of sandwiches and chips along with paper plates and plastic cups waiting for us. We sat down and helped ourselves to the food. Mom and dad sat in the dining room and talked with my aunt and uncle. I did my best to listen in and even motioned to my brothers to keep their voices down. I could hear them talking about the jobs that mom and dad had found with help from dad's brother. I heard my uncle say that he would help us find a house the next day. I was excited about that comment. I could hardly wait till we got our own home in the wonderful community. I heard dad say that he was going to check on us so I told my brothers to start talking a little louder.

Dad walked into the kitchen and gave us all a mean stare. "Who rang the bell?" he asked. I looked up and he knew the answer. "Pendeho!" he growled. "Don't ever ring that bell again!" I looked down and dared not meet his gaze. He walked to the refrigerator, opened it and found a beer. He walked by us as he went back to the conversation in the dining room. My brothers looked at me and they both shook their heads. "Sometimes you just can't win," Carlos said. I nodded and suddenly the bologna sandwich didn't look appealing anymore. I gave Jose the signal and he reached down and finished it off for me. I swear that boy had a tapeworm.

The evening passed and we made our beds in the living room and my brothers and I climbed into our makeshift beds. I had the couch again and curled up in the warm blanket. My aunt came in and asked us if we were comfortable with the temperature. I told her it was a little warm. She walked over to the wall and moved a dial. I instantly heard a noise like air blowing. I was confused and crawled out of the couch and asked her what she had done. We had used box fans and window air conditioning units to cool our houses but this was new. She explained that the way they cooled and heated their home was through a central air unit. I stood there with my mouth open as she explained it the best she could. "You mean all you do is set how cool you want and it just does it?" I asked in amazement. My aunt nodded and I turned towards the couch again. They sure did things in Texas different.

I felt the temperature drop as I wrapped myself tighter in my blankets. It was getting cooler and the blankets felt so warm. I thought to myself, "No wonder people in Texas are friendlier, they all sleep so comfortably." I felt my breathing settle down to a slow rhythm and I knew sleep would soon come. The dreams would soon follow; I only wished they would be good ones. The happenings of the day always set the tone for my dreams. Today there would be no telling what my dreams would bring. Would they bring me visions of a little golden-haired girl or the pain of being hurt by the classroom bully? Either way I would deal with the pain if need be. I would prefer to have Debbie in my mind while I slept. I forced a smile on my face as sleep finally came. I hoped this would lead to friendly dreams tonight. I was wrong.

My eyes opened to a metal bathroom stall much like those in school. There was a door and it had a doorbell on it. I had never seen a stall door with a bell. I looked up and down and realized I was sitting on the toilet with my jeans around my ankles. I kept turning my head to get a good look at everything and found that I could see beyond the stall because the door had a gap of about one foot on the bottom, it did not reach the floor. I started to stand so I could pull up my jeans when I saw shadows approaching the stall. The shadows turned to sneaker-covered feet. There was about four to five pair of feet waking directly to the stall. I quickly buttoned my pants when the doorbell rang. I did not want to open the door so I asked loudly, "Who is it?" There was no response. The bell rang again. I questioned those outside the door once more and still no answer. I lowered myself to my knees so I could look outside the stall and I spotted Rudy and Brian. They had other boys with them and they did not look happy.

"Open the door coconut!" Rudy yelled.

"Wetback!" Brian yelled. The pain started to come back

"Pendeho!" I heard a familiar voice call out.

"Dad?" I looked under the door and saw his sharp pointed boots outside the door. One of the boots was tapping quickly. He always did that to warm his toes up so he could kick us. The bell rang again and more names were called. There was no way I was going to open the door. The name calling was getting louder and louder and then the walls started to close in. The stall began to close in on me, slowly at first then faster and faster. It seemed that the walls and the people outside were working in unison. The louder they yelled the faster the walls came.

I felt the temperature rise and I began to sweat. I began to push the walls back with no success. I tried using my legs when my arms tired. Nothing was working. I felt tears welling up as fear began to take over. My breathing increased and it came in gasps. I gave up pushing and began pounding on the door. The name calling was like a crescendo building into something that I did not know. I pounded harder and louder on the door to cover the name calling that was also getting louder. I fell to my knees and then my hands. I wanted to cry. "Leave me alone!" I yelled. Tears fell from my eyes like water.

"Sissy!" I heard someone call. "Vieja!" I heard dad's voice call out.

"No!" I yelled loudly as I picked my hands up from the floor and used them to cover my face. Then the cold wave hit.

I felt it in my heart first. Then it began to cover my arms and legs. I put my hands in front of my face to see if the coolness was visible. Yes it was. My skin was changing colors as it cooled down. My pain, sadness and sorrow were leaving me. I was growing cold and green! My forearms thickened as did my legs, chest and neck! The larger I became the colder I felt. I tried to stand and I fell back on the toilet. From a sitting position I could see my body changing. I also saw that the walls had stopped closing in. I put both my arms out in front of me and saw my muscles growing and thickening. Veins were pumping beneath my skin. My jeans became very tight as did my tee shirt. Then there was a ripping sound and cloth gave way to growing mass of muscles. I stood and noticed I was growing in height also. I began to see the stall shrinking as I grew to see over it. The change stopped and all became quiet.

I looked down and saw five frightened faces looking back at me. The boys and my dad had their mouths open as they looked at the massive creature facing them. I had seen this in my comic book. What were these pathetic people going to do now? They had brought out the worst in me. No longer was I a nice fifth grader with feelings and tears. I was now a giant green creature that was cold and willing to strike back. I reached down and grabbed the door with one hand and ripped it out of the stall. The boys took off running in one direction and dad took off in the other. "Where's your coconut now?" I growled at them. "Where's your pendeho now?" I stepped out of the stall and my massive shoulders barely cleared the confined space. With every step I felt colder and colder.

I began to walk towards Rudy and Brian as they scrambled for the door of the bathroom. With every step I could feel the cold concrete beneath my bare feet. Part of me was excited about crushing the boys, but somewhere deep within this huge beast a warm spot was still burning. Every step on the cold floor caused a flinch in the monster. Not noticeable to its victims but evident in the body of the dream creature. I stepped closer and closer to the frightened boys until the last step on the floor was almost freezing on my feet. I raised two huge arms as the boys began to yell and my real body came to life. I was no longer in the boy's bathroom and I was no longer green. My feet were still cold however. I looked down at my body that was wrapped like a cocoon except for one thing. My feet were poking out of the blankets. I wiggled my toes and laughed out loud. The cold was from not having my feet covered!

Chapter 11
Surviving

Fifth grade was not easily forgotten. I was beginning to change in many ways. Physically I was getting taller and starting to develop into an athlete. I continued to excel in sports and in the classroom. During our Physical Education classes I was always the last one picked for the teams but seemed to be the standout in every sport. It hurt being the last one chosen every time but that was okay. I did not cry any more and I guess I would have been shocked if I would have been picked first. I soon realized that being picked last was a blessing. People expected me to be a poor athlete, and they were very wrong. I developed a sense of fierce competition that I still have to this day. I gave every event, every sport all I could and hated to lose. This drive is a piece of me that started to form during this time in my life. It was not enough to just win. I wanted to completely annihilate the competition. It sometimes got me in trouble though.

I recalled a game of kickball in fifth grade. I was again chosen last, as usual. I was playing third base and Rudy and Brian were on the other team. Rudy had kicked the ball and was rounding first base headed for second. I caught the ball on the first bounce and headed for Rudy. I could have easily tossed the ball to the second baseman but I wanted to prove something. I threw the ball as hard as I could at Rudy. He tried to jump over my throw but did not make it. The ball caught him on the left foot and caused him to spin in the air. He landed on his head and cut his forehead. Rudy was very popular because he was a "normal" Mexican. All the girls ran to him and the blood made some of them cry out loud. Even Debbie was misty eyed. That led everyone to dislike me even more. I lowered my head and walked back to third base. What they couldn't see was the smile on my face.

In the classroom I was just as competitive. I read as many books as I could and pushed myself to make the best grades possible. I was checking out books from the library at every opportunity. I took them home and read one almost every weekend. I remember the teacher would give us a gold star on a board for every book we read. I had the most and let the Brian and Rudy know it. To prove we had read the book the teacher made us get in front of the class and give a summary on what we had read. This was the first time I realized that I liked getting in front of an audience and performing. I was on my way to becoming a ham. I had no problems standing in front of the class and talking about a book. I even began walking and talking, like a businessman giving a presentation. There was no lack of confidence for me in school. The same could not be said at home.

We lived with my aunt and uncle for about two weeks. I was excited about getting our own house. I just knew it was going to be like the brick home my aunt and uncle had. I was hoping for nice neighbors, a backyard and a sidewalk running through the front yard. What we got was something totally different. We came home from school one day and mom and dad were waiting for us. They loaded us up in the truck and headed out of town. Once again we were in the back of the camper sweating in the heat. Mom had opened the back window to circulate the air, even though it did not help. I asked mom where we were headed and she responded that they had found a house for us to live in. I was a bit excited but apprehensive because the nice suburban homes were giving way to countryside and mesquite covered woods. As we drove I told my brothers we were probably going to live in a house as bad as the ones we had in California or Plainview. If I only knew how right I was.

We pulled into the pressed dirt driveway of this dilapidated old white frame house. Parts of it were white and others were yellow. There were no neighbors, sidewalks, or fenced in back yards. I didn't even want to get out of the truck. Mom and dad were already out and walking around it when dad gave us the "look." We knew that it meant to get out and start looking like we were impressed. Dad had walked around to the back of the house when a man walked across the street in our direction. On the other side of the street was a big brick home that had a manicured lawn and a big wooden fence. I could see a big barn and cattle pens farther behind the property. He walked up to me and shook my hand. "Hola," he said. "Donde esta tu pappa?"

"My dad is walking around the house," I responded. "Is that your house?" The man smiled and ignored my question and walked towards the rear of the house. "I guess he doesn't speak good English," I told my brothers.

My brothers and I explored the area around the old house. We had definitely lived in worse. We saw the man give dad a key and a handshake as he walked away. He smiled at my brothers and me as he headed across the road. We continued to explore as mom and dad entered the house. Behind the house was a wooded area of mesquite trees and cactus bordered by a barbed wire fence. We walked to the fence and could see cattle trails leading into the woods. I was tempted to jump the fence and continue our adventure but I knew that a whipping would be my reward if mom and dad called for us and we were not available. We decided to head back towards the shack, I mean house, and see what the inside looked like. It was no surprise when we went inside. It looked just as bad. I thanked God for the roof over our head at the time, but I was sure it leaked. The house had one bedroom and one bathroom. I remember the floor sloped in the bathroom. You could make a down-hill run to toilet, literally.

We left our uncle's house the next day and moved in. It took at least an hour to finish moving in. We didn't have much, so moving was pretty easy. Once we were done I asked permission from mom to go exploring beyond the fence. Dad had overheard and told us to go. "Maybe it will make a man out of you to go into the woods!" he said. I don't know what that meant and I didn't hang around to find out. My brothers and I ran to the fence and crawled through it. We found a cattle trail and began to follow it. The mesquite brush was very thick and dense on either side of the trail. The path led us through brush and to an open meadow. There we walked off the trail and explored the edges of the brush. We each found a walking stick and headed back to the path. We followed it a little longer and came to a creek. The water was flowing over rocks and boulders. It was very beautiful: the site, the sounds, the aroma are all still in my memory.

We spent the weekend getting settled in and Monday morning we had to wake much earlier to catch a bus back to school. We loaded in the bus while it was still dark and it brought back memories of the migrant camps and the frosty mornings. In the bus we got stares and looks from the White kids. We were the only Mexicans in the bus. It was no problem for me or my brothers. We had gone through this before. I recognized a few kids from school and they gave me a nod or a wave. No one wanted to be the person that was affiliated with the "Mexicans." I wasn't torn up about it, neither were my brothers. We had each other to keep us company. Once we arrived at school we left the bus area and headed to class.

It was April or early May when we moved outside of the city limits. School was winding down and there were a lot of outdoor activities. There was an excitement in the air because our fifth grade class was going to be competing against other classes in a track meet. Our teacher's name was Mrs. Mahoney and we were going to be called Mrs. Mahoney's Ponies. We each had to bring a white tee shirt and the girls had cut out a stencil with the shape of a horse jumping on it. In class we had to pick who would compete in events that would give the class the most points so we could win a small trophy. I thought is was funny, I was always the last pick during PE for teams but now the class wanted me to compete in almost every event. The teacher would call out an event and the class would select the person to represent the class. In almost every instance I was picked. I sat in my chair and didn't say a word. Debbie leaned over to me and said, "Now you're the popular kid."

Deep inside, I was very excited about the track meet. I would be competing in the sprint races, long jump, and softball throwing events. I ended up winning a blue ribbon in every race. In the long jump and softball throw I won a second place red ribbon. After each event I had to report what ribbon I had won to the class and our points were added up. I came in with ribbons and the point total was growing. That was when I noticed something. It doesn't matter what skin color you are when it comes to sports. If you can run and jump or throw a ball you quickly become an asset. All sense of me being Mexican faded as long as I was bringing in the points. The girls in the class began to talk to me, the boys started following me to my events. They all cheered and jumped on me when I won. I found this really odd. I hadn't changed. Neither had they; they all of the sudden needed me for my athletic skills. I felt important for a day.

Our team won the track meet. I was a hero for a day. The next day everything was back to normal. The only person that never changed was Debbie. She was my friend every day. Brian and Rudy started disliking me more the day after the games. I had won more ribbons than anybody in the class. I was pretty sure they were jealous of me and would like nothing better than to catch me in the boy's bathroom. They knew better however.

I took my ribbons home and showed them to mom and she just nodded and went about her job of fixing dinner. I didn't even bother showing them to dad. When I went to show them to Jose he laughed. He had five blue ribbons to my three. He had won first place in every event he had entered. He has always been a better athlete than me. Carlos had a first place ribbon for the softball throw. He was always stronger than me.

Summer was upon us before we knew it. School was over and we spent the summer staying at home alone. Mom was working at a local nursing home. Dad was working for a local nursery. He took care of trees and plants. He had missed a couple of days work already because of his drinking. I spent the summer exploring the woods behind the house and reading. I had found a handful of paperbacks in a garbage pile in the woods. Someone was dumping their trash in a gravel pit and I had spotted the books. They were very long and did not have any pictures. I found them very mushy and had a lot kissing and hugging. Still it kept my mind fresh and the learning continued. I still had the box of comics under our bed. Since our house had only one bedroom, my brothers and I shared a bed that we placed in the living room.

The times were hard. Poverty is a relative experience. Since you do not know what it is not to be poor, you only have one experience to relate it to. We always had food, even though it was rice, beans and potatoes. We had tortillas at every meal. Mom and dad bought a few chickens so we always had fresh eggs. Mom even planted a garden in the area next to the fence. She had tomatoes, squash, green beans and herbs. It was a good thing too: dad lost his job at the nursery in June of that year. Dad kept complaining that they didn't like him because he was Mexican. He had mom convinced. Mom always agreed with him. I was a little smarter. I figured it was the fact that he was missing at least one day a week because of his drinking. Pop took time to watch us work in the garden during the days since he was not working. He would stand in the shade and direct us to pull weeds or plant his peppers. We already had experience in working the fields and I was wishing he would find a job soon so I could go back to my books.

It took mom fighting with dad every day to get him to do something. I'm pretty sure he had worn out his welcome with my uncle. I recall the man from across the street walking over one day and beating on our door. Dad was home and answered the call. They talked for a while and I could overhear the man asking for the rent. We did not have it of course. They talked for a while and then he left. Dad lounged around the house for a while and then left. I took the opportunity to grab a book and head for the woods. We had built a small tree house in a mesquite tree. It was just big enough to lie down in and was covered with shade. I would lay there for hours and read. During the afternoon it was pleasantly cool and always had a breeze. I could also see the backyard from this vantage point. When mom called us for dinner I could see her stepping out the back door. I stayed in the tree until noon then walked back to the house. Carlos and Jose enjoyed watching television so they were glued in front of the set all morning. I chose to get out of the house.

One day, I went inside to get something to eat and drink. I opened the refrigerator and grabbed a bowl of yesterday's leftovers. We had beans last night again so I made two burritos of cold beans and headed back to my perch in the tree. I ate the cold lunch and continued to read. The book was really sappy but it was all I had. I liked the way the story unfolded from black and white ink to wonderful colors in my head. The book was about a woman lost at sea with a ship full of pirates. From the look of the cover one of them was lifting weights. The man was very muscular and was holding the woman very tightly. The story involved lots of kissing and hugging and words that sounded like the two were on fire. One line described that the man's heat was on fire. I read the line two or three times and could not understand it. I just kept on reading. Surely there had to be parts where the pirates would fight like I had seen on the television. I stayed in the tree for a few more hours then came back down. I was getting tired of reading and the story was really boring. I climbed down the tree and headed for the house.

Carlos and Jose were still in front of the television. There were plates on the floor where they had also eaten cold bean burritos and empty glasses. I cleaned the plates and glasses off the floor and took them to the kitchen sink. Mom would be home soon and I didn't want her to get angry. She would fix dinner for us, even though dad was supposed to do it because he was not working. That might have been the case but dad had not cooked dinner at all for us. He was usually too drunk to do that by the time evening came. I wanted to help mom out a little so I walked into the living room and turned the TV off. I asked my brothers to follow me and they slowly came to life and followed me outside. We went to the garden and looked over our patch of vegetables and decided on what we wanted for dinner. We chose the green bean Mexican casserole. It was one of Jose's favorites. We picked the green beans, tomatoes, and one jalapeno pepper. I wasn't sure if we had any meat in the house so I grabbed a few extra tomatoes just in case. We took dinner into the house and cleaned it and prepared for mom to come home.

Mom arrived a little later than usual and dad was still not home. She rested for bit and asked us about him. We shrugged our shoulders and she headed for the kitchen. We showed mom the big bowl of vegetables and asked if she would make the casserole we had wanted. She agreed since we had everything ready. I knew we were out of meat when mom brought out the potatoes and began slicing them. We always had them when we were out of meat. She sliced them into medallions and tossed them into the pot with the other vegetables. She added the other ingredients and then added the magic touch: a large helping of flour. She said this thickened the broth and made it taste better. I'm pretty sure we call that "filler" now. We had our hot meal for the day and mom sat with us and asked us about our day. She apologized for running late. She said she was working extra hours to make more money. We listened to her story of how her day went and we smiled back at her as we cleaned our plates. After our meal my brothers and I took turns washing, drying and putting away the plates and glasses. After our chores we went outside to walk off our very filling dinner.

One of favorite games as the sun went down was chasing bats. They would begin flying out of our attic as the sun went down. They would come out one by one then the entire colony would come out in a big cloud. We would chase them with sticks and throw rocks at them. We never caught or hit any. I never understood why people said, "blind as a bat." The little animals were very hard if not impossible to catch. Once the sun went down we would walk to the edge of the fence and listen to the sounds of the south Texas nights. We could hear owls, coyotes and insects. The darker it got the louder the sounds of the night became. We headed back into the house just in time to see the headlights of dad's truck pull in. Mom instantly pounced on him then froze in panic. Dad had blood all over his shirt and arms.

Dad began barking orders at mom and she sprang into action. She ran inside and came out with a handful of knives. Dad walked to the back of his truck and pulled a big buck deer out of the bed. It had the throat cut and was still dripping blood. Dad carried it to the back yard and hung it off the pole that supported the clothes line. Mom turned on the backyard lights and brought out extra lights. Dad barked more orders and she turned them off. He wanted just enough light to do his work and not draw attention. Dad began his gruesome work. He was very good at this. He hung the carcass with the back legs open wide and head dangling. He started at the top and worked his way down. While he was doing his work he yelled at me to get a shovel and start digging a hole by the garden. I did as I was told and started digging. The ground was soft and I dug for almost an hour. Carlos was helping mom, Jose was helping dad. I was glad I was digging. I hated watching dad gut animals. I had helped him with goats before. I can still smell that awful odor.

I knew what the hole was for and here came Jose with the items to be buried. Dad had placed the guts and head in a large bag he had made from the skin. He had tied it shut with the guts. Jose dragged the remains into the hole then we began covering it. Dad came over and told us to make sure it looked like nothing had happened. He had us spread bits of grass and twigs over the hole and even dragged a few squash vines over the hole. I was exhausted by the time I walked back to the house. I came in the back door and the odor was overwhelming. Mom had every pot and pan on the stove cooking deer meat. Dad had a big knife and hammer on the kitchen table and was chopping huge chunks of meat into manageable portions. He was wrapping them in foil paper and placing them in the freezer. At least we would have meat in our casseroles now, I thought to myself

Mom and dad continued to work in the kitchen while my brothers and I washed up and headed for bed. I looked at the clock and it was very late. I heard dad yell at mom that he was hungry. He was telling her what a great provider and hunter he was. Mom didn't say a word. I knew she did not have the heart to tell the great hunter he had used a pickup to kill the deer. The truth was that dad was driving drunk and had run over the deer because he did not see it. She continued to cook his dinner even though it was close to midnight. I knew she was tired but the great provider had to be fed with the blood of his kill. I giggled a bit as I was falling asleep. I thought to myself, "The great drunk hunter." I lay in bed and waited for Jose and Carlos to join me. I hated sleeping with my brothers. We were getting bigger and barely had enough room to get comfortable. I was tempted to sleep on the floor but there were spiders and scorpions that came out at night.

I fell asleep wondering why dad had us bury the deer remains and do our best to cover them up. I felt like I was covering up a murder the way the evening had ended. During the night my dream came the way they always did. First it was complete darkness then light. Not just a glowing light but a light so bright it engulfs everything. Then the colors of life began to fill in like a coloring book. This dream was different. There were no comic book heroes, no costumes, just our poor house. I was still in bed and my brothers were still asleep. The sound that woke me was a knocking noise coming from the door. I rose and walked to the door. I slowly turned the doorknob and opened it. Everything was moving in slow motion and the sunshine coming through the window as a reddish yellow tint. There was an odor of death in the air, like blood and treachery hanging in the shadows of the morning. The knocking continued even though I was opening the door. Two large men in uniform seemed to cover the entire doorway. Their badges were reflecting light even though the sun was at their back. The men had sunglasses on their faces and I could not see their eyes, but I could feel their piercing stare.

"Step outside!" one of the men shouted. I slowly stepped outside. I was standing in the moist grass and my bare feet cringed and made my toes curl. I looked up at the two men with one eye closed. Their backs were to the sun. The morning light kept me from getting a good look at their faces. "Yes," I said in a mousey voice. There was no response from the men. They stood like statues in front of me. They didn't move and I guess they didn't blink either. I felt guilt welling up inside of me, an urge to cry was starting to creep up my throat. I felt a tear begin to form in my one open eye. I began to move back inside the doorway. I took one half-step, then another. The men saw this and one reached out and touched my shoulder. It was all I could stand.

"I didn't do it!" I yelled as I tried to break the grip of the man holding my shoulder. "I swear I didn't!" The more I struggled the tighter the grip became.

"Did what?" the man holding my shoulder asked. His voice let me know they were on to me.

"I don't know," I said while I continued to wiggle and squirm in my vain attempt to lose the grip on my shoulder. "Let me go!"

His grip just tightened. Then he started to shake me. "Wake up!" I heard him say. The shaking continued. "I said wake up!" His voice sounded like Carlos now. Then I felt two hands on my shoulders. This time I opened both eyes. The sunshine as well as the two big men were both gone. They were replaced by Carlos. He was trying to wake me up. He had both hands on me and was shaking me. "I'm awake!" I said.

"The landlord's at the door!" Carlos said in a whisper.

"I think he knows we're here," Jose said from under the sheets of the bed.

I got out of bed and went to the front door. It was mid morning and both my parents were gone. Mom was at work and dad was gone. I stepped out and there was the landlord. He had both his hands on his hips and a scowl on his face. "Where's your father?" he asked firmly.

"I don't know," I said while I looked at the ground near my feet.

"You tell him he better pay me the rent or I'll be throwing your asses out!" He turned and walked away before I could respond. What was I going to respond with anyway? I watched him walk away and both his hands were clenched in fists. I knew what had happened. Dad had borrowed money from my uncle to pay it but had spent it on beer and cigarettes. Now we had no money to pay the bills and we were about to be homeless. I turned and walked back into the house and told my brothers everything was okay. "He just wanted to know if we had seen a dead deer near the road," I said. They both started to giggle. They knew about the great drunk hunter and how he had single handedly killed a huge buck, with a pickup truck. I walked through the combination living and bedroom into the kitchen and saw a huge piece of deer meat thawing in the sink. Well at least we would have meat for dinner.

I spent the day back in my tree reading the novel I had found. I was nearing the end and the plot had not changed. There was way too much loving and kissing in this book. I read it anyway and imagined Debbie as the heroine and me as the pirate. I put the book down and lay on my back with my eyes closed. I pictured the ocean and sea breeze in my face, my woman in my arms as we sailed across the sea. No landlord to ask for rent. No venison to eat. That would be the life, sailing the seven seas and chasing fortune and fame. I smiled while I lay there and dreamed. Anything was better than this.

Mom came home late again and worn to the bone. She looked so tired. She was leaving for work before the sun rose and coming home after dark now. She was working as much overtime as she could get. At minimum wage, she would never get ahead. Dad still had not come home. She asked if we had seen him and we shook our heads. I didn't have the heart to tell her we were starving. We had eaten the leftovers from yesterday and there was no food in the refrigerator. Mom read our mind and started grilling the deer meat that had thawed. It smelled funny but we ate it anyway. It was that or nothing. As we finished dinner dad pulled up. We heard his truck pull into the yard and close the door. He came into the kitchen and began to demand his dinner. He was drunk again and mom did as she was told. We left the table and left it to the king of the house. We knew he did not like sharing his table with us.

My brothers and I prepared for bed. We headed for the bathroom to take our showers. I listened to dad tell mom how no one would hire him because he was a Mexican. I knew inside he had probably spent the day drinking at a bar. He told mom that he had spoke to his brother in Chicago and he could get him a job making ten dollars an hour. My ears perked up and I strained to catch every drunken word my dad said. I wondered what rent cost in Chicago and if landlords came to your door asking for money.

We finished getting ready for bed and I fell asleep wondering where Chicago was located. I had trouble sleeping and no dreams came that night. I had a strange feeling things were about to change again. I was ready to start sixth grade in the same school. Debbie was there and the kids were starting to accept me as an equal. There was talk about going to the local junior high and playing real football, with pads and helmets. School would be starting in a few weeks and I was getting excited, but cautious.

I awoke the next morning and something was different. Dad was home and he was boxing up things in the kitchen. He had large amounts of deer meet thawing in the sink. "Get up!" he yelled. "Wake your brothers now!" In the kitchen were cardboard boxes. I knew what was about to happen. "Start putting all your clothes in the boxes." I listened to him but kept walking to the bathroom to brush my teeth and take a shower. We always did that in the morning. I was still half asleep as I walked to the bathroom. I raised my arm to open the bathroom door and all the sudden the door slammed into my face. Dad had walked up behind me and kicked me in the rear and launched me into the door. I fell in a heap against the door. "What did I tell you to do?" he yelled at me. My head was still foggy from sleep and now dazed, I could not answer. I felt a boot come across my ribs as I rolled in the direction of our bedroom. "Start packing now!"

Carlos and Jose jumped out of bed and began to get their clothes out of our drawers and boxes from underneath the bed.

I lay on the floor for a minute. I dared not move and expose myself. I heard dad's footsteps walk back to the kitchen. I realized that I had closed my eyes so I did not have to see the beating I was getting. Somehow that made it hurt less. I slowly opened one eye then the other. Dad was back at the stove cooking his breakfast. I got up and started to put my clothes in the box Carlos and Jose had started to fill. Between the three of us we hardly filled the box. I had tears roll down my cheeks as I put my underwear and blue jeans in. I was grimacing in pain but would not cry out loud. That would invite more kicks and show weakness to my brothers. I needed to stay strong for them. It only took a few minutes for us to pack. We only had about two blue jeans each and a few tee shirts. During the summer we rarely wore shoes so socks were in short supply. I looked in the box and realized I only had three pair of underwear. Since we didn't wear socks, why use underwear?

Dad came into the room and started yelling at us to start packing all the blankets and pillows. After we had done that he began to disassemble the bed. He had us put it all against the wall. He then had us fill boxes with pots, pans and dishes. This went on for a few hours and I realized we had not showered or even brushed our teeth. While we were packing the kitchen utensils there was a knock at the door. My brothers and I froze. We knew who it was. I guess dad did to. He walked out the back door and walked around to the front to meet the landlord. I took this opportunity to run into the bathroom and brush my teeth. Carlos and Jose followed behind me. We brushed and washed our faces in the sink. Jose watched for dad as Carlos and I finished up. We walked into the front room where we could hear dad talking with the landowner. Both their voices were getting louder as dad tried to convince him that he would have the rent tomorrow. The talking stopped and we knew dad would be coming back inside. We ran back into the kitchen and started packing again.

Dad came back in but not before we heard his truck door open and close. He returned with a can of beer. We dared not look at him but continued to load a box with spoons and forks. We heard him pop the can open and walk back to the stove. He continued to order us to pack and soon we had all our belongings in boxes stacked near the kitchen. It was close to noon now and my stomach was starting to growl. Dad had been cooking and eating at the same time. We also knew that when he drank beer he did not eat much. He called us over to the stove and handed us each a taco of grilled deer meet and a can of soda. I was starving and took my lunch to my tree with both my brothers behind me. We climbed up our tree house and sat with our bare feet hanging off the edge of our platform. We opened our sodas and took a bite of our tacos. The meat was so tough we could not chew it. The stuff was as tough as leather. We ate the tortillas and threw the meat into the brush. I was still hungry as were my brothers. We made Jose run into the garden and grab a few tomatoes. He grabbed one for each of us and we ate them fresh off the vine.

From our tree house we saw dad repeatedly make a trip to his truck until he finally brought the ice chest inside the house. As long as dad was inside the house my brothers and I would stay outside. We stayed in the woods till mom came home. She arrived earlier than usual and we met her at the door. She came in and was not at all surprised to see the house in boxes. She looked at the stove with a skillet of cold deer meat in it and lowered her head. She looked at us and knew we had not eaten well. She walked around the kitchen and there was dad. He was sleeping on the floor and had a pile of beer cans around him. She said nothing but went back into the kitchen instead. She instructed us to go pick vegetables from the garden so she could cook dinner.

I walked outside and my brothers followed. Summer was coming to an end and the garden was starting to wither in the south Texas heat. We walked through the plants and managed to find a jalapeno pepper, tomatoes and a few zucchini squash. We took these into the kitchen and washed them. Mom had taken the cold cooked deer steak and sliced it into thin strips. She filled the skillet with water and heated the water to a slow boil to soften it. She added a few pieces of the pepper and the rest of the vegetables. While it was simmering she added my favorite part: the fideao. In English we call it vermacilli noodles. It will always be fideao to me. I can still remember the smell of this dish cooking. We usually used chicken but any meat will do. Mom let the dish simmer and she set about the task of making tortillas.

She used an extra large helping of flour this time and I knew we were in for a trip. We would be eating tortillas all the way to Chicago, wherever that might be. Mom asked us to go outside until the food was ready so we would not wake our father. We complied and took our last walk around the little house. The sun was beginning to set and the bats would soon begin their flight to hunt for food. We did not bother them this time. There was an air of fear tonight. Once again we would be on the move. We had no idea what the next day would bring. Where was Illinois? Would there be friendlier kids there? There were so many questions yet no one to answer them for me.

Carlos and Jose did not share my concern. They walked around the old house and talked about how much they hated it. I have seen pictures of the old house and my brothers and I dressed in tattered clothes. It still amazes me to this day that we survived that summer. We made it by eating fresh vegetables and road kill. Mom worked overtime at every opportunity to make extra money and dad drank it as fast as he could. I guess the old saying that people don't get rich on overtime is true. The landlord that owned the old house did not make any money off of us either. While he slept that night on the promise of dad paying the rent the next day we left for Chicago, Illinois.

Chapter 12
The Ghetto

The drive to Illinois was uneventful. I think it was because I chose to block out many of the things that happened. My one recollection is stopping at a truck stop. I remember stopping to buy fuel and to use the bathrooms. I was in a toilet stall and dad was in the bathroom waiting for me. I heard two men talking as they washed their hands about how Mexicans smelled when they used the toilet. Dad did not say a word and the two men eventually left. I finished my business and exited the stall. Neither one of us said a word as we left for the highway again.

I was stuck with dad again as we drove north. The surroundings were so different from south Texas. The mesquite had given way to tall pine trees as we headed north. I did not speak to dad. Summer was beginning to end and everything was green from the rains and humidity. Our truck did not have air conditioning but it was still better than riding in the back of the truck in the middle of the desert. I kept looking out of the window and stared at the endless forests. In the early morning, steam and mist was rising out of the canopies. I looked into the dense growth and wondered if trolls, goblins and troglodytes lived there. I continued to stare for what seemed hours into those woods. From time to time I would smell the whiff of tobacco as dad lit up a cigarette. I would pretend not to notice.

I looked forward to the pit stops we took, not only to stretch my legs but to talk to my brothers. I tried to get them to switch with me and get them to ride with dad. It did not work. Carlos and Jose made it clear that since I was the oldest it was my duty to ride with dad. They also said that since they were younger they needed to ride with mom. Regardless of the reason, I rode the entire trip with dad. We hardly exchanged any words during the thousand mile trip. He would drive and I would stare at the woods bordering the highway in hopes of catching a glimpse of monsters and heroes. I never saw either one.

We arrived at our uncle's house in Harvey, Illinois late at night while I was sleeping. I remember someone jerking my arm and telling me to get out. The pain was enough to wake the dead. My arm felt like it was being ripped out of the socket. I gave no indication of how bad it hurt but I got out of the truck quickly. I was groggy and had one eye closed as I located my brothers and followed them. We were led into a strange home and directed to the couch with pillows and blankets piled up on it. Some things never changed; I grabbed a pillow and a blanket and took one end of the couch and covered my head. Sleep came very easy and quickly. The soreness in my arm was subsiding as a gray mist consumed my mind. Some time during the night I might have cried. I already missed Debbie and Texas.

The next day came sooner than I wanted. The blanket I was curled up in was jerked off of me as I was told to get up. This time it was mom that rudely woke me up. I rolled off the couch to a crouching position. I sharp pain in my shoulder sent a jolt through my side. I was instantly awake now. Mom instructed me to follow my brothers to the bathroom where we were to get cleaned up. She had laid out clothes for us to wear. That was easy enough. I think I had two pair of jeans during that time: one with holes and one without. I got to wear the ones without today. It must have been a special day. My brothers and I showered and got dressed quickly. We were on our best behavior, no towel snapping today. I wanted to get Carlos so bad but the throbbing in my shoulder told me to behave. There would be a next time. All three of us walked into the kitchen where my mom was calling. Breakfast was ready for us. My aunt, who was my dad's sister, and her husband were seated when we entered. They stood as we came around the table and acted like they were so excited to us. I put on my best happy face and acted just like they did. We introduced ourselves and went through the same routine: name, age and serial number. Well, maybe not the serial number.

My Aunt Rosa looked like a female version of my dad. She had a dark complexion and a thick stocky build. Her black hair lay on her shoulders with no particular style. She looked tired and her face showed she was not excited that we were here. Her husband, Uncle Pete, was a thinly built man. He was as tall as Rosa, but she had at least fifty pounds on him. His skinny face had whiskers that he was trying to grow into a mustache, beard, or something. His face was pleasant however and did not give off any negative feelings. As I watched my aunt and uncle it became very evident she was in charge. I never saw my aunt smile the entire time we were in Illinois.

We had cold cereal in little bowls for breakfast. I looked at the small serving and knew that Jose's tape worm would starve today. I glanced at Jose and he had a look of utter disbelief. He never had a bowl that small. Dad gave us a glaring look. He knew what we were thinking. I was able to catch Jose's eyes and he saw me give him the warning look. He looked up and thanked my aunt for the generous amount of Tony the Tiger Flakes that would fill him up for about ten minutes. We ate breakfast quietly and were still hungry when we finished. I heard my aunt ask mom if we wanted more. Mom said we were fine and the box of cereal was put away. I could see Jose's eyes follow the box all the way to the cupboard as it was put away. Then I heard his stomach growl. "It must be the worm," I told Carlos. We walked to the sink and placed our empty bowls in the sink and walked to the couch where our uncle was watching the morning news.

"You boys play baseball?" he asked. The three of us shook our heads. Dad had never let us enroll in little league. We were never anywhere long enough to get started, actually. "I'll teach you guys to play when I get a chance," he stated. I was thinking to myself that we would probably be moving again before I learned how to bat. We sat and watched the sports report and my ears perked when the announcer started talking about football. My uncle saw the shine in my face and asked, "So you like football?" All three of us nodded our heads. My uncle broke out in laughter and said we reminded him of the Three Stooges. I did not get the joke, but I guess he did. We sat and watched more of the news with him and then he got up to go talk to my dad who was still in the kitchen eating breakfast with his sister.

I looked at my brothers and asked if they thought it was safe to change the channel on the television. Jose asked, "How's your arm?"

I told him, "It still hurts."

"Then you better leave it alone." The television remained on the same channel and we watched the boring news cast. As the anchorman gave his report I kept one ear on the grownups as they talked about work and housing. I heard dad and my uncle say their goodbyes as they headed out the door. Mom and my aunt sat at the kitchen table and talked about women's stuff so my attention drifted back to my brothers.

We stayed on the couch and chatted about what school would be like in Illinois. "Do you think there's Mexicans here?" Jose asked with a curios look in his face. I shrugged my shoulders in response. I really didn't know. The fact was there were plenty of Mexicans in the area where we would live. We were to settle in an area of Harvey, Illinois that was populated by large numbers of Hispanics that worked the factories and service industries. Today that area would be called a slum, barrio or the ghetto. The house we would move into made the shacks in Texas look really nice. Once mom and my aunt were finished talking they called us over and we walked out the door and down the street.

We walked through an alley that didn't look bad at all. All the houses had huge fences that were probably ten feet high. You could only see the second story of most of the houses or just the roofs. As we walked, the houses began to change from middle class blue collar dwellings to broken down homes subdivided into multi-family houses. It looked like someone had taken a two story house and split it up so three families could live in the house to maximize rent. As we walked down the alley I became aware of an eerie feeling, like I was being watched. I looked at a window and I could see a face behind a towel that was being used as a curtain. The further we walked the closer my brothers and I got to our mother. My aunt quickened her pace also. I saw a look of relief when we neared a long house that was very oddly shaped.

The house was long like a rectangle and at the rear toward the alley it had a second story, but only on the back one-third. Stairs led up to the second story. I looked up and saw a pregnant Mexican woman standing in the doorway with two babies under three years hugging each leg. As we walked past the middle third of the building we came across a screen door with another woman standing behind it. She watched us as we walked by. I looked at her and waved and she waved back. I gave her a smile as we walked by. We came to the front of the house and found our new home. We had the front part of the long house. The front door faced a main street that was fairly busy. Across the street was the rear of a huge plant that made mattresses, according to my aunt. I walked to the front door and noticed two big windows on either side of the door. I looked at mom with a puzzled look. She wasn't smiling much right about now.

It turned out the front part of this building used to be a store. That's why the two windows were so big; they were used to display products that were sold there. I looked up and down the street and guessed this "house" actually used to be a bar. This was easy to figure out since there were a few more still in business down the street. It made sense now as I scanned the entire "house." This was the entrance and the middle where the other family lived was where people drank. The rear and upstairs of the home was where people ate or lived. My aunt pulled a key out of her pocket and unlocked the door. We walked in and counted our blessings. At least it did not have an earthen floor. That was about all this new home was blessed with.

The inside of the "house" really showed that it used to be a bar. The front room had a kitchen, living room and bedroom all in one space. A wall had been made out of sheetrock to make another room behind it. The master bedroom was small and it had the only bathroom connected to it. In the bathroom there was a toilet, sink and a tub. There was barely enough room for one person. The tub looked like it had been placed there after the fact. I scanned the tiny room and wrinkled my nose. It did not smell good at all.

My brothers were also looking around the tiny house. It was going to be easy to divide the rooms up. Mom and dad would get the only bedroom and we would get the rest of the house. At least we wouldn't have to walk far to get to the kitchen. Mom motioned for me to follow her as we walked out and my aunt locked the front door. I was going to tell her to leave it open. There was nothing to steal anyway. She mentioned that there were lots of bums that walked around the area. I pointed down the street to man sitting on the sidewalk. "Like him?" I asked. My aunt ignored me and started walking back towards her home. Her pace had definitely quickened when she saw the drunken bum lie down. When we arrived back at my aunt's home, mom took the key from her and loaded us up in her car and we drove back to our new home.

We spent the rest of the day cleaning the bathroom and the kitchen. We unloaded the car and made the best of our situation. With our belongings moved in, mom began to fix lunch for us. I took my sandwich and stepped outside to look at what we had moved in to. It was nothing like Texas. Cars and trucks drove up and down the busy street. Huge tractor trailers pulled out of the factory. There were so many strange noise and smells. Gone were sounds of cicadas and birds. There were no birds singing or wind blowing through the mesquites. The only sounds and smells being made were all of industry. Trucks were billowing out smoke as were the smoke stacks of the plant across the street. It smelled like trash burning in the fifty-five gallon drums of the migrant compound. This time the smoke was worse and it was coming straight to our front door. Part of me wanted to cry, but I knew what would happen if I did. I also knew dad should be home soon.

When dad arrived he was not happy. He had already had a few beers and was on the verge of getting drunk. He was upset more than he usually was. He began yelling bad words in Spanish as well as English. From what I could make out the job his brother-in-law had arranged for him had been given to someone else. I listened to him recount the story to mom and as far as I could make out, his sister had told management that he was a drunk and would cause trouble at the factory. It was making sense now. My aunt and uncle both worked at the plant where dad was to work. She did not want to put their job on the line by getting dad hired. I wish they would not have invited us here at all. As confusing as this sounded, it made sense when dad explained it to mom. The bottom line was my dad was a drunk and he would cause trouble. He was actually drunk now and causing trouble.

Dad yelled to my mom about the way he was going to whip his sister when someone beat on the wall in the bedroom and yelled for him to shut the "you know what" up. Dad yelled back some obscenities and continued to drink and yell. That's when someone began to beat on the door. Dad looked out from behind the sheet mom had on the front window and his head looked shocked. I ran to the other side and peered out. There were three big men standing outside the door. Dad ran into the kitchen, it only took about three steps and came back to the door with a butcher knife. Dad opened the door slightly and began to talk to the men. He laughed and talked about the bad day he was having. Dad talked some more to the men and handed the knife to mom and he stepped outside. Mom clutched the knife, worried. I pressed my ear against the door and could make out the men and dad beginning to joke. I went back to the window and grabbed Carlos and pushed away from the window where he was looking out. I took his place and watched as dad went to his truck and grabbed a bag from the front seat. I knew what was going to happen. He handed each of the men a beer. Then came the familiar sound; "pfft."

Mom handed us each a blanket and a pillow and we slept on the wooden floor. I lay there wrapped in my blanket and strained my ears to listen to dad and the men talk outside our front door. Everything was so strange now. Texas and Debbie were gone for good. I knew I would never see either one of them again. I thought about which one I missed more and my eyes grew heavy. My eyes were to reopen when dad came back into the house. He fumbled with the door and made his way to the bedroom where mom was waiting for him. I could hear as he used the bathroom and flushed the toilet. I felt the floor move as he fell on the floor. Mom and dad were also sleeping on the floor.

I was too sad to dream that night. I was scared I would dream of a blonde-haired, blue—eyed beauty. I might also dream of a beautiful state with wide open meadows, birds and deer. Somewhere in the night I slept and then awoke, scared. The sun was not yet up and strange voices were outside our front door. I heard men and women talking about the price of a party. Two men were wanting to party with this woman who was asking for money or dust. I didn't get it. The street lights from the road silhouetted the people on the sheets mom used for curtains. They haggled about some price and walked off. Other people would walk by and some of them walked like dad did when he had drank too much.

The next morning I awoke and found mom and dad sitting at the kitchen table talking softly. They were looking at me and my brothers sleeping on the floor. Mom looked like she had been crying all night. Dad looked like he had not slept either. Mom said something to him and she pointed at us. Dad lowered his head and covered his face with his hands. He then got up and walked out.

Mom fixed us breakfast as we took turns cleaning up and folding our blankets. She did not yet have a job and neither did dad. I knew money had to be running short and we had no more relatives to turn to. I asked mom where dad had gone and she ignored my questioning. She served us breakfast tacos of eggs and beans. I looked at her face and it was still red and so were her eyes. After we ate she went to the bedroom and closed the door. We could hear her crying out loud now.

We stayed inside and read our books that we had brought on the trip and around lunch time dad came back. He had a stack of papers and some folders with pictures of army men and green colors on them. He sat at the table and began filling out forms. I knew better than to bother him. Mom came out and I heard dad tell her it was done. He had re-enlisted into the army, for a four year tour. I sat there confused. I knew dad had been in the army before, but now he was going back in?

Within a few weeks dad got his orders to leave for boot camp. He was now in his thirties and was an old recruit. I guess mom and dad decided this was the only way to get dad cleaned up, and get us out of Illinois. I remember when dad left, mom cried all day. My brothers and I shed no tears. I don't even recall hugging him goodbye. Before we knew it, we were alone.

Mom got a job at a factory and was making barely enough money to buy groceries. Dad's army paychecks had not yet started coming in. We lived off of eggs, potatoes and beans. We drank tap water and our best lunches came from school. I only attended school in Illinois for a few months. We started there in early September and were gone by October. I was so glad to leave. It was growing colder every day.

Early October brought a few cold fronts that made the "blue northers" from Texas seem mild, it is indescribable. We had no winter clothes and could not afford to buy any. We also did not have a heater in the house. Mom would take us to malls on the weekend and would stay there all day to keep warm. When we finally came back home, she would put a pot of water on every burner of the stove. The steam coming up was to warm the house. I'm not sure it worked. There were times you could see your breath inside the house. Mom kept telling us that dad would be coming home soon and we would move somewhere warmer.

I was excited about moving to a warmer place but not about dad coming home. Mom received letters from dad about every two weeks. He kept her informed on his progress and when he would be coming home. I remember mom getting a letter and she started jumping up and down. Dad was on his way home and we were headed back to Texas.

Chapter 13
Tejas, the Friendly State

It was great to be going home, wherever that was. I was once again stuck in the truck with dad. This time we were driving south. Behind the truck, my brothers were in mom's car. The windows on the truck were rolled up and I was choking. I didn't show it, though; I knew better than to show any pain. Dad was smoking and had his window was rolled down about one inch. That was not enough to keep the cab free of smoke. It was November and cold. Not as cold as it had gotten in Illinois. When the wind comes in from Canada, across Lake Michigan it feels like an ice dagger going through your heart, especially if your heart is in Texas.

Dad had received orders to report to Fort Hood, Texas. Mom and dad were so excited. It was closer to home than Illinois and dad was guaranteed a job. I had to admit, I was very excited. I did not enjoy Illinois one bit. The cold was very unpleasant and the people were not friendly at all. As we drove I was reading dad's brochures about the army base. It showed how big the base was and how the Tejas Indians had inhabited that area before the state was colonized by the Whites. I continued to read more about the base and I guess I must have begun to drift off to sleep

My eyes opened wide and tried to focus. I was kneeling on the floorboard of the cab. I rubbed my forehead and felt a lump. Dad had jarred the breaks and I had been thrown forward into the dash of the truck. My dad looked down at me and said, "por ser pendeho!" I crawled back into the truck seat and looked straight ahead. For almost twelve years I thought my name was "pendeho." Being called that by my dad didn't hurt, but the knot on my head did. My conditioning of not showing pain kicked in and I forced myself not to rub the growing lump on my forehead. I went back to reading the brochure and picked up where I had left off. I read that the word "Texas" came from the word "Tejas," which means "friendly." I closed the brochure and tried to visualize friendly Indians. Whenever I saw cowboys and Indians on the television they weren't very friendly. I reopened the pamphlets and continued to read, feeling the truck slow down, this time I braced myself.

We had stopped in Temple, Texas to refuel. I heard dad tell mom that we were very close and would be there within an hour or two. I opened one of the brochures that had a map and found where we were. Dad was correct. Fort Hood was only about fifty miles away. I walked out of the truck and headed to the car to see my brothers. I showed them the map and tried to tell them we were almost to our new home. They just kept staring at my head. "Does that hurt?" Jose asked. He was pointing at my head while he stared at me.

"Yes!" I said. "Now let me show you where the base is!"

Carlos kept staring at me and finally asked, "How did you get that goose egg?"

"I fell," I told him.

"In a truck?" he asked. I got tired of being quizzed so I walked back to the truck.

I went back to looking over the brochures when I looked in the side view mirror of the truck and saw mom talking to my brothers. Her head snapped up and she came over to my side of the truck. I rolled down the window and she grabbed my head. She looked my head over and over and looked up in time to see my dad walking to truck with a six pack of beer. She ran around the front of the truck and slapped the beer out of his hands. Dad put both hands in the air and declared his innocence. They walked over to the truck and dad asked me to tell mom what had happed. I knew I better have my story right. I told mom I had fallen asleep and fell forward. Dad picked up his beer and got into the truck. We headed south again. Dad didn't look at me and never said a word.

We entered the base through the main gate and stopped at a guard shack. Dad showed a soldier manning the site his orders and they spoke for a few minutes. The guard gave dad directions and we were on our way. As we drove through the base I instantly fell in love with the military. There were tanks, helicopters and cannons on display everywhere. I pressed my face against the cold glass of the truck and stared in wild amazement at the war pieces on display. I can still visualize them to this day. There was something about those old tanks and guns that stirred a memory in my brain. I guess it comes back to the dreams that I have where I am in combat. Somehow those items were familiar to me and made me feel at home. Dad continued to drive until he found the building we had been searching for. He parked the truck and entered the offices that were closest to the parking lot.

The movement of the flag caught my eyes. Two soldiers were lowering the American flag and another was playing an eerie tune on a trumpet. I was spellbound. I froze and my gaze could not leave the soldiers. The flag continued to drop and the sound continued to come from the brass instrument. It was a sight I never forgot. I kept staring and watched the ceremony until the flag was lowered, folded and taken inside the building where dad had gone in. I then caught sight of soldiers marching in step as they came around the corner. They marched by and froze in the middle of the parking lot. I couldn't make out what the big soldier in front of the formation was saying but it must have been important. All the other soldiers lifted their hands to their head about the same place I had my bruise and then lowered their hands sharply. The big soldier then yelled one word and all the troops started to walk away. I must have looked like a dog being driven around in a pick up truck. There were so many sights to take in!

Dad came out of the building and had several manila folders and big envelopes with him. He motioned mom to follow him and he got in the truck and drove off. I continued to stare out and take in as many sights as possible. I saw soldiers jogging in formation and it reminded me of ants moving in a column. Then I heard a sound I had never heard before. I lowered my head thinking the base might be under attack. I ducked my head as the sound got louder then began to grow faint. I looked out and saw two slender helicopters fly overhead toward the horizon. All I could see were their blinking lights after a few seconds. I wish I had someone to ask questions. There were so many things I needed to know. I knew not to ask dad. I doubt if he would even know anyway. Dad continued to drive and the sights began to get less interesting. We passed a two huge buildings that I would later find out were the army department store and grocery stores. We turned the corner and I saw my new school. It was huge! It was two stories high and had football fields around it! I was getting really excited now.

We continued to drive and we entered an apartment building complex. It was the biggest I had ever seen. There were rows and rows of them. They all looked alike. Dad drove very slowly and looked at a piece of paper that must have had the address on it. He looked at the paper then the numbers on the buildings. I then became very sad. I was hoping to live near the woods again like we did in San Antonio. There were no trees here, only very big buildings. They were two stories high and had four units to each one. It almost reminded me of what we had just left in Illinois.

We parked the truck and mom's car and headed to the front of our new home. Dad opened the front door and we walked in. This was the biggest home I had ever seen. There were separate rooms for everything! The kitchen was huge. It already had a stove and a refrigerator. We walked around and opened doors. We found closets and one bathroom. I was a bit concerned because it had a sink and a toilet but no tub or shower. My worries were put to rest when we went upstairs and found the rest of the house. I learned I was going to get a room of my own! I had never had an entire room to myself. It was not very big but it was mine! I didn't have to share it with anyone. Mom walked into the room with me and smiled. She ran her hand over the bruise I had forgotten about and told me to go downstairs and start unpacking.

Dad and I unloaded the truck and my brothers helped mom. It took a couple of hours to get the truck and car empty. By that time I was exhausted and hungry. Mom opened up a bag of tortillas and opened up containers with boiled eggs and potatoes. I gladly made a few burritos and ate them. We each got a soda and sat at our table and ate quietly. We were all tired. Mom handed us each a blanket and we walked upstairs. She had set out a few towels with our soap and toothbrushes. We took turns using the shower. We figured it out even though we had always used a tub to take a bath. After my shower I headed to my room and curled up on the floor with my old blanket, which smelled like the trunk of my mom's car. I was so tired I didn't care. I wrapped myself up like a cocoon and sleep came quickly. I awoke a few times in the night when my bruise hit the carpet after my head fell off the pillow.

During the night the visions of army tanks, cannons and helicopters came back to me. This time they weren't parked for people to admire but were moving through the battlefield. The tanks roared and fired their guns as troops ran for cover. The cannons boomed as their rounds impacted in the soil. I looked over the rim of the smoking crater and squeezed the stock of my rifle. My trigger finger felt the warmth given off from the metal parts of my gun. I eased my head farther up to get a view of my surroundings. The sounds of battle raged on but I felt the urge to see the destruction. Through the smoke I could see the tanks coming towards me. The ground trembled and dirt began to fall into the crater and cover my boots. I had to get out.

I let my body fall back into the hole and then tried to crawl out the back of the crater. It was like trying to swim in sand. The harder I tried the more the dirt fell in and over me. I went into a swimming motion to try and get out. My boots could not grip the loose soil and my hands had nothing to grab. I stopped crawling when the ground began to shake. The fog somehow got darker and the roar of the battle got louder. I was still face-down in the dirt when I felt the war chariot come closer. I somehow knew not to move and I lay very still.

The tank moved slowly towards the edge of the crater and its treads began to move over the hole. I rolled over so I could see underneath the tank. The metal beast rolled forward but I wasn't scared. I lay still and watched as it went over me. I wanted to touch its belly but I kept my hands on my rifle. Part of me wanted to shoot the monster. Another part of me admired this machine. I smelled the bitter exhaust as the beast finally rolled on. I grabbed a grenade and told myself to wait a few seconds until it got far enough away, and then lob the small bomb on the rear end of it. I knew that was its weak point. That's where the engine of the monster was hidden. I felt the small metal bomb and tried to pull it from my belt, it would not give!

I released the grip on my rifle and used both hands to try and pull the grenade off its clip. It just would not come off. I began to roll in the dirt trying to get the darn thing off and could not do it. Then the tank stopped moving. It began to rotate its turret. It turned to the right and kept coming. I could not take my eyes off it. It continued to come around and the large cannon resembled a sword coming around to cut me in two. I had no choice but to get away so I started to roll away from the tank like a tire in dirt. I rolled and rolled and the tank turret continued to turn. I rolled and rolled until I hit something hard. I knew it couldn't be dirt because it was flat and cool. It also kind of hurt. That's when I opened my eyes and found I had rolled into the wall.

I was once again wrapped up in my blanket. I had actually rolled into the wall and hit my head. I had to roll in the opposite direction to free my arms. I lay on the floor for a while until I heard my mom beat on the door for me to get up. I made my way to bathroom and got ready to start my first day in Texas with a home that was not a truck.

We spent the day moving our sparse furnishings around so it looked like it was more than we had. Mom had us move the table around a few times and the same thing with our one old couch. I did not see the point. I was never allowed to bring friends over, and dad had no friends. So who was going to come over? Anyway, I wanted to get to school and check out the football field as soon as I could.

The next day I got to see the field and I loved it. Jose and I went with mom to the junior high and registered for school. Carlos went to the elementary school directly behind our apartment building. The drive to our school was very close and we could see kids from the neighborhood walking to school. I was so excited all I could think about was playing football. After mom finished our paperwork I was led by a student to my first class. The boy who took me to my class was smaller than me and skinny. I asked him about football and he said the tryouts were going on this week and if I wanted to play I had better get to the coaches quickly. Tryouts?

During class my mind kept wandering back to the word "tryout." I was getting a little nervous. I had seen a lot of big kids in the classes and hallways at my first day of school. I also saw a lot of Black kids. Growing up in migrant work areas I had never really been exposed to Blacks. In South Texas there is not a large Black population. Even in the seedy part of Chicago there were not many either. Regardless, I was determined to do my best. I had not waited all my life to get the opportunity to play and not make it. There was, however, a small bit of doubt starting to grow in the back of my mind. Could I compete with these kids in Texas and play football?

In reading class I sat next to a Black kid about my size and weight. I leaned over and asked him if he was going to try out? He leaned over and answered me in Spanish! I was shocked. He introduced himself as Miguel. I stood upright in my chair and must have looked pretty goofy. Miguel chuckled and asked me my name. I gave it to him and stressed the "R" in Rodriguez to make myself sound even more Mexican. His last name was Gomez. He told me he was from Puerto Rico and spoke Spanish. He talked to me in Spanish and threw in a couple of English words to make it even more confusing to understand. Some of the Spanish words I could not understand. We continued to talk until the teacher came in. Once she walked in and the bell rung everyone sat up straight in their chair and stopped talking.

Mrs. Faber was very tall and very skinny. Her glasses sat on the tip of her long nose. She looked over her glasses and she noticed me right away. She walked over to me and extended her long bony arm. "Your papers please," she said. I handed her my class schedule and she handed it back. "Welcome Mr. Rodriguez. Welcome to our class," she announced. I had never been called Mister in my life. I beamed a little and sat up a little straighter in my chair after being given the title of mister. Mrs. Faber gave the class an assignment and once the class began it, she motioned me to come to her desk.

At her desk she handed me a small workbook and a form and asked me to complete it. She told me it would test my reading comprehension. I sat back down and started the assignment. I read a short story I still remember to this day. It was a science fiction story about aliens abducting an astronaut and holding him prisoner. The aliens held the hero of the story in their ship and he eventually escaped to warn earth about the impending invasion. I finished the story and answered the questions in about twenty minutes. I took the completed test to the teacher and she looked at me over the top of her glasses.

"You're already through?" she asked.

"Yes Ma'am I am," I responded. She took the paper and put a template over it that revealed the correct answers.

She looked it over and over and then looked back at me. "You got them all correct Mr. Rodriguez." she said. I wanted to tell her it was very easy and needed to be given to third graders. Even my little brother could handle that type of easy reading. Mrs. Faber reached into a file cabinet and handed me another short story to read and questions to answer. I sat back down and completed the assignment and carried it back to her. She graded my responses and once again told me I had answered them all correct again. By that time the bell had rung to signal lunch time. I didn't need a bell to tell me it was time for lunch: my stomach was growling.

I left reading class, and let the herd of hungry kids lead me directly to the food. I found the line and fell into place. I stood with all the other kids and brought out the lunch card they had given me at the office. They said I qualified for free lunch. I didn't pay attention to it. All I knew was the food was free. I handed my card to lady taking money at the end of the line and she punched a hole in it and handed it back. I smiled at her and thanked her but all she did was say "Next." I took a tray and followed the line and ladies piled food onto my tray. At the end of the line I was handed my full tray and then I looked for a place to sit. I looked around and found Miguel sitting by himself so I joined him.

Miguel was already eating his hamburger when I sat down. I put mine together and started eating as he began to ask me questions about where I came from. Miguel could talk more than I could and somehow he was asking me questions and answering them for me. I kept chewing and looking at him as he talked and ate French fries. I finally got a word in and told him I had just moved in from Chicago. He then went on to tell me it was very cold up there and how it was a lot like New York City where he was from. "I thought you were from Puerto Rico?" I asked. He just nodded and kept on talking. I asked him who were his friends and he shook his head.

"I don't have a lot of friends," he said softly. He began to explain to me that he was Black, but not really Black. He was considered Latino, but not really. At this point I was getting a bit confused.

Miguel and I finished our lunch and turned in our tray. He went on to explain that his mother was really pushing academics on him and he was taking a lot of honors classes. He had to explain the whole "honors" program to me. He then dropped a bombshell on me. He told me a lot of his Puerto Rican relatives and acquaintances called him a "coconut." I froze in my tracks. He told me he did not run with gangs and act like other kids his age. Instead he concentrated on his studies and spent time with his family. I had no idea how Puerto Ricans were supposed to act so I took his story at face value. It was all too familiar. I told him of my challenges and he was surprised to find out that coconuts know no boundaries.

We walked the schoolyard and chatted about classes and eventually about sports. He told me he did not like any sport, he would rather study and make straight "A's." The bell rang and we headed off to our classes. I pulled out my class schedule and found speech class was next. I found the class and unfortunately the only chair open was in the front row. No matter, I sat and waited for the teacher to come in. Mrs. Todd finally came in and sat down.

She had closed the door and began to call role when the door reopened. I looked over my shoulder and saw the biggest kid I had ever seen walk into class. He was about a head and a half taller than me and his large hair made him look even bigger. I would learn later that his hair was called an afro and the thing sticking out of it was called a pick. He probably weighed over two hundred pounds. I was tipping the scales at about one hundred and twenty in seventh-grade that year. "John, you're late again," Mrs. Todd stated without looking up. John looked for a chair to sit in and could not find one. He walked over to a kid in the back row and gave him a mean look. The little boy stood up picked up his books and got out of John's new seat. The teacher looked around and pointed to a chair next to a table and the boy sat down there instead of a desk. Somehow I knew this big guy was going to be trouble down the road.

Once class got started I became really excited. Today a few of the kids had to stand up and give speeches. That's why it was called speech class. I found it fascinating. I instantly wanted to get up and talk in front of the class. After the kids finished talking the other kids had to give feedback and "constructively" criticize the speech. John in the back of the class would just laugh or give a few smart remarks. The teacher just ignored him. Towards the end of class the teacher handed me a sheet of paper and told me I had two days to prepare for my first speech so she could help me determine where I was at this stage of the school year. I nodded and then the bell rang for PE.

I followed the big kids to the football field house and found the coach walking around talking to a few of the biggest kids I had ever seen. John was among them. I walked up to him and told him I wanted to try out. He stated that the tryouts were almost over and that I needed to be here a week earlier. I told him I was in Chicago and apologized for being late. A couple of the kids that were listening laughed and so did the coach. He told me to follow him and he dug in a box and handed me a pair of shorts and tee shirt. He then asked what size shoe I wore and handed me a pair of cleats. My mouth dropped open and must have looked shocked. The coach asked me what was wrong and I told him I had never owned any cleats before. The coach told me not to get too excited because I might have to give them back by the end of the day. Those words brought me back to reality.

On the football field kids were getting into groups to try out for different positions. I did not know which group to join. I saw John in a group with all the large and heavier kids. I saw another group of kids lining up and running for passes. They were a lot smaller than me. The coach that had given me my training clothes came up and asked me what position I played? I shook my head and I lowered my face. I felt like crying. He put his hand on the back of my neck and asked me if I liked to hit. I lifted my head with a big smile. "All I need you to do is knock the crap out of the kid with the ball. Can you do that?" I nodded my head and he pointed to a group of kids practicing on the far side of the field.

I ran to the group and fell in line. One of the coaches looked at me and smiled. He asked me my name and I told him. "Rodriguez, well that's a good name for a linebacker! Fall in line," he yelled. The coach made us run left, right, and in circles. I found I was one of the fastest kids in the group. As we practiced the coach would call over some of the slowest kids or those that could not run well over and whisper something in their ear. The kid would start walking to the field house. I overheard one of the boys say that they were getting cut. So this was what "trying out" was. I pushed myself a little harder after I saw a kid that was about my size get cut. We must have practiced drills for about two hours then the coach called over another group of kids that were a lot smaller than us.

The coach gave us instructions that we were to try and prevent the smaller kids from catching the ball. We lined up and the receiver took off running. The coach would throw the ball and we had to try and get it. I watched as kid after kid was not able to keep up with the smaller and much faster boys. In fact some of the receivers were laughing at the linebackers. Our coach came over and told us we had to "jam" the receiver at the line of scrimmage. I raised my hand and asked him to show me what that meant. He had me stand in front of him and he demonstrated by jamming his forearm into my chest then began to run backwards. That hurt! Years of putting up with pain allowed me to brush it off and I nodded to the coach that I understood. It was my turn for the passing drill.

I had noticed other boys stand in front of the receiver and bent their knees and push the boy across from them and then try and keep up with them as the receiver ran down the field. I had different plans. The boy came to the line of scrimmage with a big smile on his face. He had already received the signals from his coach and knew which way to run and when the play would start. He didn't know I had my coach give directions on how to prevent him from scoring. I squared off from the kid in front of me and watched his eyes. He blinked as his coach yelled "hut one!" I could see the coach out of the corner of my eye raise the football. That's when I exploded into the chest of the wide receiver. His feet took off but the rest of his body did not. He was now flat on his back and his coach had already thrown the ball to where the receiver was supposed to be. I took a few steps backwards and caught the ball. I tucked it under my arm and ran forward to where the real receiver was trying to get up.

My coach began to yell. "That's what I want!" Right there! Did you see that?" He kept yelling as I ran back to the end of the line. Now the other linebackers were ready. The receivers on the other hand were a little skittish. They knew what was going to happen when their coach gave them the signal. Once I got back in line our coach patted me on the back and told me I had done a good job. I liked positive reinforcement. It was better than being called "pendeho" and kicked in the rear.

After practice I changed back into my jeans and tee shirt and headed home. I was so pumped about my first day of practice I forgot it was a tryout. I wasn't cut so I could not wait till tomorrow. I did not dare tell mom and dad about my day. I knew they didn't care anyway. I went to bed that evening dreaming about football but strangely my mind kept focusing on the assignment I had been given in speech class. I brought out the sheet of paper and read it over. It said I had to act out the part of a reporter on the street. It said to stop people on their walk and ask them specific questions. It was a role play. I had to be a journalist. I had no idea what this was about. I decided to ask my teacher the next day.

I went to bed that evening with dreams of Texas football in my mind. I didn't sleep well at all, tossing and turning with excitement about practice the next day. I kept reminding myself that is was still a tryout. I knew I would be crushed if I were to get cut and I lay in bed with my sheets wrapped around my head wishing for a dream, any dream because that would mean I was asleep. Sleep finally came but without dreams that night. I awoke ready for the day to begin, riding the wave of adrenaline from the previous day's football practice and the thought of being a journalist. I made my way to school that morning at a quick pace. I probably wanted to run but I didn't want to waste any energy.

At school I was still the new guy so I didn't have any friends yet. Miguel was nice enough but I had not seen him this morning. I walked in the hallway and found my locker and started going through it to find the books for my first class. John walked by as I closed my locker he had three other kids with him that I recognized from practice. I waved and said hi to him but he did not respond. I was used to this so I went about my way. When we crossed paths he stepped in front of me and looked down at me. "I don't like Panamanian's on my football team," he said in a low voice.

I smiled back at him and told him, "No problem, I'm Mexican," and walked around him and his friends. I did not feel scared or threatened by them because we would probably be on the same team anyway. I headed off to reading class and found a seat.

Mrs. Faber called me to her desk and opened up the quiz I had taken the previous day. She started telling me how I had a very high reading comprehension level. I sat there and pretended to be interested. I liked to read but my mind was on football. She handed me a thick book and asked me to read it. It was pretty thick and I really didn't want to read it. She told me that the books the other kids had would bore me and that I had no choice in the matter. I took the book and looked at the cover. "The Hobbit." What the heck was a hobbit? The book didn't have any pictures so I guess I would have to read it to find out. I walked back to my desk and saw a few kids in the back that looked like they might be Mexican and gave them the Mexican nod. They did not return the favor.

I gave the Mexican kids another nod and once again they did not return the favor. One of them stood up and gave me a nod with a double arm throw back. I knew this meant trouble. I decided not to start anything and went to my seat. I heard one tell the other, "He thinks he's so smart, pinche coconut."

Well, there it was. Now the even the Mexicans were giving me trouble. I had no idea what the problem was but I wanted to find out. After the bell dismissing our class rang I followed one of the Mexican boys and tapped him on the back of his shoulder. He spun around and gave the reverse nod with both arms bent back. I raised my arm to tell him I didn't want any trouble. I asked him what the problem was and he kept his hands behind him and head tilted to the right. "You think you're bad don't you?" he said.

I responded by asking. "What?" I was a bit confused.

"You play football and read big books, Whiteboy!" he said as he turned around and walked off. I stood there speechless. I was totally shocked. I had never been called that at all. I guess he saw how I was spending extra time with the teacher and the large book she had given me. Those guys had also seen me walking towards football practice. I wanted to chase that kid down now and show him how a Mexican Whiteboy handled himself but I changed my mind. All of the sudden someone pushed me from behind.

Big John had walked up to me while I was thinking about how I had just been called a Whiteboy. He pushed me square in the back and I fell forward. As I got up he called me a Panamanian again. I got up and told him I was Mexican. He laughed and his friends started giggling. I turned and walked away. John kept calling me Panamanian. Was I a Mexican Whiteboy, or a South American? What a day; at least there was football!

Chapter 14
Are You Ready for Some Football!

"Rod Get over here!" The coach had already given me a new name. Today had been strange. I had been called a Whiteboy and a Panamanian. Now I had a new name: Rod. Not bad. Rodriguez was too long for a football player, I guess. I had made the cut and I was starting on the "A" team as a middle linebacker. All I knew was to stand in the middle and hit who ever had the ball. I was totally lost at first. The coach tried to explain to me what to do when the tailback was in this position and when the fullback was in a strong formation. Well I just did not understand and my look gave it away. He reached over to the other linebacker and told him to help me.

The other linebacker was not as big or as fast as me but he was football smart. He coached me along slowly and helped me understand. "I've never played football with a Mexican middle linebacker before," he said in the huddle.

"I've never played football before," I responded.

"No kidding!" I heard a couple of the other kids say. We all laughed in the huddle until the coach started yelling at us.

"Get in position!" We obeyed and got in the defense Carl, the other linebacker, called.

I scanned the offense like Carl had showed me and bent my knees and had my arms in front of me, almost like a boxer. I started bouncing on my toes as the quarterback called his signals. The ball snapped and I stepped forward and saw that he had handed off the ball to the runner. It was like all this was happening in slow motion and I was running at full speed. I shoved

186

the lead blocker out of the way and hit the runner with my face mask on his face mask. I loved it! I didn't realize I was screaming when I hit him. The next thing I knew the coach had grabbed me by the back of the shoulder pads and launched me in the air. "That's how you hit!" He was screaming at the top of his lungs. I thought I was in trouble or something. He bent down to look at me in the face and started yelling again. "Rod I want you hit him again!" I got caught up in the moment and I started yelling again and I slapped Carl on the helmet. We both started jumping up and down and celebrating. "Huddle up!" the coach yelled. Carl gave the signal and we fell into place. He got the signal he received from the coach and relayed it to us.

I was in place again and the offense formed up on the ball. Something was different this time. The quarterback was looking right at me as he called the signals. Something was wrong; I couldn't tell what but I could feel it. The quarterback received the ball and faked the ball to the runner. I saw the fake and didn't fall for it. He then pitched the ball to the left. That's when the lights went out. All I remember was stepping sideways towards the play and then the bright light.

I heard a whistle blow and the coach lifted me off the ground. "Rod!" he yelled. "Are you okay?"

I wasn't. I had never been hit that hard, not even by my dad. Slowly the fog lifted and I regained my sight. "I'm fine!" I tried to jump up on my feet but my knees weren't ready.

Carl helped steady me and said, "John gave you a cheap shot." I thought to myself, that wasn't cheap; I got the full price hit. I cleared my head and fell back into place with the defense.

I looked across the line to the offensive huddle and John was rolling with laughter. The other linemen were laughing also. I was furious. I could feel my temperature going up. Carl leaned over and gave me some pointers. "When he goes for your helmet again lower your head and throw your helmet into his belly." I nodded in response and I got in position again. The offense came to the line and I gave the quarterback my meanest look. He barked out the signals and Carl and I studied the formation. The ball was snapped and the ball was faked to the runner again. It was the same play! I knew what to expect. This time I turned in time to see Big John running towards me. I ran towards him as fast as I could. He went for my head and did what Carl told me.

I faked like I was going to hit him in the head and at the last moment I ducked and my helmet hit him right under his shoulder pads. I heard him gasp as all the air left him. On the way down I saw the runner try and leap over the pile John and I had made. I reached up and grabbed his ankle. This slowed him down in time for Carl. The runner was out of position when Carl hit him in the helmet. The contact was right on the ear hole of the helmet. The poor guy went down hard. I rolled out from the pile and jumped on Carl. The coach came running out and celebrated with us.

The offensive coach and his assistant ran out on the field. One was helping the runner and the other was helping Big John. They had loosened his pants and were helping him breathe. The coaches looked over at me with a little hate in their eyes. The rest was probably pure joy to see someone had put John in his place. I was too busy jumping up and down with Carl and the rest of the defense. The coach called for silence and he had us kneel around him and he gave us a pep talk while the other coaches helped John and the other kid off the grass. The coach praised us for the hard practice and told us the first game was next week. I was so excited! He told us a few more practices and we would be ready. Then he told us to hit the showers and go home.

As I ran towards the gym I looked over the B team. I smiled. I was "A" team material. As I looked even more I slowed down. There were about five Mexicans on the B team. I realized I was the only Latino on the A team. I sped up again. "So what," I thought to myself. For that brief moment I did not care that I was an "A" team Mexican and that those guys were "B" team Mexicans, it was their problem, not mine. I could see the look of envy in their eyes. I ran by and cheered with Carl and the other "A" team members and pretended not to notice them. I could feel their eyes on the back of my head as I ran by and thought about turning around and giving them the Mexican nod but decided against it. My head still hurt from the shot John had given me anyway.

The next day in school I went about my classes as usual. Speech class was a lot more fun now that John did not give me any problems. I was really starting to enjoy this class. It was now my favorite. I jumped at any opportunity to get up in front of the class and talk. My teacher had to tell me to give the other kids an opportunity to present material. I was taken aback at first but understood. My teacher called me and asked me to stay after class. She asked me if I would be interested in participating in drama and poetry.

I was shocked. She told me she would like to see me in the school play or poetry recital. I told her I would think about it. As I walked out of class and headed to football practice I had made up my mind. No "A" team middle linebacker could be seen reading poetry and being in a sissy school play.

I made it to the locker room and started putting on my football pads and noticed this big kid walking around with the my coach. He was the same size as my coach. This was the biggest White kid I had ever seen. He had blonde hair and blue eyes. I thought I had muscles, this kid made me feel small. The coach had his arm around the boy as he led him to his locker which was next to mine. The boy smiled at me and extended his hand in a shake. Once again I wanted to give him the Mexican nod but I was sure he wouldn't understand. I shook his big hand and he introduced himself as James. He was nice enough. He began to talk to me as he dressed in his pads. I eyed his biceps as he was pulling his shoulder pads on. I looked at mine then his again. Well, at least I was the starting middle linebacker. "James what position do you play?" I asked. "Linebacker," he said.

I asked James where he had come from and he told me his dad had just been transferred from Germany. He had been playing football there. As he continued to put on his pads I noticed this kid was definitely all football. I probably looked a little funny, the way I was staring at him. This boy had muscles on muscles! Then it hit me, he looked just like Captain America in my comic books. James kept talking about all the awards he had received while playing in Germany. When he sat down to put his cleats on he asked me what position I played. I paused and was starting to wonder that myself. I was about to answer when the coach walked up and put his arm around my shoulders.

"Rod, I have some great news for you," the coach said. "You are now the defensive captain, of the B team!" The coach said with a big smile. He was spinning me around as he talked. He had a hand on my shoulder pads and spun me around in the direction of the "B" team. "James will be taking over your duties on the "A" team."

"No kidding," I said. He slapped me on the rear and pushed me in the direction of the "B" team practice. I had overheard kids talking about how James was an all star middle linebacker from a school in Germany. I had also heard he had cracked a helmet when he hit a kid real hard. Well, so what, I thought to myself. I could hit too, just not as hard. I kept trotting to the kids I had run by the day before.

I reported to the "B" team defensive coach. "Rod!" he yelled. He then called a defense huddle and broke the news to the "ex" captain. I was going to run the defensive unit. I scanned the group and the first thing I noticed was how small everyone was. I looked over my shoulder and was already missing the "A" team. The kid I replaced was still a linebacker but no longer the captain. He came over and shook my hand. "I'm glad you're here, we suck!" he stated. I was so happy to hear that.

The coach started barking out commands and practice got back underway. I lined up and waited for the offense to line up. The quarterback came up behind the center and looked me over. I knew him. He was one of the Mexican boys that had been staring at me the previous day. I saw him smile at me as if to say, "Look at you now." He got up under the center and gave me the "Mexican nod" before he started calling his signals. I began to call out the defensive signals and waited for the ball to be snapped.

The ball was snapped and handed off to the running back and he was coming right at me. The lead blocker tried to hit me but I was practically twice his size. The little offensive guard was so small! I hit the little guy on the side of the helmet and he was knocked off balance. This allowed me to hit the runner with a full head of steam. I connected with him before he had gotten to the line of scrimmage. I knocked the poor guy backwards and was laying on him when I heard him yell, "Get off me maricon!"

I rolled off and looked down. It was another Mexican kid. His helmet was almost off his head and the chin strap was under his nose. I instantly gave him the Mexican nod with the two arm throw back, and headed back to the defensive side of the ball. The other players on defense were screaming and yelling and slapping me on the butt and head.

A "maricon" is something no Mexican man wants to be called. I have even heard it used by Puerto Ricans and other Latinos. The word translates in to "fag" or "queer" and not in a nice way. I didn't appreciate being called that either. I let the poor kid know that every time he got the ball, he would never get past the line of scrimmage. I made a personal note to that effect. I saw the offensive line coach chewing out the linemen because they could not block me. It really wasn't fair. I was "A" team material. I had to make the best of it. We lined up again and I got into my zone. I loved this! I was releasing all my pain and frustration! I was ready to hit anyone that had the ball. I loved it!

After practice I headed to the locker room with my new team mates. We all laughed and cut up. In the showers I felt like the big boy. I was more developed than most the other kids. As I showered the other Mexican kids came in and we gave each other the "nod." I stayed under the refreshing feel of the shower and then walked by the Mexican boys. I was definitely more developed than them. The evenings when I lifted weights and did pushups in my room had paid off. I left the showers and got dressed before heading home. While I dressed the Mexican kids walked to my locker and we started talking.

I found out that the Mexican boy that had been running the ball was actually Puerto Rican. His name was Valdez. "Isn't Valdez a last name?" I asked.

"Yeah, so is Perez, he said.

"Valdez Perez?" I asked. He nodded and I apologized and giggled. The quarterback was Mexican. His name was Jesse Montana. "Just like the pro?" I asked. He nodded and I laughed out loud. All three of us started cutting up now. We found out we all lived pretty close to each other so we walked together. In front of our school was a walkway over a main road that was four lanes wide. We were not allowed to cross the street but had to use the walkway that went over the road. Everyone called it "the bridge."

The story went something like this. If you got in a fight on the other side of the bridge you wouldn't get in trouble. But if you got in a fight on the school side of the bridge you would. It was silly but I knew it to be law in seventh grade. Valdez, Jesse and I walked over the "bridge" and noticed a group of kids on the other side. They were players from the "A" team. I knew them all and I thought they were just waiting for me to join them on the walk home. As soon as we started down the bridge I knew that was not the case. The group of kids started walking to the bottom of the walkway to meet us.

Big John was in front of the gang of boys and he walked up to me as I came out of the bridge. He got right in my face and the other boys surrounded me in a circle. A few of them were pounding their fists into their hands. They all had on their meanest faces. Valdez and Jesse both started backing up and the gang let them pass untouched.

John looked at them both and said, "Let the wetbacks go." Valdez raised a hand and said, "Excuse me, but I'm a Puerto Rican."

John looked at him and with a very low voice said, "Good you're next!"

Valdez got a look of fear and started walking backwards until one of John's friends grabbed him. Most of the kids were the linemen on the offense from practice. These were big boys!

Big John was now in my face. He looked down at me and I could smell his breath in my face. His big hands were both balled up now. This was nothing new to me. I had been beaten up so many times this would be no problem at all. I was not scared and I stepped up to him and looked up into his face, actually his nose.

John said, "My daddy said it takes more pride to walk away from a fight."

I stood on my tip toes and said, "Then you better start walking." I gave him the meanest Rodriguez stare I could muster. I felt my leg muscles twitching; if this didn't work I knew I had to jump on him quickly. John took a step backwards and I saw a brief glimpse of fear in his eyes. He took another step back and I took one forward. John's expression changed and he said "Okay." He turned his back to me and started walking.

The kids in his gang were more shocked than I was. Their mouths fell open and they looked at me like I was some kind of plague carrier. They couldn't get away fast enough. I heard John tell one of his friends. "That Mexican's crazy! I'm not fighting a crazy Mexican. You know he's got a knife anyway." The mob moved off and Valdez and Jesse came up to me and asked what I had told Big John. I looked at them and told them I had told John I was a maricon and wanted to kiss him. They busted out laughing and I thought Valdez was going to choke. I laughed with them and we continued our walk home. I looked at Jesse and said, "Can you believe John thought I had a knife?" I shook my head and talked about the stereotype of Mexicans and knives. Jesse smiled and showed me the knife in his pocket. Valdez started cracking up again and waved as he headed to his house. I waved at Jesse as he departed also. All my energy was about to be sucked out of me now. I was entering my home. I wished I was still at school.

I hated coming home. I took up sports as an escape. Sometimes you can't escape far enough and you have to come home. This time it was different; dad's truck was not home. Yes! I walked in and mom was in the kitchen. She was getting dinner ready. I could tell she was tired from her new job. Mom was working in a sewing factory making blue jeans. She told me pop was not coming home for a few days. He had called and he had been sent to the field. Instantly I though of being back in the fields of west Texas and California, this was not the case however. The field was where the soldiers went to go train, like going in the woods to practice. I nodded when mom told me this and headed up to my room. She told me to get ready to eat in about an hour. I ran up the stairs and just knew today was my lucky day, but first I need to rest.

I collapsed on my little twin mattress. I hurt so badly! I stood up and took off my shirt and looked in the mirror above my dresser. I had bruises all over my body. There were black and blue marks on my rib cage and lots of bumps on my arms. Even though I hurt everywhere I cracked a smile. I couldn't wait to show these off tomorrow in school. To me these were badges of honor I had earned on the field of battle. I turned around and looked over my shoulder and saw a big bruise on my lower back. That one really hurt. I poked the purple and blue mark and thought about how I had gotten it. It was where Big John had fallen on me. I lay back down on the bed and tried to relax. I heard mom call for me and I got up and put my shirt back on. Mom would not understand how hard I had worked to earn my marks.

The next day at school I wore a tee shirt that was a bit too small. It revealed all my bruises as well as my developing body. I wanted the other football players to see my bruises and hopefully it would also attract a few girls. I walked through the hallways and noticed a few girls looking at me and that made me walk a little taller and a stick my chest out a little farther. I didn't have a girlfriend at this time but I sure was on the lookout for one. I noticed one girl that was close to my locker. She reminded me of Debbie. I walked up to her as she was closing her locker and said, "Ouch!" My lower back all of the sudden erupted in pain! Petra, the girl I was hoping to talk to, just laughed and walked away. Meanwhile I was hunched over in pain.

I heard a familiar laugh and then someone say, "Yoras como una nina! (you cry like a little girl)" It was Valdez. He had come up behind me and slapped me on the biggest bruise I had.

"You didn't have a problem knocking the crap out of me yesterday," He raised his tight tee shirt he had on and revealed his bruises to me. There was a mark on his ribs that looked exactly like a face mask on football helmet. "Hoto! (fag) you did that to me," He said. Valdez's voice was getting a little higher as he complained abut the hits I had given him yesterday.

"If you ran a little faster I wouldn't catch you!" I told him. We both laughed and then focused our stare as Petra and another girl walked by us on their way to class.

"She's way too cute for you maricon," a voice said from behind us. It was Jesse.

"Why do you two keep calling me that?" I asked.

"It's because you hit like a girl!" Jesse said, as he punched me in the shoulder. Once again I winced in pain. Jesse had hit another bruise. I swung back and hit him on the arm. He writhed in pain. I had hit him on a bruise also. I stood back and looked at Valdez and Jesse. All three of us had tight tee shirts on and were covered in bruises. It had to be a funny sight. We all started laughing at the same time. I guess we all had the same idea. All through the school boys had on tiny tee shirts or had their sleeves rolled up so they could show off their marks from football practice. As silly as it sounds now, it was a big deal back then.

I made my way to speech class and watched as kids struggled to speak in front of the class. I waited for my turn to speak. We had to get give an oral book report to the class today. I had read a book about the ocean and the food cycle. I got in front of the class and found myself in my zone. I talked about how plankton was a food source for small fish, which in turn fed bigger fish and so forth. To me it was fascinating. I don't know if I enjoyed the material or the speaking better. As I spoke I noticed kids losing interest so I began to accentuate my voice a little higher then lower. This brought a few back to paying attention. I then began to talk about the top predators in the ocean like sharks and whales. This brought the entire class back into focus. This was great! I was really enjoying public speaking. I don't know where I got this talent, but I do know this class helped me identify it.

At the end of class the teacher gave us all constructive criticism. She told me I needed to stay in one place and not pace so much. I was a bit disappointed at that. It was not natural for anyone to stand in one place and talk. I got on "A" for the report but was a bit troubled by the teacher's comments. Next time I decided to stand still. No matter, football practice was next.

In the locker room before practice Jesse and Valdez horsed around with me. We snapped towels at each other as we got undressed and put our pads on. I had to be careful; I had been hit with the towel on the bare rear by Valdez and it really stung. I was really enjoying having two "Latino" friends. I had never really experienced this before. I guess it was the camaraderie that was creating the friendship. Whatever the reason it was great. It made practice fun and I finally had someone to talk to and enjoy junior high. This did not mean I took it easy during workouts.

"Get off! You're heavy!" Valdez would yell. Jesse was smarter. He would just fall before I hit him. I laughed and would help them up. I laughed at Valdez a lot during practice. I kidded him that I could outrun him and how could he score a touchdown if he was that slow? It was still a lot of fun. Days like that made it fun during football practice. Afterwards we would walk home together. We would talk about girls and football just like any normal American kid. We never discussed the fact that we were Mexicans; well, just me and Jesse. Valdez kept reminding us he was a "PR," I always reminded him that he was a "very slow PR."

I don't think Valdez scored a touchdown that year. He was slow, but very competitive. In fact we only won one game all year. We beat Copperas Cove by two touchdowns. Both were scored by the defense. I caused two fumbles and both were returned for touchdowns. I won the best defensive player award for that game. The rest of the season was a disaster. We got pounded every game. I led the team in tackles every game and gave it all I had. It was still a release for me. Putting on a football helmet was just an excuse for being able to hit other people.

There were a few games where an opposing player would call me names. There was one particular game where the quarterback and running back kept calling me "wetback." I made it a point to hit them as hard as I could every time they had the ball. I even hit them when they didn't have the ball. I got a few penalties called on me, but who cares. Our offense couldn't score and we were getting beat really bad. I also got really hurt during that game.

The running back broke a long run and I chased him down the sideline and was able to catch him from behind. We both went out of bounds and got tangled up in the down markers. The chain that held them together got wrapped around my arm and cut me in the bend of my arm, where the bicep and forearm meet. It was a nasty gash, and in a hard place to tape. The coach taped my arm the best he could and I finished the game. Once again we got beat really bad. The coach kept telling us that it was not about winning or losing, but how well we competed. By looking at the scoreboard we didn't compete very well.

The season was winding down and we held on to the feeling of our one big win. I kept joking with Valdez that the defense had more points than the offense, which was true. It really wasn't fair. They had all the "scrubs" on their team. That's what we called all the kids that were small and slow. All the big kids were on the "A" team or "B" team defense. It didn't matter. It was all fun. I had found two new loves: public speaking and football. Football was a lot more painful however.

I ended up getting a slight staph infection from the cut on my arm. It was so hard to tape that it got dirty every game and it took a long time to heal. After every game and practice the coach would wash my arm with a sanitizer and then spray this painful germ killer into the wound. He would always warn me that it would hurt and that it was okay to cry out. To cry out only invited more pain. I was a veteran to hurt and pain. I prided myself by not showing any emotion.

Chapter 15

Hicks in the Sticks

I had no idea where we were. Pop had made a deal with a big businessman outside of Fort Hood. The agreement was pop would work forty hours a month and we got room and board for free. Dad had two years left in the army and he was already looking to get out. Being in the service was really putting a damper on his drinking. He had to run every morning and stay in shape. That made it harder to enjoy his vice. The businessman had a huge ranch south of Temple, Texas that needed someone to live on it. Dad jumped on the opportunity. So here we went again, we would work the cattle ranch while dad waited for the day his military career would end. I knew we were in for some hard times as we pulled into the driveway of the old house.

By the looks of the house the rich guy should pay us to live here. The house was brick but it was in the middle of nowhere. There were four hay barns around the house and a fence around it. That was the good thing, I guess. We got out of dad's truck and started walking around. It sure was different than living on the army base. No neighbors close by at all. I walked over to the west side of the house and about a half mile away I could see a house. At least there was someone else in this part of Texas. I heard dad start complaining about how close we were to another house. Of course, he said that as he swigged down a beer and threw it on the ground.

We continued to explore around the house and hay barns and it made me very sad. On post I could walk across the street and visit with my friends or go behind our apartment and play basketball. Here there was nothing,

nothing at all but work. I could see it coming now: my brothers and I would work our tails off again, just like we had in the past to carry pop's part of the deal. From the house I spotted three small ponds and that was good. I loved fishing, even though I didn't own a fishing pole. I asked permission to go check out the ponds from mom and was shot down. She told me to go get dad another beer instead.

The next day we began moving in. The house was very small and only had three bedrooms. I got my own, Carlos and Jose had to share. The move took us a few trips in the truck but dad had a few of his army friends help out. Within one day we were through. Once the house was situated dad had us outside. "You see that shed? I want it cleaned out and all the trash burned over there," he said while he pointed to clear place where we could burn rubbish. Mom was at work so we were at his mercy. We started to work and he jumped in his truck and left. My brothers and I stared at each other and sighed. We knew what would happen if we didn't do as we were told.

We worked all day on the shed. Since it was summer and we were burning wood and trash, it was very hot work. We worked until mom got home from her job. She pulled into the dirt driveway and looked mad. "Where's your dad?" she asked. We all shook our heads and continued to work.

"This feels like California," I said. Mom went in and started to cook dinner while we finished burning the last of the trash we had dragged out of the shed. I did not want to add to the fire because it was getting dark. The other sheds had hay in them and did not want to start a bigger fire. My brothers and I sat on the ground and watched the smoke billow up into the night sky.

The darkness surrounded our home but it was overshadowed by the noise of the night. Because we had farm ponds all around us there were frogs croaking near the water. In Texas we called the ponds "tanks." I don't know why but I bought into calling them "tanks" also. My brothers and I scanned the horizon and off in the distance we could see the neighbor's house. It was lit up against the night sky. In the direction of the road that led to our house we saw a pair of headlights coming down towards our house. There was only one reason to come down Stagg Road: either you lived in our house or you were lost. We kept watching the headlights and noticed they would speed up then slow down. At one point they stopped and turned off. "Dad's taking leak," I said softly. The lights came back on and started down our road again.

The closer they got the more we noticed they were swerving all over the narrow road. We followed the lights until they pulled into the driveway and we sat quietly in the dark. The fire had died down by now but a new one was to erupt inside.

Dad's truck pulled into the driveway and he turned the lights and motor off. We sat in the darkness and kept quiet. Dad opened the door and fell out. We didn't move and kept our giggles to ourselves. We watched him use the truck door to help himself up. He got back to his feet and started walking to the back door. "Vieja! Tengo ambre!" Dad was hungry and mom was expected to have food ready. Dad disappeared into the house and we stayed outside sitting cross legged around the fire like Indians. We could hear the fight raging inside. We were numb to it so we decided to put more wood on the fires to see if we could get it going again. We fed the fire and talked about what our new school would be like.

"Do you think there's Mexicans in the school?" Carlos asked.

"I know of three," I said. We continued to talk about school and sports. I would be in eighth grade. Jose would be in seventh. That meant we would both be playing junior high football. Carlos would have to wait another year. We talked on about football and girls, mostly about girls though. It was so nice sitting on the dark. It seemed like all our worries were a million miles away like the stars in the sky. We could see them but they were so far away. We eventually lay on our backs and stared at the Texas night sky. The smoke from the fire was keeping the mosquitoes away so it was very pleasant. The noise from inside the house had died away and only the insects and frogs were competing for the loudest noisemaker in the night. Eventually mom called us in and we were forced to exit the wonderful evening.

The next morning mom had driven off to work and dad was outside behind the barn ridding his system of the previous day's alcohol. We got dressed and wondered what the day would bring. We fixed our breakfast and were at the table when dad came in. "Hurry up and finish eating!" he said, as he walked toward the bathroom. As soon as the door closed we giggled and kept eating our eggs and bacon. After we finished dad loaded us up in the truck and took us down a gravel road on the ranch. We drove through a few cattle gates until we came down a steep hill. Once at the bottom a large field opened up and then dropped off into a huge river. He drove us close to the edge and we could see the water swiftly flowing over rocks and tree stumps.

The edge of the field connected to the banks of the river. Where they met there was a jungle of briars and small trees. It was very thick and you could not get to the water. It was about ten yards deep of brambles. I was wondering why dad had brought us here then I knew why when he stopped the truck. "Get out!" Dad said.

We were once again hard at work, clearing all the briars, trees and undergrowth and burning it in piles. Dad wanted the "river bottom" cleaned out so the cattle could get to the river to drink. I stared into the tangles of prickly vines and poison ivy and wondered how in the world we could do this. Dad pulled out a couple of axes, hatchets and a bucket of diesel. He tossed me a box of matches and told me to get to work. He told us he would be back with lunch later. My brothers and I did not own a watch so we had no idea when lunch was or what time it was. Dad got back in the truck and drove off. We stood there and watched him drive off then turned and looked at the mass of jungle behind us. Carlos looked back at the truck in the distance and said, "at least he'll have to open his own gates." I laughed and reached down and grabbed an axe and headed to the thicket.

My brothers and I did not own any gloves so within a few minutes first blood was drawn. I remember the vines having huge thorns on them as we pulled them out of the under growth. We could not grab them with our hands but we soon discovered a way to clear them out. Carlos would cut the vine as close to the bottom as possible then Jose and I would wrap it around the longest axe we had. Then the both of us would pull on the handle and drag the vine to the brush pile. We would then carefully walk in a circle around the growing bush pile. The vine would tangle around the branches. We then cut the vine off the axe handle with a machete. It kept us from tearing our hands up more than they already were.

The hot Texas sun was already heating up the river bottom. We kept on working and wondering when dad would come back with lunch. He had left us a jug of ice water but that was getting low. We wanted to conserve what we had so we drank sparingly. We worked for hours and hours and the brush pile kept getting higher and higher. We had built the stack of green vines on top of old logs we had drug out of the mess so the fire would have something to start on. I poured diesel on the logs and then the green branches and used a match to start the pile on fire. The pile went up quick. We continued to feed the flame with more and more brush and vines. The fire became too intense to wrap the tough prickly vines around so we got a new idea. We rolled the

200

vines into a wheel and tossed them into the fire. Soon the pile was about ten feet high and getting very hot. We decided to take a break at that point and sat under a huge pecan tree. We shared the jug of cool water.

We looked up the hill that led out of the bottom and saw dad's truck slowly making its way toward us. We thought about getting up but were too tired. At this point I did not care if we were going to get in trouble. Dad pulled up and stopped the truck. He took a swig of beer and got out of the truck. Just as we expected he yelled at us for being lazy and called us a bunch of girls. He threw a small grocery bag at us and told us to get back to work. As we got up I looked at my brothers. We were soaked in sweat down to our jeans. It looked like we had been wading in the river. All three of us were bleeding from the scratches from the vines and our tee shirts were ripped. Dad was not bothered by this sight but I was. He climbed back in his truck and sat there as he watched us go back to work. He finished off his beer can and threw it into the bed of the truck. Dad had a collection of aluminum cans he would sell to buy more beer.

He drove off as he started into a new beer. As soon as he was out of sight we went back to the shade tree and looked into the brown bag. There was a loaf of bread and a package of bologna. We looked at each other and tears wanted to come out of my eyes. I knew I had to be strong for my brothers so I began to make sandwiches for Carlos and Jose. We had nothing to put on the bread except the cold cuts so it was easy to fix. We sat under the Texas pecan tree and had our lunch or dinner since we had no idea what time it was. After we ate we went back to work.

We worked a lot slower now. We knew dad would be too drunk soon to do anything about our pace anyway. The heat from the sun was getting unbearable and we were running out of water. We decided to build another fire in the shadow of another huge pecan tree. The sun was going down in the western sky and the shade was nice. We had to drag the brush under the shade and it helped. We kept the pile smaller so we would not damage the tree. I looked into the horizon and figured it had to be around five in the evening and called my brothers out of the thicket. We eyed our work. There was a huge swath of clean land leading directly into the river bank. It was actually very beautiful. The grass under the brush was a deep green in color. The cattle would like that. It would be a nice place to put a picnic table. We walked back under the tree where I had hung the bag of bread and cold cuts and decided to have dinner. I had put the bag on a piece of bailing wire I had found and hung it from a tree branch to keep ants from getting in it.

We sat under the tree and ate more of the dry sandwiches. We were out of water so it was tough going getting the bread down. I looked down at my hands and saw a bloody mess. They were coated in dried blood and dirt. I picked at a few splinters and used my teeth to pull out pieces of the vine thorns. My brothers did the same thing. It was starting to get dark when we saw the truck coming down the hill towards us. Dad was slobbering drunk when he came to pick us up. I was just glad he had not forgotten us. In the passenger seat next to him was mom. I was a bit shocked. I thought she would get angered because pop was drunk again. He would be getting his discharge from the army soon. Mom wanted him out looking for a job now, instead of waiting until the last day of his discharge. When he had time off he would hang out with his buddies in Fort Hood and drink all night with them,

Mom motioned us to get into the bed of the truck. I lowered the tailgate and we climbed in. We tossed in the tools we had used as well as the empty water jug. Dad drove slowly back up the road and we hung on as we made our way to the house. I looked at my brothers and realized how bad we looked. I guess it could be worse. We could still be in West Texas picking vegetables. We arrived at our house as the sun was setting. We had to help dad out of the truck. He was very drunk. My brothers and I carried him into our parent's bed room and threw him on the bed. We then went to the kitchen to eat. Mom had heated up some leftovers and cooked some bacon and eggs. We ate them as fast as the chickens lay them, I bet. We were starving. The tortillas tasted better that night than they ever had.

We continued being a cheap source of labor for dad that summer. As long as work was being done he put it on his time card. He kept telling mom he was looking for a job but we knew better. His military time was winding down and he was supposed to be using his vacations to look for a job. Dad would rather drink than look for a new job. We were too scared to say a thing. Summer made its way to fall and we were ready to get back to school. A couple of weeks before school started pop took us to the school offices to register. While dad was talking to the secretary I heard her ask him if we were migrants. Dad said no. She then told him that if we were we would qualify for free lunches. Dad said yes this time. I guess he took it as more money for beer. I also heard the lady say that she had a daughter in the same class as I was going to be in. Great, before school even started I would already be known as a migrant. We continued to sit in the office when a man dressed in football coach's shorts and shirt came in. He looked us over and asked me if I played ball. I told him yes and he asked me where I had played before. I told him that I had been the seventh grade starting middle linebacker in Fort Hood. He smiled and walked over and shook my dad's hand. They chatted for a few minutes then the coach walked out. After we finished registering we left and drove back to the ranch.

Dad dropped us off and he left for Fort Hood. We were on our own and were shocked that he did not have work lined up for us. My brothers and I went into the backyard and took our football with us. We started throwing the ball back and forth and having fun until a new pickup truck pulled into our drive way. It was Mister Bee. He owned the ranch we lived on. He got out of the truck and shook all our hands. He asked where our dad was. We shrugged our shoulders. He then asked us about school. I told him we had registered today. He asked if we wanted to make some spending money and I nodded. He told us he was going to bring a hay bailing machine over and he wanted us to haul hay. I had no idea what that was. He smiled and drove off. Later that afternoon a tractor pulled into the field next to our house and it started cutting the tall grass and left it in rows. I thought that was odd. My brothers and I argued back and forth about what were supposed to do.

Mr. Bee came back around that evening looking for my dad, who still wasn't home. He drove off and we cleaned up and got ready for mom to come home. She arrived later than usual and had a few bags of groceries. We helped her unload them and then she had a surprise for us. She handed us a bag of hamburgers and French fries. We were in hog heaven! We never got to eat food from town. Each of us had two burgers and two little packs of fries. Mom gave us each a cold can of coke. We sat at the table and put the food away fast. It was a special treat for us to get food like that. Money was always short and it is cheaper to feed three big boys with groceries instead of fast food.

Dad came home drunk again, of course. He probably had hung out with his army buddies after completing his day. It was getting to be old news. That night I lay in bed and imagined what school would be like in this little hick town. When we had registered, the school building that housed the high school and junior high were the same. My bet was that is was going to be small. I hoped I could make the tryouts for the football team. I fell asleep going over drills that I used to do when I was in Fort Hood. Sometime during the night I became a pro linebacker. I could see myself chasing down running backs and chasing down receivers. I knew I could be good. My dream ended when I heard a strange noise outside my window.

It was already morning. In the field where the rows of cut grass lay a tractor was pulling a weird machine. It was swallowing the cut hay and spitting out a bale of hay out the back end. So that's where hay bails came from, I never knew. Dad came by and banged on the door. I knew I had better get up and get dressed. When I went into the kitchen my brothers were already there. Carlos was frying bacon and eggs and Jose was making Kool-Aid to drink. They said that dad was outside talking to Mr. Bee.

We ate breakfast and went outside. Dad was pulling out of the drive way and Mr. Bee was looking at us. "You boys ready to haul some hay?" he asked. All three of us nodded. We had no idea what he was talking about. He asked us if we had any gloves and we shook our heads. He reached into his truck and threw a paper bag at us. Inside were the nicest leather gloves I had ever seen. Well actually they were the only gloves I had ever seen. He then asked us to climb in and he drove us into the field. "Jose, you get behind the drivers seat. Carlos you stack and Albert, you're the biggest so you throw." He then gave us the two-minute training on hauling hay. The concept was easy, but the job was very difficult.

Mr. Bee got us started and told us his wife would be around shortly to pick him up. He wished me luck on dad's job interview in town. I nodded. Yeah, right.

I threw about five bales into the back of the truck. They were heavy! I now know they weigh anywhere from eighty to one hundred pounds. The field we were in was huge; it was about fifty acres. All I could see across it were little squares of grass. Carlos was stacking the bales and doing a good job. Once we had a full load in the truck we drove slowly to one of the barns and Mr. Bee taught us how to unload and stack it. While this was going on his wife drove up in a big car. I was told it was a called a Cadillac. Before he left he told me he was going to pay us a quarter a bale of hay we put in the barn. I continued to unload the bales. As soon as he left I started to do the math. Mr. Bee had told me there were about two thousand bales in the field. That was five hundred dollars! Wow! Mr. Bee had said that it would help us buy school clothes. I was excited and so were my brothers. We had never had new school clothes.

We made trip after trip in and out of the field that day. Every pickup load had twenty-five bales in it. We filled one barn and started on the other. We talked about all the money we were going to get as we worked the hay field that day. We took a break for lunch in the late afternoon. I did not realize that we were soaked to the bone in sweat. I guess the excitement of the money made it unimportant. After we ate we headed back into the field and saw the tractor pulling out of the field. An old man was driving it and he stopped to talk to us. "Boys, there are twenty-one hundred bales out there. Have fun." He hopped back on his tractor and drove off. We attacked the field and at one point I was running from bale to bale. I figured the faster we got done the faster we got paid. We hauled hay till dark that day, and went home tired, hot and sweaty.

Mom came home and fixed us dinner as we were using the water hose to wash up. I had hay everywhere on my body. Mom fixed us dinner and we told her about all the money we were going to make. She didn't even ask us about dad tonight. I could tell she was defeated. Dad came in drunk once again, ate and went to bed. I had no problem sleeping that night. I was so exhausted I literally passed out in bed. My hands and arms were in pain from grabbing the hay bales by the two wires that holds them together. That night I kept thinking about the clothes I was going to buy. For once I was not going to wear clothes from last year that did not fit or have holes in them. I wouldn't look like a migrant.

In the morning we started up again. My brothers and I traded positions so we could keep up a fast pace. We were covered in sweat after the first load. I didn't care. I told Jose to speed it up. I was running from bale to bale. We kept up a fast pace all morning. During our second load we saw dad drive off. I guess he was going in for his second interview. We kept on going. When it was getting close to lunch time we could see the last row of bales. We decided to skip lunch and we kept on going. We had started at the crack of dawn and now it was about four in the afternoon. We had not stopped for lunch and it was the last load. We were through! We unloaded the last of the hay and headed for the kitchen. We were starving. As we washed up we decided that I would hose down first and start cooking bacon and eggs. It was the fastest food to cook and most plentiful. We had about fifty chickens so there were always plenty of eggs.

By the time my brothers had washed up I had fried about three eggs for each of us along with tortillas. We ate pretty fast since we were starving. After we ate we went outside and sat under our shade tree. We talked about all the money we had made. I actually had a piece of paper and pencil and I was figuring out the exact amount. My figures came up to five hundred twenty-five dollars. I took that number and divided it by three and got one hundred seventy five dollars for each of us. I had a smile from ear to ear. We laid back and talked about the stuff we were going to buy. School was a few weeks off so I was looking forward to buying some clothes. I was tired of being the poor kid in class that wore the same clothes over and over again. It was getting close to dusk when mom pulled into the yard.

We told mom about our hard day and she smiled as she walked into the house. She quit smiling when she saw the mess we had left in the kitchen. She started screaming and slapping us. We ran outside and she told us she was going to get pop to whip us. As we stood outside we decided who would sneak back in and wash the dishes. I was the oldest so I waited for mom to leave the kitchen so I could get to work cleaning.

I walked in the back door and started in on the dishes. I filled the sink with hot water and started scrubbing. Without warning my hands came out of the hot soapy water. I was in pain! My hands were blistered and bleeding from hauling all the hay. I winced and stuck my hands back in the water and started scrubbing. Mom came back in the kitchen and saw my eyes watering. She looked at me and said, "That's what you get for being pigs!" I ignored her like I usually did and continued to wash the pots and pans. She started on dinner and we did not speak. Later that evening pop came home.

We could tell pop's interview had gone well. He was drunk again. As soon as he came in the door mom started in on him. Not about being drunk but about how we had made a mess in the kitchen. He looked at me and my brothers and a scowl came over his face. He rushed into me like a linebacker making a tackle. I was thrown backwards and landed on my back. I received a kick to the ribs that sent me rolling towards the living room. My brothers ran for their bedroom where dad cornered them. I could tell from the screams that they did not get away. I crawled to my room and lay on the floor. I knew dad would be too tired to come hit me again. I lay on the wood floor and the hot night air came over me. It was the only way to handle the burning in my side.

Morning came with a loud yell. "Get your lazy ass up and find something to do!" It was dad again. I guess he had already thrown up his beer from yesterday. I had fallen asleep fully clothed so I made my way to the bathroom and brushed my teeth and headed out the door to find something to do. My brothers were working in the garden so I decided to feed the chickens. While I was spreading the feed out I heard Mr. Bee pull into the driveway. Dad walked out of the house and met him. The old man stayed in his truck and talked to dad. I saw him point to me and then handed dad some green paper and then they shook hands. Pay day! I tossed the rest of the feed into the chicken coop and ran towards dad. He was waving as the old man pulled away. My brothers were also headed towards dad. They had wide eyes as they also knew we were about to get our reward for the hard work we had done.

As I made my way towards dad I saw him put the bills into his pocket. The three of us came together around our dad and he stopped. "Que!" (what) he said. "We got paid right?" I asked. He reached into his pocket and held up six one hundred dollars bills. "Pa la casa!" (for the house) He shoved them back into his pocket and headed into the house. "Pa la cerveza!" (for the beer) I yelled. He turned back around I was amazed at how quickly he caught me. This time I did not have the luxury of crawling back into my room. At least he kicked me on the opposite side this time. I did not scream in pain but in frustration this time. "You're only going to use it to get drunk!" I yelled. By this time mom came out and pulled dad away from me. I was on the ground in the fetal position. Mom pushed dad away and I got to my knees and tried to get up. It hurt but I managed. I had tears of pain streaming down my cheeks and I headed towards one of the hay barns.

I lay on the bales of hay we had hauled yesterday and I could still feel the heat they held from the hot summer Texas sun. I managed to lay flat on my back and put my hands behind my head. I closed my eyes and took in the aroma of the barn. It was a cross between the bales and dirt. It was still better than the house where the smell of misery was always present. I heard my dad start his truck and drive away. "Second interview my ass!" I thought to myself. The mean thoughts I was having about my dad faded as it grew dark in my mind. I began to have visions of California and my uncle who always knew what to say when it hurt. I recalled the desert we drove through and the heat as it blew into our camper. The heat was not hard to forget because it was what woke me up. I was covered in sweat when I heard my brothers calling for me.

"Are you alright?" Carlos asked. I did not feel like speaking.

"You need to keep your mouth shut," Jose said. They told me that mom had headed into town to pick up some groceries. We were supposed to stay home and clean the kitchen. Mom had left us lunch. I found out I had fallen asleep through breakfast and it was now lunch time. We went in and had lunch and between the three of us we cleaned the pots and pans. We talked about how I could not keep my mouth shut. I told them it was a gift I had, and would use it at every opportunity.

I would receive many more beatings from our dad because I would speak my mind. It was abuse, but when you live in the sticks, who hears you? We would work in the woods and pastures of the ranch for over two years. We made a good bit of money but never saw it. Dad drank it twelve ounces at a time. The funny thing was he would have us crush the cans and then sell them for aluminum. If that did not add insult to injury, what did? We ended up being the poor Mexican kids with only a few old clothes to wear, fitting the stereotype I was trying to avoid.

Chapter 16
Back To School

Eighth grade arrived. We had made it through a rough summer on Mr. Bee's ranch. It had definitely hardened us. I was on the long yellow bus headed to school. I sat in a seat by myself and my brothers sat in front of me. I eyed every person that came aboard but spoke to no one. We made pickup after pickup as we got closer to town. I was glad once we got off the gravel roads and on to asphalt.

At school, the bus emptied and we headed to class. Jose and I went to one building and Carlos went to the elementary school on the other side of the street. I thought that was odd. In Fort Hood you had to go to Killeen for high school and they were huge. This building was tiny. I went in and found out that the eighth graders had to meet in the science lab. When I finally found it I was really shocked. There were only about a dozen kids in the room. I sat on a stool and looked around. A big red-haired kid looked at me so I asked him where all the eighth graders were. He looked at me and said, "This is it, wetback." He turned back around like it was no big deal.

I got out of my stool and headed for him when a big hand came down on my shoulder. "Sit down please," a voice said.

"Welcome, I am Coach Tye," the big man said. He walked in front of the class and wrote his name on the chalk board. I looked him over and he looked like a coach. He was blonde-haired and blue-eyed, purple polyester coaching slacks and a matching purple and white shirt. He started telling us how he was going to be our teacher for science and would coach the football team. While he talked I eyed the back of Red's head. He must have known

I was looking at him because he turned around and winked at me. That made me angrier. Coach Tye had us all give a brief story about ourselves and he decided to start with me, so I told the class the usual stuff. I had the routine down from all the schools I had gone to. I had to stand off to the side to give my introduction and this gave everyone the opportunity to see my old clothes.

I was the epitome of a poor Mexican, wearing old jeans and sneakers. The tee shirt I had on was a purchased for less than two dollars because the picture on the front was off—centered. I felt like a big loser. I noticed everyone was looking me over from head to toe. Thanks to my dad all the money we had earned had gone to beer instead of clothes for school. The only saving grace for me was that I had developed big shoulders and arms from all the hard work. The coach asked me if I had played football in Fort Hood. I nodded and he began to ask me more questions related to sports. I told him I was the starting middle linebacker. I did not mention that I had been moved to the B team. I also told him I played basketball and ran track. The coach explained to the class that in bigger schools you had to try out. The kids looked at me again and were surprised. Red whispered something to a cute girl sitting next to him and she began to giggle. I gave them both a mean look and Red just winked at me again. I was getting madder by the minute.

The last kid gave his story, but I did not hear. I was still mad at Red. How dare he call me a wetback. What even made it worse was that he was getting the best-looking girl in class to laugh with him. There were only five girls in the class and ten boys, including myself. None of the girls would win a beauty pageant and none of the boys would either. I could not believe this was all the eighth graders in the school. It was so small. There were two Black boys in the room and the rest were White.

As I thought on how to deal with Red, the bell rang. "I'll see the boys at football practice!" the coach said.

I waited for Red to walk out first. He was a lot bigger than me so I had to be sneaky. He was six feet tall and close to two hundred pounds. We all walked out to the hall and headed to our lockers. Red had a handful of books and was trying to open his locker when I tapped him on the shoulder. He turned and I reached out and grabbed him with a pinch hold to the throat. His eyes opened wide as did his mouth. With the pinch hold I had on him he could not utter a word; he tried but only gasps would come out. Since his hands were full of books he could not fight back. I moved my other arm back to punch him when a big hand fell on my shoulder. "Don't!" I heard a deep voice say.

I released my grip and turned around. I was looking directly into someone's belly. I had to look straight up to see the face. This was the largest man I had ever seen. He squeezed my shoulder and forced me to turn sideways. He told Red to put his books away and he grabbed him by the shoulder and marched us down the hall. "You're new here aren't you?" he asked.

"Yes sir," I said.

"I see you've met Red." We walked down the hallway and other kids stared at us. This was great: now I was poor, Mexican, and a trouble maker.

We were led to the office where the principal looked us over. He was getting angrier by the second I could tell. "Aren't you two late for football practice?" He yelled.

We both said, "yes sir."

"Get out and don't come back!" he bellowed. We both turned and ran out. We kept running out the front of the school. I don't know where we were running, I just followed Red. I figured he knew where we were going.

"Ya stupid Mexican, we're late for football practice!" he said as we ran.

"You're pretty fast for a fat boy, Red," I replied. He laughed and we kept running to the gym. We got there as Coach Tye was looking over his new junior high squad. We took a seat with everyone else.

"How many running backs do I have?" A few kids raised their hands. He kept asking position questions and I kept my hands down. I only knew linebacker. I would like to run the ball but I did not know how to. I knew how to hit, and I liked that! The first day of practice was just listening to the coach talk. He also had us pick out our pads and helmets. I was shocked at the equipment. The helmets did not match and neither did the pants. Some of the pads were very old and falling apart. I kept my mouth shut and selected the pads I needed. I remembered the high-quality equipment at Fort Hood, and wanted to laugh but didn't. Jose was also there and he was trying to find a helmet that fit. I helped him select one. The face mask was a different color than mine. After we picked out our stuff it was time for lunch.

Jose and I headed for the cafeteria and got a surprise when we left the

211

gym. Red and a few of his friends were there. "Wetback!" he said out loud. He was posturing for a fight. His chest was out and his hands were clenched in big fists. This kid could hurt me. "I don't want to fight, I just want to play football," I said. I extended my hand for a shake.

He looked me over and I expected him to take a swing at me. The other boys behind him started patting him on the back and told him to shake. I heard one kid tell him that we needed the big Mexican on the team. He took my hand and leaned forward. "Don't call me fat boy again or I'll whip your ass," he said just loud enough for me to hear. He turned and headed for the lunch room.

Jose and I walked with the rest of the boys and we all sat together. We talked about football and how good we were going to be. I was making friends that shared the same things I did: football and girls! After we ate we walked around the small campus and Red filled me in on all the details of small town life in Texas. I found out my brothers and I were the only Mexicans playing sports and the other Mexicans in the school were really wetbacks. They were here illegally. He was not being mean when he used the "W" word. He really thought we were related to the other Hispanics in the school. I quickly set him straight on the issue and let him know that my brothers and I were coconuts and not related to the other minorities. I guess at times I did not mind being a coconut. After school my brothers and I rode the bus back home and our escape was over for the day.

Dad was already home and drunk, of course. He had been waiting for us. We were forced to quickly fix a sandwich for dinner and change into older clothes. We were already wearing our "old" clothes to school. Pop loaded us up in his truck and took us to the cattle pens. In the corral were all the cows and calves that had pink eye. There were over a dozen calves and about ten cows that needed doctoring. Pink eye in cattle is similar to the infection humans get in their eyes. The only difference is the cows can't go to the doctor. For these cows we were the doctor. We had to spray a purple spray directly into their eyes as well as around the eye. The only problem was the cows did not like it and the spray was deep purple, the color of grape juice and it did not wash out.

Dad sat in the truck and yelled at us until he passed out. He had beer in his ice chest that he always kept handy. After he fell asleep we kept working. We had to get every cow and calf into a squeeze chute one at a time. It took all night. We were tired, hungry and our hands and faces were purple. We looked like we were turning into Smurfs. We ended up finishing the evening by using the headlights from dad's truck. He didn't mind, he was already asleep. We just pushed him over to the passenger seat. The only good thing that came out of working the cows was our tackling ability. The older cows were easy to get into the chute. The calves were a different story.

We treated all the cows first. They had done this before and seemed to know what we were trying to accomplish. After we treated them they were easy to spot. Their face was purple, but the breed of cattle was called the Whiteface Hereford. It was actually quite funny to see them look at each other and see them look over their purple faces. For the calves, we had to tackle each one and hold them down so we could spray them. I had Carlos and Jose funnel the calf towards me and I would literally tackle it like a football player. It was not easy. By the end of the night not only did I have purple hands, I also had a busted lip, bloody nose and a slight black eye. I was so glad when I tackled the last one. I was worn out.

We drove back home, actually I drove the truck back home as dad continued his drunken sleep. We parked the truck and mom came out to greet us. She made us strip down in the back yard. Not only were we purple but we also were covered in cow crap. During this time of the year the cattle were grazing on fresh new green oat sprouts. That's when the oats are only about ten inches tall and very green and moist. It gives the cows a lot of nutrition, and a lot of diarrhea. In the dark it was hard to tell just how much poop we had on us, but now that mom had the back yard light on we looked as bad as we smelled. We stripped down to nothing and took a shower outside.

Mom brought us a bar of soap and we tried to get the purple and green off of us. The green came off pretty easy. The purple did not. We looked like we had some type of disease with all the spots we had. We had fun that evening running around in the back yard naked with the water hose going. It made up for the beating we took from those cows. After we dried off we went in the house and mom had dinner on the table. It was very late but we were very hungry. After dinner we headed off to bed. Mom came by my room and asked me where pop was. We had totally forgotten about him. We had left him in the truck. I told her where he was and she looked surprised. "Why did you leave him in the truck?" she asked. I told mom I really didn't care, it wasn't my problem. She gave me a very nasty look and took a slap at my face. I easily dodged it and went into my bedroom and crawled into bed.

I fell asleep very quickly and the dreams came back. In my dreams I was no longer the poor Mexican kid in school. I was popular and had nice clothes. I could see me and Red walking around our campus with the prettiest girls. We were the jocks of the eighth grade football team. We were supposed to be cool and all the girls were supposed to like us. This only happened in my dreams though. The truth is it never happened. I would go on to be a very good eighth grade football player just like Red. He was big with red hair and freckles and I was a Mexican. What a combination! We never got the girls and were never popular. However, tonight in my dreams I was cool, popular, rich, and had the cutest girls. I wished that night would go on forever. It felt like I had been asleep only a few minutes when my mom woke me up to get ready for school.

Once again we rode the bus to school. This time a few of the kids talked to us. I was anxious to get to practice so I could wear the pads and hit someone instead of cows. In class people kept asking me if I got into a fight with a Smurf. I had purple spots and bruises all over my body and face. I just grinned and avoided the question. During my classes I began to check out the girls in the class. I had an easy way to talk to them because they were also inquiring about my purple paint. It was so different from Fort Hood. There were probably four hundred eight graders there. Here there were only eighteen kids.

I learned the names of the girls quickly. The prettiest one asked me if I was a migrant wetback. That stung, and would leave a bruise. I knew she wasn't trying to be cruel, just asking a question the only way she could reference it. I explained to her that I was not a "wetback" or a migrant. She wasn't buying it. She just turned up her nose and stared at my purple hands. The other girls followed her lead and avoided me. I think she told the other girls that the purple marks were contagious. I decided to show them what I was made of on the football field.

After suiting up in pads Jose and I walked onto the practice field and it became evident I was used to playing on a different level. The coaching I had received in Fort Hood was stronger than what was going on here. My technique and form pleased the coach and he kept using me as an example on how to hit and tackle. A few of the boys on the squad were not impressed but did not want to face me in tackling drills. We went through drills and ended practice by running sprints against each other. The team soon found out what I already knew. Jose was fast! He outran everyone on the team very easily. Even without turning his speed on full throttle he won every single sprint. The coach started calling him Speedy Gonzalez. Jose told him his last name was not Gonzalez. I thought it was funny. So did the coach. He got tagged with just "Speedy" for the rest of his high school career.

During lunch a bunch of the football players sat together and we talked once again about sports and girls. While we practiced football they were working on volleyball. They came in after us into the lunchroom. We all stared at the few girls there were and made good eighth grade boy comments about them. I'm sure they were doing the same with us.

Full contact practice finally came and I ran out to the practice field and looked for someone to hit. I found Red and we started bouncing into each other and doing head butts. As the other kids made their way to the field we greeted them with a helmet to helmet hello or a flying tackle. The coach soon came out and put a stop to that and got us organized for a real practice.

This was my favorite part of the day. Since I only played defense, I practiced against the starting offense. I was getting to hit as hard as I wanted; that is until I almost hurt our quarterback. The coach made me hold back. The coach worked with me and showed me how to read the eyes of the opposing players and determine where the ball was going to be ran to or passed. I learned a lot from that man. I wished I could have a father that showed me things like this. I often wonder what could have, should have, been, but never was. We practiced in pads for another week and learned our positions well. Coach taught me a lot. I still remember one phrase he always said: "If you only had some speed."

I would always reply, "I have deceptive speed: I'm slower than I look." Later I would tell him, "I have three speeds. Slow, neutral and reverse. He would laugh along with the other kids and then slap me on my rear. As slow as I was, he made it fun for us, until game time.

The first game came up quickly. We had practiced two weeks in pads. We did not even have our numbers until that day. I remember girls asking us if they could wear our numbers on pins or jackets. The evening of the game while we were getting into our pads the coach came by and started giving us our jerseys. The coach gave me number 44. He said I would play offense later in the year if I could become half as fast as Jose. I laughed and held up that jersey like it was made of gold. I remember the light shining through the mesh material. I looked around and every kid was doing the same thing. Then the fireworks started.

"Put those damn war shirts on ladies!" I ducked my head and started to look for the mad man that was yelling. "You heard me!" Coach yelled. He had turned into a lunatic. We all quickly put on our shirts and he was on top of us. "Rod, are you ready to hit!" he yelled. I could feel spit flying out of his mouth and landing on my face. "Answer me, dammit!"

"Yes sir," I said softly.

"That's not good enough!" he yelled again. This time his head and neck were red and his veins were popping out. "Get out there and hit!"

Coach screamed and yelled at us all the way out to the field. The people in the bleachers must have been in shock. Our town was always quiet and here came a bunch of screaming junior high kids. We barely had enough time to warm up and set up for the kick off. The coach picked me and Red to be captains and we were late to the coin flip. The referees were motioning us to get over. We yelled "heads" before we got to the center of the field. We won the toss but coach had told us that he wanted the other team to get the ball first, something about us getting in the first hit I recall. When we kicked off, Coach was still hollering. The other team made a short return and that's when the fun started.

I watched for Coach to give the signal and I set up the defense. I could feel butterflies in my stomach and a knot in my chest. I was playing middle linebacker just like I had done in Fort Hood. This time I was faster and smarter. I knew more about reading eyes and motions. My leg muscles felt like springs and they exploded when I saw the quarterback hand the ball off. The runner was coming right for me! Red was playing a lineman in front of me and he stood the blocker up and made the running back go around him. I connected with him as soon as he got to the line of scrimmage. My helmet caught him right below the chin strap. I guess no one taught this kid to run low. I wrapped my arms around his waist and lifted him off the ground. I arched my back like Coach had taught me and kept my forward motion. The impact caused the back of the runner's head to be the first thing that came in contact with the ground. I could feel his body contort when I landed on top of him. Red added to the pain when he landed on top of me. That's when I felt all the air leave the running back's body. The referee began to pull us off and by the time he got to me, the poor kid at the bottom he was gasping for air like a fish out of water.

The game stopped and I called the defense to line up. Red started something that lasted all year. He slapped his thigh pads twice and then clapped his hands twice. He did this over and over again. Soon, every player on our team was doing it. The kids on the sideline jumped in. The fans joined in after the hurt kid had been taken off the field. I still remember the sound, thump, thump, clap, clap. No one said a word. All you could hear was thump, thump, clap, clap.

While the offense was huddled up we continued the rhythm. The entire game would follow the impact of the first hit I got on their running back, and I could sense the fear we had created from that first blow. We completely dominated the game and the rest of the year. We never lost a game in eighth grade, and had only two or three touchdowns scored on us all year.

Our success came from Coach. He fired us up so much from the field house to the playing field that our emotion started high and never faded. During the game he was the fiercest man I have ever seen; off the field he was so calm and pleasant. That's how he wanted us to be. I wanted so much to be like him and admired how he could turn it on and off. By the end of the season we had more fans coming to watch us play than the high school. I remember the varsity squad lost every game that year. The high school players resented us and were very jealous of our success.

Our seventh and eighth grade class wound up being a powerhouse in junior high competition that year. We won the district championship in football, basketball and track. I didn't contribute much to track however. Jose looked like an Olympic champion with all his medals after every meet. After track the school year started to wind down and the coach started talking about how the varsity team would be much better with the new freshmen coming in. Once the current varsity players heard this they were very unhappy. They were even more upset when the coach was interviewed for an article in the local newspaper.

In the article that came out in the paper he talked about his disappointment in his season where he lost every game. He then mentioned his excitement in the upcoming freshmen class and how we were creating a winning tradition since we did not lose a single game in football and dominated every sport. He even mentioned a few of us by name. He did not mention any of the returning upper classmen. You can imagine that did not sit very well with some. I would get the brunt of that frustration soon.

The last few weeks of the school season were very relaxed. The coach asked the eighth grade boys to work out after school with the varsity football team. We were in shorts and basically running and going through drills. Red and I could sense the hostility during the workout. Coach had left the quarterback for the high school in charge to help him develop his leadership. He broke us up into backs, receivers, and linemen. I was told to go with the wide receivers. He had me line up outside and told me to run a "ten and in." I knew what that meant so I ran ten yards down the field and turned in and there was the ball. This guy could throw a rocket. I caught the ball but it stung. I thought it was going to go right through me. The next couple of kids ran the same route and he did not throw it near as hard. In fact he threw a couple of lobs. I thought to myself, "No wonder they lost every game." These guys had terrible work ethic.

I lined up again and was told to run a ten and out. I lined up and took off. When I got about ten yards down the field I felt a sharp pain in my back that launched me forward a few feet. The quarterback had speared me in the back with the ball. I got up and saw all the varsity boys laughing and joking. I picked up the ball and threw it back to the quarterback, whose name was Mark. I lined up again was told to run the same route. I ran eight yards down the field and turned. There was the ball. I caught it and tossed it back to Mark. He did not like that and started yelling at me. "Mexican, you do what you're told to do!"

I laughed and got back in line. I got back in line and he asked me to run a five and in. That was really a short distance. I lined up and ran a five and out. Mark threw the ball about forty yards down the field. I trotted back in line and waited for my turn to go again. Mark started calling me names and ordered me to get the ball. I told him that since he threw it he needed to go get it. If he could not hit a five yard pass he did not deserve to be the quarterback. Not only that, I called him a 0 and 10 loser. Mark stormed off towards the linemen workout. I blew it off and started talking to some of the other eight graders. Mark came back with help and it got worse from here.

The entire varsity team had been rallied by Mark and they formed a circle around me and the other eighth graders. They started taunting us and calling us names. We had two Black kids in our class and they were also catching a lot of heat. The biggest lineman on the team stepped out of the group and walked up to me. "You're a wetback!" he yelled.

I was scared. This kid was big. Zack was about six foot three and about two hundred fifty pounds. I was topping about one twenty.

"Chili choker! taco bender!" he continued to yell. The other boys started yelling also. "Kick his ass!" "Wetback!"

I tried to be funny and asked, "What's a taco bender?

Zack got madder. "You dumb wetback. You're the Mexican at the taco shop that bends the tortillas to make tacos." I laughed and he did not.

The next thing I remember, I was flat on my back. I blacked out for a minute. I finally came to my senses and all I could see was sunshine and the beautiful Texas sky. My mouth hurt and I could taste something in my mouth. I tasted like under cooked meat and had a coppery taste. I ran my hand across my mouth and I pulled back a blood covered hand. Zack had ripped my mouth open. I still bare the scar to this day. My mouth actually became about a quarter inch bigger on the right side. I got up on one knee and let the blood drain. I could see the kids continuing to call me names but I could not hear a thing. I saw Zack lifting his arms like he had just won a pro wrestling match. He continued to pump his arms up and down and point in friend's faces. Slowly my hearing came back and my bleeding was slowing down. I looked down at the pool of blood and I thought I was going to heave.

Zack continued to jump up and down and my hearing came back. "You niggers are next!" The other boys called out. There were only White boys on the varsity that year. Slowly the jeering stopped as I started to walk towards Zack. I had been beaten before, and beaten worse. I clenched my fists and stepped closer to the big lineman. Now the name calling stopped. "You want more, wetback?" Zack yelled. He telegraphed his haymaker punch. He got lucky last time and it would not happen again. I took a step and spit out more blood. I kept an eye on Zack's chest and arm. This was going to be easy. He came around with a big punch that started way behind his head. I knew he was aiming for my face. This time, I was ready and I would hit the homerun.

I remember his punch going over my head and the look in Zack's eyes as I ducked. Then I remember the look of terror as my fist connected with his crotch. I went to a kneeling position and drove my legs and hips up as hard as I could. My fist came up with me and all my power connected on his "family jewels." As he went down I stepped back and reloaded. I took a step back and then propelled myself forward. I had been taught by my uncle that the power for punching comes from the hips and legs, almost like a golf swing. I used that technique and hit Zack right on the lips. I recall it looked like a tomato that was too ripe being squished. Blood shot out and he went down on his back. I would not make the same mistake he did in letting me get back up. I dove on him and landed on his chest. I sat on him and put both my knees on the inside of his elbows. He was pinned!

I lost all track of time, space and reality. All I did was strike out, and strike hard. I pummeled Zack's face with everything I had. I hit him on the nose, mouth and eyes. I remember looking down and seeing bumps form on his brow and cheeks. I remember blood flying out from a gash above his eye. I also remember the silence. I could see the damage being done but I could not hear a sound, not even Zack's pleas for help.

Zack managed to free himself and rolled over on his stomach. I stayed on top of him. I knew if he got up he would kill me. I sat on his back and grabbed a handful of hair with my left hand and swung my fist around with my right. I was catching him on the ear and cheek. I pulled his head back as far as I could. It must have been a sight. I was riding this big horse like a Texas cowboy. I switched hands back and forth for what seemed hours, even though it was only a few seconds. Suddenly I stopped and released Zack. Minutes ago he had smashed my mouth open and now he was in the fetal position bawling like a baby. He had both hands over his face and blood was seeping through his fingers. I hadn't said a word since he hit me.

I stepped away from the scene and touched the corner of my mouth. I probably needed a few stitches but knew that would never happen. I sucked on the cut and spit out the blood. I never said a word to Zack, just walked away. The White kids stood there with their mouths open. I kept walking and did not look back. My Black friends started yelling and laughing at Zack as he tried to get up. The taunting had now changed. As I walked to the field house I heard steps behind me so I clenched my fists. The adrenaline was gone and pain was starting to set in. If Zack's friends wanted me, I was done for.

The noise got louder and I finally turned around. It was the rest of the eighth graders. They piled on me and we all fell to the ground. They helped me up and they started making comments about my new "bigger" mouth. We all walked into the building together and I went to the sink to wash up. I looked in the mirror and the corner of my mouth looked like raw meat. I rinsed my mouth until the taste of blood was gone. I finally looked down at my hands and my knuckles were bruised. My hands were swollen and starting to pulse. My head was starting to hurt and my stomach was starting to turn. My knees gave out and I felt cold all over.

I ran into the bathroom stall next to sink and fell to my knees. Tears finally came. I stayed there kneeled in front of the toilet for a few minutes. I puked up blood that I had swallowed and tried hard not to cry out loud. Scenes from what I had done to Zack flashed in front of my eyes. No human should ever do that to another. I stayed in the stall and I was reminded of hiding from the teachers when I was in California. That brought a smile to my face and I was finally able to stand.

I came out of the stall and went back to the sink to rinse my mouth again. While I was doing this Jose came in. "What happened to your mouth?" he asked.

"Nothing," I said. It hurt too much to talk. We stood and talked while I put moist paper towels on my cut and then Zack walked in. However bad I looked he was much worse off. His entire face was beat up bad. He had blood all over his grey workout shirt and his ears were puffy and red. I looked up at him as I continued to clean myself up. Jose saw him and started to put two and two together. He looked at me and said, "You did that to him?" I did not respond and started to walk out so Zack could use the sink. We walked by each other and did not make eye contact. Jose started making fun of him until I gave him a look to make him stop. That was the last fight I was ever in.

That was how junior high ended and I got my taste of freshmen football in Texas. I guess I was a tough coconut to crack. High school was right around the corner and we had another summer to go. Looking back at that year I still get a giggle out of being called a "taco bender." I have a picture of a little Mexican guy sitting on a stool bending tortillas in the shape of a taco shell. I got called a lot of other things that year but I also made friends that lasted all through high school.

Getting to this point had been a long hard journey. I was about to embark on a journey my parents had never taken: high school. To me and many other first generation Hispanics we see it as something normal, going to school. Education beyond a few classes in elementary is something that was foreign to my parents and many others. I consider myself very fortunate to have made it this far. I could have been sent to the fields like other relatives of mine, but I was also very lucky to have been allowed to play sports.

Athletics taught me a lot and made me physically and mentally strong.

I look forward to sharing my high school adventures with you. Coconuts and White bread is an ongoing adventure that lasts a lifetime. You have only read a short portion of a saga that is shared by thousands, maybe millions of young Hispanics in the United States of America.